FOLLOWING GOD
CHARACTER SERIES
BIBLE STUDY

An informative **12 WEEK BIBLE STUDY** of life principles for today, to guide the church and the Christian's walk.

The Acts of the Holy Spirit

GUIDANCE FOR THE CHRISTIAN WALK

AMG
PUBLISHERS

BOOK 1

EDDIE RASNAKE

Following God

THE ACTS OF THE HOLY SPIRIT
BOOK ONE

Published by AMG Publishers. All Rights Reserved.

ISBN: 978-1-61715-529-1

Manuscript editing, text design, and layout by Rick Steele
http://steeleeditorialservices.myportfolio.com

Cover illustration by Daryle Beam/Bright Boy Design

Printed in the United States of America
2019 First Edition

This book is dedicated to my
paternal grandparents:

John Ezra Rasnake
and
Golda Ball Rasnake

They followed Christ and blazed a trail for the
Rasnakes to follow.

ACKNOWLEDGMENTS

This two-volume work constitutes the fifteenth and sixteenth installments for me personally in the series I was privileged to launch with AMG Publishers and my fellow authors, Wayne Barber and Rick Shepherd, two decades ago. Though the publishing industry has changed much since then, the enduring nature of these studies is a testament to the fact that God's Word is an inexhaustible ocean, with neither beach nor boundary, and God's people will always look for ways to study these living Scriptures more deeply. I am especially grateful to the body of believers at Woodland Park Baptist Church in Chattanooga, Tennessee, who have walked through this and many other studies I have written and have been a continual source of encouragement as we continue to develop new ministry tools together. Thanks to all the folks at AMG, especially Steve Turner and Amanda Jenkins, and to my long-time collaborator, Rick Steele, who always does a great job with editing, layout, and text design. Most of all, I remain grateful to the Lord Jesus, who saved me and continues to teach me and lead me in what it means to follow Him with a whole heart.

THE AUTHOR

Eddie Rasnake

EDDIE RASNAKE graduated with honors from East Tennessee State University. He and his wife, Michele, served 7 years with Cru at the University of Virginia, James Madison University, and the University of Tennessee (as campus director). Eddie left Cru to join Wayne Barber at Woodland Park Baptist Church, where he still serves as Senior Associate Pastor. He has authored dozens of books and Bible studies and has published materials in Afrikaans, Albanian, German, Greek, Italian, Romanian, Russian, and Telugu. Eddie and his wife Michele live in Chattanooga, Tennessee.

PREFACE

The book of Acts is a pivotal book of the New Testament, yet sometimes it gets neglected in study because of its length and narrative nature. This is unfortunate, for these accounts of the first-century church show how by the power of God, the early believers impacted the culture around them despite their minority status. Now more than ever, the church needs such examples and reminders as we seek to turn our world upside down (or perhaps a better way to express it is turn our world "right side up"). Like the early church, we believers must live our mission in the context of an antithetical and sometimes antagonistic culture. Like the early church, we do not have social leverage, political clout, or military might to change society by force, but we do have the name of the risen Christ, the person of the Holy Spirit and the life-changing power of God the Father on our side. It is my prayer that as you study this impactful New Testament narrative, you will do so with faith that God can do in our day what He did in theirs!

Following Him,

Eddie Rasnake

EDDIE RASNAKE

Contents

LESSON 1

WAITING FOR GOD TO MOVE
ACTS 1:1–10

What do you think would happen today if Jesus physically appeared on the streets of Los Angeles or the beaches of south Florida? How do you suppose He would be greeted? Do you think any would recognize Him? Maybe, but I doubt it. Would He receive the honor and glory He deserves? Most definitely not, for Jesus will not receive the honor and glory He truly is worthy of until every knee bows and every tongue confesses that He is Lord. My suspicion is that if Jesus came to earth for a visit, most would miss Him completely because they are not ready for God to show up. I wonder if I am? One thing I have learned in my years as a Christian is that God shows up when He wants, not when I expect He will or think He should. And it is for that very reason that I am called to be ready. In Luke 12:40 Jesus is speaking of His second coming and says, *"be ready; for the Son of Man is coming at an hour that you do not expect."* Are you ready? Don't be too quick to answer. If you take a moment to reflect honestly on the question, I think, like me, you will admit that you are not quite sure. In fact, sincere and frank reflection ought to keep our answers quite humble.

Why do we struggle with being "ready" for God to show up? Let me share the results of my own honest reflections. First, I do not know *when* He will show up. Second, I don't know *how* He will show up. And third, I don't know *why* He will come. You see, I don't think of God showing up as only being related to the second coming of Christ. I believe Jesus will come again because that is what the Word of God says, but I also believe God can "show up" at any time He chooses, however He wants, and for whatever reason fits His purpose. And I believe He DOES! Hebrews 13:2 instructs us, *"Do not neglect to show hospitality to strangers, for by this some have entertained angels without knowing it."* If God's *messengers* can show up at unexpected times and in unrecognized ways, how much more is this true of God Himself? As a case in point, consider some of the ways God "showed up" in the past. He showed up for destruction in Noah's flood and at Sodom and Gomorrah, and few were ready. He showed up for direction in the midst of Moses' wilderness experience as He spoke from a burning bush. He showed up for discipline when He met the prophet Balaam and spoke through the mouth of a donkey. He showed up for deliverance at the shores of the Red Sea.

God shows up all the time, but quite often we are not ready for Him, and sometimes we miss His appearance altogether. Jesus showed up after the crucifixion to encourage the despondent disciples, but Thomas missed out because he was not there. Our Lord walked with two disciples on the road to Emmaus, but they did not recognize Him until afterward. When God shows up today, some are there and experience it, while others miss it or are there and do not recognize it. In 1970 God showed up at a tiny Methodist college in the rural hamlet of Wilmore, Kentucky. It all began at a typical chapel service that ended up being anything but. The normally brief (and sometimes boring) service of speaking and singing became a continuous, round-the-clock encounter with the living God. Classes were canceled, and agendas were shredded. My uncle, Henry Howell, was a Biology professor at Asbury College at the time, and he was in the chapel service. As God began to move, he ran to a phone and called his wife, and said, "You'd better get over here, God is doing something in the chapel service." My aunt, Irene Howell, later related to me that as she walked up the steps to the chapel—before she even entered the building—she experienced an overwhelming sense of the presence of God. What started at the college spread like fire-seeds of awakening as the students went home to their churches to give testimony, and then revival broke out in place after place. Lives were changed. Sins were laid aside, and the works of God were taken up. While the intense emotions and the tangible experience of God's presence did not last, the changes in people's lives did. But this encounter with the living God was missed by many. One student at the college who skipped chapel that morning confesses that when he arrived at class to find the room unlocked but empty, he thought at first that the "rapture" had occurred and he had missed it. Believe me, you don't want to miss it when God shows up.

The book of Acts is all about God showing up in people's lives. It is not a doctrinal treatise on what God can do or plans to do. It is an historical record of what He *HAS* done! It is the living testimony of lives that are altered when God decides to move. The big "bang" of the story happens in chapter 2 with the coming of the Holy Spirit at Pentecost. Chapter 1 looks tame in comparison. But in Acts chapter 1 we see what God's people do to get ready for God to move. As we look this week, we will see in their lives lessons for ours.

DAY 1

PONDERING GOD'S MOVING IN THE PRESENT: ACTS 1:1–11

The four Gospels—Matthew, Mark, Luke, and John—give us four different vantage points on the life and ministry of Emanuel, God with us. After four hundred years of silence since the last prophet, Malachi, God Himself visits His people. Though Jesus' earthly ministry only lasts three years, it changes all of history. John fittingly ends his Gospel with these words: *"And there are also many other things which Jesus did, which if they were written in detail, I suppose that even the world itself would not contain the books that would be written."* The book of Acts comes next in your Bible for obvious reasons. It picks up where the gospels leave off. We refer to it formally as the "Acts of the Apostles," but in reality, it is the Acts of God, the Holy Spirit as He works through His followers.

Chapter 1 of Acts gives us a glimpse at that brief transition from the Gospel events—the culmination of the work of God the Son—and Pentecost, the coming of God the Holy Spirit. Let's look at what we can learn.

God can "show up" at any time He chooses, however He wants, and
for whatever reason fits His purpose

📖 Compare Acts 1:1–3 with Luke 1:1–4 and write down what you learn about why Luke writes his Gospel and the book of Acts.

_____

_____

_____

_____

Both of Luke's writings are addressed to a man named Theophilus. His exact identity is unknown, but his being called *"most excellent Theophilus"* (Luke 1:3) suggests that he is probably a Roman official. Luke makes mention in Acts 1:1 that his "first account" (the Gospel of Luke) records all that Jesus *"began to do."* While the work of the cross, purchasing our redemption, is a finished work, the proclamation of the availability of that redemption is not finished. In some ways the book of Acts is about how Jesus' work for people and with people becomes His work *through* people. In the Gospel, Luke gives us a sense of how he writes—by carefully investigating and recording chronologically the eyewitness accounts of those who were with Jesus. His aim for Theophilus is that he might *"know the exact truth"* about the things he has been taught of Jesus.

DID YOU KNOW?
Theophilus

Luke addresses his writings to a man named Theophilus. The name literally means "lover of God" or "friend of God." Luke calls him "most excellent Theophilus" indicating he is an individual of some official dignity perhaps from Rome or Greece (see Acts 23:26; 24:3; 26:25).

📖 Now reread Acts 1:1–3 and write what you learn of Jesus' focus with the disciples after the resurrection.

_____

_____

_____

_____

Acts 1:1–3 relates the forty-day period of Christ's post-resurrection appearances, and lets us know some of what this time is like for the disciples. A primary focus is proving His resurrection from the dead *"by many convincing proofs."* Much of His conversations with the disciples in these days regards giving orders to the apostles and speaking *"things concerning the kingdom of God."*

DID YOU KNOW?
Many Convincing Proofs

In the forty days following the resurrection, Jesus makes many appearances to prove that He is indeed risen. In 1 Corinthians 15:5–8 Paul gives us a summary of those appearances. *"He appeared to Cephas, then to the twelve. After that He appeared to more than five hundred brethren at one time, most of whom remain until now, but some have fallen asleep; then He appeared to James, then to all the apostles; and last of all, as to one untimely born, He appeared to me also."*

📖 Reflect on Acts 1:4-8 and answer the questions that follow.

What does Jesus command the disciples to do (1:4)?

_____

What does He say will soon happen (1:5)?

_____

What will be the results of being "baptized with the Holy Spirit" (1:8)?

_____

_____

Just before He ascends to heaven, Jesus commands the disciples to not leave Jerusalem, but to wait for the promised Holy Spirit, which they have been hearing of ever since the ministry of John the Baptist. Jesus tells them they will be *"baptized"* with the Spirit, and that it will happen soon. As proof of the Spirit baptizing them, they will receive power and be witnesses of Christ in an ever-expanding circle to the ends of the earth.

In Acts 1:6–7 the disciples ask an interesting question of Jesus: *"Is this the time of the kingdom?"* We can understand why they ask this. Before His death and resurrection, Jesus had been teaching them about the kingdom. I imagine they are a bit frustrated with His answer though. He basically tells them, "when my kingdom comes is not yours to know." In other words, your focus doesn't need to be on the benefits you will enjoy in the kingdom, but rather, on getting as many people into the kingdom as you can. Like the early apostles, we tend to think in terms of self, while Christ thinks in terms of the whole world.

📖 Look at Acts 1:9–11.

What do we learn here about the ascension?

_____

_____

_____

What promise is given for the future?

_____

_____

It is difficult to really visualize what this scene must have been like or all that goes through the disciples' minds. After giving them instruction, Jesus is *"lifted up."* One imagines that perhaps He gradually begins to float away like a released balloon, until He disappears in a cloud. In a special act of encouragement, God sends what appears to be two angels to help them absorb the event. These messengers offer the promise that Jesus will one day come back in the same way He has just left.

What do the disciples know at this point? They have had three years of instruction at the feet of Jesus. They know much of the ways of God. They know Jesus is alive, yet in heaven now. They know the kingdom of God is coming and Jesus will return. They also have a clear sense of what they are to be about until those things take place. They are to wait on God to give them power by His Spirit and then speak of God to all who will listen. In a practical sense, this is what the Book of Acts is all about.

 DOCTRINE
Jesus' Return

There are two parts to Jesus' return: the "rapture"—when He meets believers in the clouds (see 1 Thessalonians 4:13–18), and the "second coming"—when He returns to earth to make war with the Anti-Christ and unbelievers (see Revelation 19:11–19). Some Christians see these events as occurring simultaneously, while others believe the two parts will be separated by a period of up to seven years.

DAY 2

PATIENCE FOR GOD'S MOVING IN THE FUTURE (ACTS 1:4, 12–13)

I cannot imagine what it would be like to be one of the apostles at this point. I don't think any of us can fully appreciate what a traumatic few weeks this has been for these followers of Jesus. In less than two months they have gone from the triumphal entry of Jesus into Jerusalem, to the devastation of the cross, and then the glorious hope of the resurrection. As if that is not enough to have their minds reeling, after only forty days of resurrection glory and hope, Jesus leaves them again. They would not be human if this emotional roller-coaster leaves them calm and unchanged. They cannot possibly grasp the full impact of what awaits them at Pentecost, yet they do have a clear sense of what they are to do. As we will see today, they do as they are told. There is good wisdom in that. Regardless of what you do not know, make sure you do what you know to do.

> *"Gathering them together, He commanded them not to leave*
> *Jerusalem, but to wait for what the Father had promised..."*
>
> —Acts 1:4a

📖 Review Acts 1:4. What exactly does Jesus command the disciples to do and not to do?

_____

_____

Jesus' words to the disciples before His ascension are not vague or ambiguous. He says to wait! He commands them to stay put. "Don't leave Jerusalem—just wait!" He also reminds them of what they are waiting for—the promise they first learned of by the shores of the Jordan River from the lips of John the Baptist. His promise is about to be realized. They are going to be *"baptized with the Holy Spirit."* They are about to enter into a new way of relating to God, and all they have to do is be patient. It is frustrating how often that word "wait" appears in Scripture, but there is much spirituality woven into this simple term.

📖 Read Acts 1:12–13 and compare this with what Jesus commands the disciples to do in 1:4.

How do the disciples do at obeying Jesus' command?

_____

_____

How many of the disciples are obedient?

_____

_____

Jesus has clearly communicated His will to the disciples, and it is obvious that they do what He asks. They go directly to Jerusalem and wait. A quick count of the names listed in verse 13 shows us that all of Jesus' disciples, except for Judas Iscariot, are gathered together to wait on what Jesus promised. There is a powerful and practical lesson for us in the disciple's simple act of obedience. Blessing comes on the heels of obeying what God tells us to do.

📖 Compare Acts 1:1–13 with Luke's account of the ascension in his Gospel (Luke 24:50–53) and write down any additional details you find.

_____

_____

_____

_____

We learn from Luke's other book that just before His ascension, Jesus "blesses" the disciples and then parts from them. Luke tells us in his Gospel something of the disciples' attitude. He states, _"And they returned to Jerusalem with great joy."_ It may not seem like a big deal, but after all they have been through, joy is not something to be taken for granted. We also learn in Luke 24:53 that one of the activities they engage in during this period of waiting is in spending time at the temple worshiping God. There is another important lesson for us here. When you are waiting on God, make sure you are spending time with Him and worshiping Him.

In America, convenience is king. When we want instant breakfast, we just add milk. Dinner goes from the freezer to the microwave to the table in less than ten minutes. When we need instant cash, we have automated teller machines available twenty-four hours a day—and when we do not have cash saved up, we use credit. If we want a letter to go overnight, we send it via overnight delivery, and if that isn't fast enough, we fax, email, or text it. From coast-to-coast jet travel to quick-dry nail polish, there is little in our culture that cultivates patience. Yet God quite often calls us to wait as He called His disciples to wait in Acts 1. They waited—will we?

DAY THREE

PRAYING FOR GOD'S MOVING IN THE FUTURE (ACTS 1:13–15)

Waiting is never easy. As children, we all experienced the delightful but frustrating period of waiting to open presents as Christmas Day approached. We longed for our expected presents, but could do nothing to make them come any faster. But waiting is not something we outgrow as we approach adulthood. We wait for a mate. We wait for children to come and then for them to grow up and move out on their own. We wait for grandchildren and retirement. When you think about it, a lot of life is spent waiting. But waiting is not something we do until life happens—it is part of life. I believe God has purpose in the waiting. There is something in waiting that draws our eyes to Him where they should be. This was true for the disciples, and it is true for us. What should you do while you are waiting for God to move? Is waiting an invitation to passivity? I do not think so. Waiting on the Lord should be an active thing. It should motivate us in what we choose _not_ to do. And it should focus us in making sure we are seeking God and staying sensitive to Him.

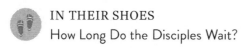

IN THEIR SHOES

How Long Do the Disciples Wait?

The period of waiting for the disciples is ten days. We know this from the fact that Jesus' ascension is forty days after His resurrection (Acts 1:3), and they wait until Pentecost. The term "Pentecost" means "fiftieth part." It is a significant Jewish feast that always falls fifty days after the Feast of First Fruits, which takes place on the day after the Sabbath following Passover (Resurrection Sunday).

📖 Look at Acts 1:13 and Luke 24:53. Where do the disciples spend their time during the period from the ascension to Pentecost?

_____

_____

Acts tells us they are lodging and meeting in "the upper room." Since the Greek word here appears with what is called the "definite article," it is rightly translated as "the upper room" (a certain specific room) instead of "an upper room." Many take this to mean it is the same upper room where Jesus observed the last supper with His disciples. It must be a large room since we find 120 persons gathered here at one point (Acts 1:15).

According to Luke 24, they also are "continually" at the temple. Perhaps that is where they spend most of their daytime hours. We do know that the temple hosts a regular time of prayer at the ninth hour which is about 3 p.m (Acts 3:1). One would expect from the context of Acts 1 that prayer features prominently in their temple times.

📖 Reflect on Acts 1:14 and write down your observations.

_____

_____

_____

The first phrase that grabs our attention in this verse is that they are functioning "with one mind." There is a unity of purpose and focus here. All are actively participating and wholeheartedly committed to this activity. The most prominent observation we receive from this verse is that the disciples are "continually devoting themselves" to prayer. This is a strong expression, denoting persistence in prayer. The disciples are joined in this activity by a group of women, including Jesus' mother and also by Jesus' brothers who apparently are now believers.

📖 Read over Acts 1:15.

Name the significance of believers meeting together in this context?

_____

_____

How does gathering with others relate to waiting on God?

Several logs in a fire burn brightly when they are close together, but if you take one of those logs out and place it on the hearth, the fire quickly goes out. As Christians, we need each other. We need the encouragement of being with each other. We draw fire from each other's faith. Apparently, the early believers recognized this. Equally important, they probably wanted to be together. The same ought to be true of us today.

IN THEIR SHOES
The Power of Prayer

One cannot separate the incredible evangelistic response at Pentecost from the ten days the disciples devote to prayer. They pray for ten days, Peter preaches for ten minutes, and three thousand souls are saved. Today, we pray for ten minutes, preach for ten days, have a few souls saved, and we think "It's Pentecost all over again!"

As you reflect on this continual devotion to prayer, for what do you think they are praying?

Obviously, as we see the disciples waiting upon the Lord, none of us knows for certain the content of these early prayers. Are they praying for the Spirit to come? Perhaps, but we cannot say for certain. Jesus has already promised that the Spirit will come and baptize them. We know from Luke 24:53 that some of their praying is simply devoted to praising God. Prayer is not asking God for stuff all the time. I suspect that much of what they pray comes from hearts that want to communicate with and be connected with Jesus. For three years they talked with Him. Now that they are physically separated because He has ascended to heaven, prayer is their only means of communicating with Him. They may be praying for Christ to return soon and usher in God's kingdom, and perhaps they are praying they would remain faithful while waiting for this kingdom to come.

First Thessalonians 5:17 exhorts us to *"Pray without ceasing."* This doesn't mean that we skip work to go to a prayer meeting, or that our heads are always bowed with our eyes closed and our hands folded. What it means is that life is to be lived in constant communion and communication with the Lord. We should talk with Him about everything as we walk through our day. Praying is an "always" activity, but it takes on a special significance when we are waiting on God. It keeps us sensitive to anything He might call us to do.

DAY FOUR

PREPARING FOR GOD'S MOVING IN THE FUTURE (ACTS 1:15–26)

There is an important order to our text here that should not be missed. It may not be obvious, but I believe it is significant. First, the disciples pray, and then they act. Action that is born in prayer is usually in response to God. It is in talking with God that we get our directions for life. We don't always know what we need to do tomorrow, but God is faithful to show us what to do today. Often the process of hearing God is hindered by our inactivity on what He has already said. Years ago, when my wife was going through a life-threatening battle with cancer, we had the opportunity to hear Elizabeth Elliot speak. While I couldn't tell you what her topic was that day, I can still remember one declaration she made that ministered then and continues to minister. In matter-of-fact simplicity she stated, "When you don't know what to do, do the next thing." If you think about it, there is a profound truth hidden in this honest proverb. We don't always know *all* that we are to do, but there is usually something we know to do that is as yet undone. Sometimes it is doing what we know to do that leads us to the knowledge of what to do after that. The disciples begin the ten days from the ascension to Pentecost by praying. That is all they know to do. Somewhere in the midst of their praying they are reminded of Old Testament prophetic scripture concerning Judas that shows them one other thing they can do. As we wait for God to move, we need to be ever vigilant and sensitive to anything we are to do that is undone.

📖 Contemplate what you read in Acts 1:15–19 and write down your observations on Peter's comments concerning Judas.

....

....

....

> *"When you don't know what to do, do the next thing."*
>
> —Elizabeth Elliot

In the midst of this gathering of Christ's followers, Peter offers some commentary on the missing disciple. Perhaps someone in the group asks a question, or in a spirit of prayer a truth leaps out from scripture Peter is meditating on or reading. In any case, Peter explains to all that David had foretold Judas' treachery centuries earlier. Speaking of Judas, what a life of wasted opportunity! Christ had given Judas three years of personal discipleship, but he failed to make proper use of this incredible benefit. The paranthetical statements of verses 18 and 19 (most likely added to fill in some specific details for Theophilus) underscore the tragic end of a wasted life.

📖 Look at Acts 1:20–22. How does God reveal to the disciples what they need to do next?

_____

_____

_____

_____

Bible study is always most fruitful when in the context of prayer. As they are *"continually devoting themselves"* to prayer, God quickly places some scripture in their minds. The prophecy of David mentioned in verse 16 probably comes from either Psalm 41:9 or 55:12–15. The references from Psalms made in verse 20 come from Psalm 69:25 and 109:8. All these prophecies occur in contexts making reference to the Messiah's death, and the last one indicates something that has not yet been done—the replacement of Judas. Prompted by the Lord, Peter shares the need with the gathered crowd to identify other followers of Jesus the Lord could have to take Judas' place as *"a witness with us of His resurrection."*

📖 Read Acts 1:23–26. How do the disciples determine Judas' replacement?

_____

_____

_____

The disciples follow a three-step process in identifying who the Lord wants to fill Judas' ministry. First, they put forward criteria for who can be called an apostle. He must have accompanied Jesus and the disciples from the beginning of His public ministry. In addition, he must have seen the resurrected Christ. Whether the two names put forward are the only men who meet these criteria or the two who meet them best is uncertain, but Barsabbas and Matthias are put forward as candidates. Second, they pray for wisdom and direction from the Lord. Third, they draw lots, trusting God to be in the outcome.

DID YOU KNOW?
Judas' Death

Here in Acts, Luke tells us that Judas fell headlong, and *"he burst open in the middle and all his bowels gushed out."* Matthew 27:5 tells us Judas *"hanged himself."* Luke is not contradicting Matthew but adding other details. Apparently either the rope broke, or the bursting open occurred when his dead, swollen body was cut down.

Theologians often debate whether Matthias being chosen as Judas' replacement is the correct approach. Some argue that Paul is God's choice. Yet there is nothing in this passage to support such a view or to suggest that the disciples are in error. It should be remembered that the twelve have a ministry primarily to the Jews, while Paul's assigned mission is as an apostle to the Gentiles. Though the casting of lots may not sound trustworthy to us, it is not without biblical precedent (see Proverbs 16:33 and Jonah 1:7). This is a unique time. They do not have Jesus' physical presence to assist, and the Holy Spirit has not yet been given. While we may tend to emphasize the casting of lots in the decision, the context places the emphasis on prayer that leads to obedience.

DAY 5

FOR ME TO FOLLOW GOD

The world is about to change forever. Something new and significant—the church—is about to be born. For each of these followers of Jesus, life will never be the same. But first they have to wait. Sooner or later, every one of us finds ourselves in the place of waiting. What we do there (and don't do) is very important. What are you waiting for? Perhaps you are waiting for that special someone to come along. Or it may be that you are waiting for revival in your church or your town or your world. Or perhaps you are waiting for such a change in your spouse or your children. Maybe you wait for God's provision for some need. Possibly you wait for a change in your job situation, or it could be you wait for a change in you. Maybe God has made you passionate about your waiting for our Lord's return—all of us should be! What do we do while we wait? How do we manage the process and ourselves? The ten days between the ascension of Jesus and the Day of Pentecost represent "wait training" for the disciples. In their lives and circumstance there is much to learn that applies to us today. Let's consider how.

Are you experiencing a season of waiting right now?

What makes this time a challenge for you?

Often in the middle of coping with life's challenges and all the busy activities people are doing, we never stop to ask, "But what is God doing?"

As we consider the disciple's "wait training" and seek ways to apply their lessons to our lives, it is important to have something specific to which we can apply these truths. As we look at the disciples' experience, they begin by pondering God's moving in the present.

They reflect on it. They ask Him questions and try to understand what is taking place. This is an easy step to miss. Often in the middle of coping with life's challenges and all the busy activities people are doing, we never stop to ask, "But what is God doing?"

Take some time to reflect on what is going on in your life right now. What do you think God is doing?

You may not be able to answer this question right away, but it is important to ask it. Often, we completely miss the fact that God is using the challenges and difficulties we face to shape our character. If we miss what God is doing, we may miss what He wants to do in us.

An important part of "wait training" for the disciples is focused prayer. They are "continually devoting" themselves to seeking the Lord. This unseen activity makes such a difference in our situations. How will we know what we are to do—or what God is doing—without talking with Him? Prayer ought to be an unending conversation we have with the Lord. As you consider your own relationship with the Lord, how would you rate your prayer life?

On the scale below, place a circle over your perceived general status in this area of prayer. Then go back and place a square on where you perceive yourself to be in praying about specific areas of waiting in your life. Try to be as honest and realistic as you can.

Not Praying At All ← 1 — 2 — 3 — 4 — 5 — 6 — 7 → Continually Devoted To Prayer

Now, before you start beating yourself up over where you are, realize that none of us are ever completely satisfied with our prayer life. There is always room for improvement, and that comes as we grow and mature as Christians. But are we making an effort?

There are several principles in scripture to help us be more devoted to prayer. One practical lesson we glean from Acts 1 is that it is easier to be devoted to prayer with others than to pray alone. These disciples pray together. Get connected with a prayer meeting or prayer chain at your church if they are available. Or perhaps you can ask another believer to join you as a prayer partner. Another way scripture shows us how we can be focused in prayer is through fasting. When we fast, our own bodies work to remind us to pray. Each time we feel hunger, we remember why, and we pray again. If you have never fasted before, maybe a good place to start is skipping lunch. Throughout the day as you feel hungry, pray. Scripture models different kinds of fasts for different lengths of time. The longest period of fasting—seen through Elijah, Moses, and Jesus—is the forty-day fast. Daniel fasts from meat for a time. Paul suggests that couples can sometimes fast from sex to be devoted to prayer. Maybe you need to fast from television or music, or mobile devices and technology. Fasting is just a tool. It is meant to serve us, not the other way around. Another way to keep devoted to prayer is to keep a prayer journal. On one side, record requests, and on the other side, record answers. Another tool is to have a specific time set aside to pray. One creative believer came up with the idea of setting the beeper on his watch to go off on the hour and uses that as a reminder to pray. Consider the list below and check an area where you would like to act.

- Join a prayer group or prayer chain

- Attend a church prayer meeting

- Fast

    type of fast _____

    time of fast _____

- Start keeping a prayer journal

- Set aside a specific time to pray

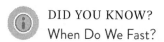 DID YOU KNOW?
When Do We Fast?

In Scripture, fasting is usually associated with either times of great distress, or great longing to hear from God (or both). The act of fasting is a sign of humility before God. It doesn't twist the arm of God, but rather, makes us more focused on seeking Him and more sensitive to what He is saying.

Another principle we glean from the experience of the disciples before Pentecost is this: as we are waiting and praying, we must be ready to do whatever the Lord shows us has been left undone. Lack of obedience to God's present direction often creates a log-jam, holding back revelation of other things that we are to do.

As you wait and pray, is there anything the Lord brings to mind that you haven't done yet?

You don't need to become anxious about this—you just need to make sure you have a willing heart. If you have decided you want to do whatever the Lord has for you to do, He will move heaven and earth to make sure you know what that is. Stay in the Word regularly and listen for Him to speak to your heart. Most importantly, when God has you waiting, resist the temptation to run off in your own direction. Jesus makes it clear to the disciples that they need to stay put. Painful mistakes often come when we start doing what God hasn't initiated because we don't see Him working. Like a water faucet, God wants us to run when He moves the handle (and only then).

As you reflect on this week's lesson, why not close it out by writing out a prayer to the Lord about your own "wait training"

NOTES

LESSON 2

POWER FROM ON HIGH

ACTS 2:1-47

How do you change the world? How do you bring about revolution? How do you change society? The world's answer to those questions is very different than the way God chooses to answer them. The world sees power externally. If you want to bring about change, you must have political or military power (or both). You need the best educated, wealthiest, and most influential people you can possibly gather. You have to be able to force people to your way of thinking. Yet though this approach may be effective in changing behavior for a time, it doesn't really change people. The only way to do that is not by force from the outside but by transformation from within. That is why the Law cannot make a man righteous, because it operates externally. But Pentecost introduces a new and different law—one written on human hearts instead of tablets of stone.

The church of Jesus Christ is born at Pentecost, and within a few centuries it dominates the globe. It has none of the components that we think are so essential for success today. It has no buildings, no financial backing, no political influence, no prestige, and no military might. Its leaders are uneducated blue-collar workers—fishermen for the most part. They come not from the political establishment of Rome, nor the intellectual elite of Greece, nor the religious hierarchy of Jerusalem, but from the common people of Palestine. Yet they are referred to as *"these men who have turned the world upside down"* (Acts 17:6, ESV). At the time of Christ, Julius Caesar, Caesar Augustus, and Tiberius are the names on everyone's lips. No one had yet heard of Peter or Paul. Fast-forward two millennia later, and the date on our calendar is given in reference to Christ, the head of the Church, not Julius Caesar. The world is different because of Jesus and His followers.

> *The power of Pentecost completely changes the disciples. Instead of men in hiding, they become "these men who have turned the world upside down" (Acts 17:6, ESV)*

It takes a lot of power to change the world. That is what Pentecost is all about. Only the resurrected Christ and the indwelling Spirit of God can explain the alteration of this motley crew of people into world-changers. After the crucifixion, they are cowering, timid souls who run from their own shadow. After Pentecost they boldly stand firm before kings and persecution and perform miraculous deeds. What can explain this remarkable transformation? Only God. These disciples bear the marks of heaven. They are endowed with power from on high. They are indwelt by God Himself.

A glove cannot play the piano. It can be laid on the keys, but it cannot strike a note. It is incapable of producing a single chord. It has no power to play. Yet when the hand of a master musician is inside the glove it is a different story. The skills of the master bring life to the inanimate glove. Suddenly sound is possible. Rhythms of beauty and grace can flow from within the piano. This is what happens at Pentecost. People become different with the life of the Master in them. This is what changed the world two thousand years ago, and it is the only mechanism that will change the world today. Humanity is not at all impressed with what we do for God. Every religion boasts devout followers willing to make great sacrifices. But the world stops and takes notice when God does through us what we could never do on our own. When the life of God is in us, we become different— we become noticeable. They see the reality of Him as He expresses Himself in us. This is what happens at Pentecost, and is what is possible for every follower of Jesus since then.

DAY 1

THE POURING OUT OF THE SPIRIT (ACTS 2:1–13)

Where is the Holy Spirit before Pentecost? Does He exist? Does He do anything at all, or is He just a spectator on the sidelines? As we consider the pouring out of the Spirit on the early church, it is important that we start with a biblical understanding of *pneumatology*, the doctrine of the Holy Spirit. The Spirit of God is not an "it" but a "Him." He is the third member of the trinity, and as such is just as much God as Jesus or the Father. He is first mentioned in Genesis 1:2 as *"moving over the surface of the waters."* In the Old Testament, before the work of the cross, He did not indwell believers. Rather, He *"came upon"* certain individuals temporarily (such as kings or prophets) to perform God's work. We see recorded in Judges that the Spirit of the Lord *"came upon"* people like Gideon (Judges 6:34) or Samson (Judges 15:14), and this wording is always associated with power from God for serving the Lord. In 1 Samuel 16:14 we have a record that the Spirit of the Lord *"departed"* from Saul, and in Psalm 51:11 David prays, *"do not take Your Holy Spirit from me."* Before the redemptive work of Jesus, no one is permanently indwelt by the Spirit. But here at Pentecost, all that is about to change.

📖 Read Acts 2:1–4 and identify what happens and the three signs that accompany the Spirit's coming.

....

....

....

We see here that the Spirit comes *"suddenly"* on the day of Pentecost, as the believers are all gathered together. His appearing is accompanied by three dramatic signs. First, there is a noise *"like a violent, rushing wind"* that fills the whole house where they are gathered. They do not *feel* a wind, but rather, *hear* a sound like a wind. Second, *"tongues of fire"* appear over each of them. Third, the Spirit gives the supernatural ability for the believers to speak in languages they have not learned.

 DID YOU KNOW?
Tongues of Fire

In the Old Testament, one of the evidences of the presence of God in His tabernacle or temple is a pillar of fire. At Pentecost, the temple of God ceased to be a building and became the human heart (1 Corinthians 6:19). It may be that these "tongues of fire" that appear over each believer are actually mini-pillars of fire communicating this change.

The text is uncertain as to exactly where the believers are gathered. Clearly at some point they are in a public place—probably at the Temple—as the manifestation of the Spirit is witnessed by the crowds. Verse 2 mentions that the *"whole house"* where they are sitting is filled. It may be that they are still at the upper room, but another possibility is that they are at the temple. The Greek word translated house is also used of the temple in Acts 7:47. Though it could be that they start at the upper room and then end up in a public place, it seems more likely that they are already at the temple when the Spirit is poured out because of the large, diverse crowd that gathers.

Consider Acts 2:5–8 and record all that you learn about the crowd who witnesses the Spirit's advent.

The first and perhaps most significant description of those who witness the Spirit's coming is that they are *"devout men."* These are Jews who are sincere and serious about their worship of God. No doubt, they are at the temple to observe the feast of Pentecost. We are told that *"every nation under heaven"* is represented in the city, though this is probably an idiomatic statement with some measure of hyperbole. The main point is that many different nations are represented. When the noise of the event is heard, the crowd gathers, and their curiosity quickly turns to amazement as they hear each language represented being spoken by the believers here. This is even more surprising considering that the believers are Galileans. This must shock the sophisticated city-dwellers of Jerusalem, as Galilee is a rural area populated for the most part by uneducated "blue-collar" workers.

📖 Scan through Acts 2:9–11a. Count up the number of countries represented and look them up on a Bible map to see where they are located.

 DID YOU KNOW?
The Feasts of Israel

Pentecost is the last of the three main annual feasts of the Jews (see Leviticus 23)—which together offer an outline of the work of Christ. Passover reflects Christ's death as the "Lamb of God" (John 1:29). The Feast of First Fruits foreshadows His resurrection as the "first fruits from the dead" (1 Corinthians 15:20). Pentecost, celebrating the wheat harvest, gives a preview of the formation of the church and the harvest of souls (Exodus 23:16).

From the list we are given here, at least sixteen regions are represented by the crowd that gathers to see what is going on at Pentecost. As you look these countries and areas up on a map you find that they make a circuit around the Mediterranean Sea. Though it doesn't appear that the whole globe is represented, most of the known world is. The Parthians are from the region of modern Iran. The Medes are a sub-region of the Parthian Empire. The Elamites live in what is now the southwestern portion of Iran. The *"residents of Mesopotamia"* make their home in the area between the Tigris and Euphrates rivers (the word "Mesopotamia" means "between the rivers"). Judea is an area within Palestine, while Cappadocia, Pontus, Asia, Phrygia, and Pamphylia are part of what is called "Asia Minor"—the region around modern Turkey. Egypt is self-explanatory, as is Libya, and Cyrene is a neighboring region in North Africa. Rome is part of modern Italy, and Cretans are inhabitants of the Mediterranean island of Crete. Finally, Arabs most likely refers to "Nabatean Arabs" in the region below Damascus.

📖 Reflect on Acts 2:11–13.

What does the gathered crowd hear?

What is their response to the activities of the believers?

It doesn't matter where you are from, someone is speaking in your language, which, as we said before, is quite surprising. The content of their speech is also significant. They are *"speaking of the mighty deeds of God."* It is clear that witnesses of this event are awestruck. Some are trying to interpret what is going on, while others are cynical and mock the proceedings.

Though there ends up being a huge response to the gospel at Pentecost, clearly not all respond positively. As we progress through the book of Acts, we will find a similar division in most of the crowds exposed to the gospel. Not all soil that receives the seed of the Word proves to be fertile ground.

LESSON TWO – DAY 2

THE PREACHING OF THE GOSPEL (ACTS 2:14–36)

Pentecost is one of the most significant days in spiritual history, and certainly in the history of the church. The Holy Spirit comes in a new and unique way. For the first time in history, followers of God are permanently indwelt by God Himself. There is much debate over the years about the role and ministry of the Holy Spirit. Some circles within Christianity elevate the Holy Spirit above Jesus and beyond what Scripture teaches. John 16:14 makes it clear that it is the goal of the Spirit to *"glorify"* Christ. Yet other churches, perhaps reacting to excessive teaching on the Spirit, swing the pendulum in the opposite direction and don't teach about the Spirit at all. One of the benefits of studying the book of Acts is that we learn so much about the Holy Spirit. In fact, other than John 14–16, Acts is one of the richest sources of teaching on the Spirit of God. One of the questions that arise with *pneumatology*—the doctrine of the Holy Spirit—is "what is the evidence of one being Spirit-filled?" We see this week, that an immediate consequence is that the believers speak in tongues—languages they have not learned. Is that the proof of being Spirit-filled? What we will see today is that one of the first results of the Spirit's advent is preaching the gospel. In fact, when this first group of Spirit-filled believers speaks in tongues, what are they saying? They are *"speaking of the mighty deeds of God"* (Acts 2:11). What does Jesus say will be the evidences of being Spirit-filled? *"You shall receive power,"* and *"...you shall be My witnesses"* (Acts 1:8). What we see from the apostle Peter, showing that he is filled with the Spirit, is someone witnessing with power.

> *"But you will receive power when the Holy Spirit has come upon you; and you shall be My witnesses both in Jerusalem, and in all Judea and Samaria, and even to the remotest part of the earth"*
> (Acts 1:8)

📖 Read Acts 2:14–36 and summarize the main points of Peter's sermon.

_____

_____

_____

What a change we see in Peter! Before the crucifixion, Peter cowers in fear. He denies Jesus three times; once to a slave girl who could not have been much of a threat. Yet here at Pentecost we see him boldly proclaiming Jesus to a crowd of thousands. How do we explain this remarkable change? First, we know that Jesus graciously picked Peter up and dusted him off after his failure. Second, his transformation is indicative of what Jesus says will happen to the disciples when the Spirit comes upon them. He is witnessing in power. The main points Peter makes are these:

First, he explains the Spirit's coming as fulfilling the prophecy of Joel.

Second, he makes his case that Jesus is the Messiah.

Third, he makes it clear that the Jews are guilty of Jesus' death .

 Look back over Acts 2:17–21.

What parts of this prophecy are fulfilled on the day of Pentecost?

_____

_____

What parts of the prophecy are not immediately fulfilled?

_____

_____

How does the message of verse 21 fit with the events of Pentecost?

_____

_____

DID YOU KNOW?
Drunk with Wine?

Some of the witnesses of Pentecost accuse the believers of being "full of sweet wine." In Ephesians 5:18 Paul contrasts being drunk on wine with being filled with the Spirit. In both cases the person is being influenced by an outside agent. With both, it is initiated by an act of the will, and both are results of the outside agent's work on the inside. With wine, it is alcohol released from the stomach into the bloodstream and brain. With filling, it is the already present Spirit released into all parts of the heart. Both result in altered personalities consistent with the altering agent.

Peter's quoting of this prophecy from the book of Joel is in response to some of the crowd's mocking him at Pentecost. We learned in Acts 2:13 that some of the Jews who congregate here are scoffing and suggesting that the believers are drunk. Peter makes it clear they are not full of wine, but full of the Spirit, just as Joel prophesied. The pouring out of the Spirit (Acts 2:17–18) is an immediate fulfillment of Joel's prophecy, but other portions of the prophecy have yet to be fulfilled. The wonders in the sky and the signs on earth (Acts 2:19–20) clearly point to events associated with Christ's second coming, not His first. The sun being darkened and the moon turning to blood are also mentioned in Revelation 6:12 as occurring just before Christ returns. Joel's reference to salvation being available to all who call upon the name of the Lord seems to point to the harvest of souls that begins at Pentecost.

📖 Examine Acts 2:23.

What is the human role in the death of Christ?

What is God's part?

Peter makes it clear that although the Jews are guilty of killing the Messiah, none of this catches God by surprise. You nailed Jesus to a cross and *"put Him to death,"* Peter accuses. But he also makes it clear that this is all according to the *"predetermined plan and foreknowledge of God."* God has proven Jesus' identity with *"miracles and wonders"* (Acts 2:22) and by raising Him from the dead (Acts 2:24). Peter reminds them of what they have witnessed because he is getting ready to tell them what they need to do about their guilt.

📖 Reflect on Peter's quote from Psalm 16:8–11 (Acts 2:25–28) and the explanation that follows (Acts 2:29–32). What is Peter's point here?

First of all, Peter's quote from the Psalms serves to prove that the resurrection of Jesus is a matter of prophecy. God already told through David what He is going to do. Second, Peter seems to be making the point that since David is speaking of the Messiah (Acts 2:31) and Jesus is resurrected (Acts 2:32) then this proves that Jesus is the Messiah.

Peter wraps up his sermon by indicating that Jesus is behind the pouring out of God's Spirit, which has just been witnessed (Acts 2:33) and makes it doubly clear that David does not speak of himself, but of his Lord. Peter concludes his address to the Jews, by instructing them that Jesus is the Christ, and reminding them that they crucified Him.

Although the Romans actually performed the crucifixion, remember, it is the Jews who rejected Pilate's offer to set Him free and instead cried out, "crucify Him!" (Luke 23:21).

Day 3

The Produce of the Sermon (Acts 2:37-41)

Have you ever wondered why we hear a sermon each time we go to church? The answer is simple—because from its very beginning, the church was founded on the proclamation of truth. This sermon by the apostle Peter is one of the first events to take place as the church is born. In Peter's words we have a model of what preaching ought to be. It instructs us in truth, it explains the Word of God, and most of all, it calls us to respond. That ought to happen every time God's people gather. The evidence of the work of the Spirit is that hearts are moved. It is not Peter's persuasiveness that cuts them to the quick but the Holy Spirit's convicting work. Remember, these who gather to witness the unusual events of Pentecost are *"devout men"*—Jews who are serious about their faith. God honors their hearts by bringing them truth, and as we will see today, they honor God by responding to that truth.

From its very beginning the church is founded on the proclamation of truth. One of the first happenings when the church is born is this sermon by the Apostle Peter.

📖 Look at Acts 2:37. How do the people react to Peter's sermon?

Notice what happens when Peter preaches in the power of the Spirit. When the multitudes hear his sermon they are, *"pierced to the heart."* Peter preaches to their minds, but the Spirit drives it into their hearts. That is the difference between preaching in the power of the Spirit and preaching in our own strength. A human agent can persuade the mind, but only God can change the heart. Paul writes in 1 Corinthians 2:4-5, *"And my message and my preaching were not in persuasive words of wisdom, but in demonstration of the Spirit and of power, that your faith should not rest on the wisdom of men, but on the power of God."* Clearly, we see this modeled in Peter. When he finishes speaking, the crowd is pierced to the heart and asks, *"Brethren, what shall we do?"* Every good sermon ought to bring us to that point.

"And my message and my preaching were not in persuasive words of wisdom, but in demonstration of the Spirit and of power, that your faith should not rest on the wisdom of men, but on the power of God" (1 Corinthians 2:4-5)

📖 Consider Acts 2:38. What instruction does Peter give to the people in telling them what they need to do?

_____

_____

_____

Peter provides his audience with four basic application points. First, they must repent. The word "repent" involves "a change of mind leading to a change of direction." Specifically, he is calling them in this verse to change their minds about Jesus and to acknowledge Him as the Messiah. The Greek verb here is plural, indicating it is an invitation to all. Next, he says *"let each of you be baptized in the name of Jesus."* Here the Greek verb is singular, making the distinction that although the call is a corporate invitation, we must each respond individually. Peter's audience will not be saved as a nation but as individuals.

It should be noted that many emphasize the act of baptism here in Peter's instruction when the emphasis should be placed on the principle behind it. The word "baptize" really means "identification." Culturally, in Peter's day it is used of dipping a piece of cloth into a vat of dye. Afterward, the cloth takes on a new identity—the color of the dye. What Peter is saying is that we are to repent and identify with Jesus as Christ and Lord. Peter clarifies in his first epistle what true baptism is (perhaps in response to questions raised over the years from his words at Pentecost): *"Corresponding to that, baptism now saves you—not the removal of dirt from the flesh, but an appeal to God for a good conscience— through the resurrection of Jesus Christ"* (1 Peter 3:21). In other words, it isn't the physical act of getting wet that saves us, but the spiritual act of dying to our old thinking—through repentance and being rebirthed by the work of resurrection.

📖 Read Acts 2:39–40 and answer the questions that follow.

To whom is the invitation of salvation made?

_____

_____

What does verse 40 reveal of Peter's heart?

_____

_____

Peter clarifies in Acts 2:39 that the offering of salvation is not for Jews only. It is for the immediate audience, but also for their children (implying future generations), and for "_ALL_ who are far off" (emphasis mine). Though the audience may not understand it at the time, and perhaps Peter himself doesn't fully understand, we see from the rest of

Acts that this includes the Gentiles as well. Certainly, that is what Christ indicates when He speaks of the gospel going to *"the remotest part of the earth"* (Acts 1:8). Salvation is not simply for the privileged, but is for *"as many as the Lord our God will call to Himself."* Clearly this passion is burning in Peter's heart through the indwelling Spirit, for he keeps entreating them to be saved.

📖 Look over Acts 2:41 and identify how many respond to Peter's invitation and how they respond.

As amazing as it may seem to us today when we compare his results with ours, about three thousand people embrace salvation through Christ in this one day. Notice how they respond. First, they *"receive"* his word. They also act publicly on that word. They are baptized in the pools near the temple, publicly identifying themselves with Christ and His followers.

WORD STUDY
Received

Luke tells us that many in the audience of Pentecost "received" Peter's word. This terminology means more than that they simply hear him. They welcome Peter's words into their heart and embrace them. The Greek word translated "received" means "to take eagerly, to receive kindly or hospitably, to embrace heartily."

What an incredible response! Imagine if your church grew by three thousand people in one day! While such response is not always the case even in Acts, it does show us that when we are Spirit-filled and share Christ, He does work in people's hearts. Truly we see at Pentecost the beginning of fulfillment of what Jesus says will happen when the Holy Spirit comes upon them—receiving power and being witnesses (Acts 1:8).

DAY 4

THE PRIORITIES OF THE CHURCH (ACTS 2:42–47)

Most everyone would say that nutrition is important, but it doesn't always work out that way in practice. If you have ever gone grocery shopping on an empty stomach and without a list, you can appreciate the tension between what we say our priorities are and how we really live. On an empty stomach everything that tastes good looks good, and before you know it your shopping cart is filled with too much junk and not enough nutrition. When you get to the cashier, it is a rude awakening to learn the cost of unplanned purchases. The worst part may not be the cost, but explaining to your spouse how you spent so much money and still didn't get what the family needed. This could be helped by a well-defined grocery list, but even with it we must still make the choice to stick to it.

According to *Webster's Dictionary*, a priority is something that we give precedence by assigning a degree of urgency or importance to it. The possible choices of what our priorities could be are like the well-stocked shelves of a grocery store. Unless we know exactly what we are looking for, we will load our lives down with "snack food" type priorities that don't really meet our needs like the nutrition of a balanced "priorities" diet. Fred Smith, the CEO of Federal Express, was asked what he considered the main thing in business. His reply was simple: *"The main thing in business is keeping the main thing the main thing."* In the Christian life, as in business, the main thing is to keep the main things the main things. Acts 2:42–47 tells us much about what these main things are and what happens when we live out of these Spirit-given priorities.

📖 Meditate on Acts 2:42.

What are the four priorities of the church after the Spirit comes upon them?

....

....

....

....

Explain in your own words what you think each of these means.

....

....

....

....

We are told that the first century Christians are *"continually devoting themselves"* to four priorities. It is essential we recognize that these priorities listed here do not represent some special emphasis week, but *these are the normal priorities, week-in and week-out, of the early church.* Translated from the imperfect tense in the Greek, the words *"continually devoting themselves"* indicate this description is always or regularly true of them. The wording here implies steadfastness. To what are they continually devoted?

First, they are continually devoted *"to the apostles' teaching,"* which consists of sharing and explaining the revelation of Christ and the Spirit along with providing commentary on the Old Testament. In practical terms, for us to be continually devoted to the apostles' teaching is to have continual devotion to the Word. Second, they are continually devoted to *"fellowship."* The Greek word *koinonia* encompasses much more than simply Christian socializing. It has the idea of "others-focused" fellowship, fellowship that moves us to meet the needs of others, not which is self-focused. Third, they are continually devoted to *"the breaking of bread,"* or communion. The principle is not just that they observe the Lord's Supper regularly, but that they practice the principle of personal worship that underlies it. Finally, they are continually devoted to *"prayer"* (literally, "the prayers"). They are continually devoted to prayer, not as a religious exercise, but as *communion* with and *communication* with God. True prayer is honest communication from my heart to the heart of God.

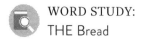

WORD STUDY:
THE Bread

The word "bread" here in the Greek is "articular"—it appears with the definite article which makes a word specific instead of general. In this case, it indicates that it refers not to breaking bread in the general sense of taking a meal, but to the breaking of the specific bread (i.e. the bread of communion).

📖 Study Acts 2:43 and identify the spiritual results of first-century church priorities.

_____

_____

_____

_____

_____

The first and most tangible result of the Spirit being poured out, and the church maintaining a yieldedness to the Spirit is that there is a pervasive sense of God. We are told, *"And everyone kept feeling a sense of awe."* The Greek word translated *"awe"* here is *phobos* (from which our English term "phobia" is derived) and literally means "to fear." When applied to God, we often speak of fear as being a "reverential awe." While this is true, there's more to it than that. True, we do not fear God in the way we would fear a rabid dog, but fear of God is more than just awe. It is a healthy respect for the holiness and righteousness of God and a genuine concern about ever doing anything that could offend that righteousness and holiness. This is motivated not so much from a fear of punishment, as it is from a fear of conscience, not wanting to grieve our heavenly Father. This fear or *"awe"* is the pervasive attitude of the early church. There is a tangible awareness of the presence of God in their midst and a healthy respect for that.

Another result of the Spirit working through the first century church is that *"many wonders and signs were taking place through the apostles."* There is no primary distinction between a wonder and a sign. They both refer to attesting miracles that motivate people toward belief. They do not contradict natural laws but instead supersede them inasmuch as God, the creator, is not bound to laws of nature. Two noteworthy observations are: a) God is working through the leadership, and b) the signs and wonders are taking place *through* the apostles, not *by* the apostles. God is doing the work.

📖 Read over Acts 2:44–47 and write what you learn about how the coming of the Spirit and the early priorities affect relationships in the church.

_____

_____

_____

_____

"They were continually devoting themselves to the apostles' teaching and to fellowship, to the breaking of bread and to prayer"
(Acts 2:42)

First, all those who believe are *"together."* One should be wary of reading too much into this, but apparently one of the results of their godly priorities is that they want to be together. Sin alienates us from each other but walking in fellowship with God draws people together.

Second, they have *"all things in common."* The word *"common"* indicates that state of communal living by which all partake equally of the resources of the group. This is true communism. Although the world system of communism espouses such equality, it cannot deliver, for a person without God is selfish. It is only through God that true equality can be achieved. As a byproduct of their commonality, they begin selling their property and possessions and are *"sharing them with all, as anyone might have need."* Acts 4:35 spells out that the distribution of these possessions is under the direct oversight of the apostles. The upshot of this communal system according to Acts 4:34 is that there is *"not a needy person among them."*

A third result of Pentecost is unity. We are told that they are *"day by day continuing with one mind in the temple."* The emphasis here is on the fact that they worship together at every opportunity. They don't skip church for reasons of convenience. More importantly, not only are they together in body, but also in their thinking. *"With one mind"* implies that they are operating from the same priorities and values. Since the temple is the unifying place for these values, it is obvious that the unity is obtained not by trying to be one with each other, but by seeking oneness with God which automatically unifies us with each other. Another result is camaraderie. They are *"breaking bread from house to house."* This differs from the breaking of bread spoken of in Acts 2:42. In verse 42 the definite article is used in the original Greek, indicating a literal Greek-to-English translation of "the breaking of the bread." Here there is no definite article, indicating that the bread spoken of is the bread of meals taken together. This is reiterated with the statement that they are, *"taking their meals together with gladness and sincerity of heart."* Because of the working of God in their lives, they want to spend time together. They take great joy from each other's company.

Yet another result of these early priorities is *"praising God."* The Greek wording implies singing praises to God. They have a song in their hearts. In these early days, they are even *"having favor with all the people."* While this is not always going to be the case with even the first century church, it is an objective to be sought. Persecution can result in disfavor with the multitudes, but as Paul puts it in Romans 12:18, *"so far as it depends on you, be at peace with all men."*

The final result we find listed here is the growth of the church body. We are told the Lord is, *"adding to their number day by day"* those being saved. Note that the credit is not given to their church growth strategies or to their witnessing, but to God's working.

If we focus on the right priorities, God will bring growth. However, if we prioritize numeric growth over maintaining integrity, any growth will be shallow and temporary because it is growth that originates with us instead of God. Notice that their growth is described not through people changing churches, but through God's working in them as a result of their priorities and of people being saved.

> *"...and the Lord was adding to their number day by day those who were being saved"* (Acts 2:47). *When we live under the Spirit's control and in His priorities, the Lord will add to our numbers.*

DAY 5

FOR ME TO FOLLOW GOD

Wouldn't you love to be a part of a church like the one in the first century? It wouldn't be hard to get up and go to church if every gathering was like that. But that was then, and this is now. We can't really expect God to work like that anymore can we? WE CERTAINLY CAN! Oh, we cannot demand that God do this or that miracle at our whim and for selfish, self-glorifying motives. However, we can pray for, prepare for, and expect His presence if each member of the church lets God, by His Spirit, be in control of their lives. The key to the early church is not their commitment, but their surrender. As they yield their lives, God is able to be in and through them what they are not. The same can be true for us today. No, Pentecost will not be repeated. The Spirit has already come. But the effects of Pentecost can be repeated in us. We can receive power when the Spirit comes upon us, and we will be witnesses of Him—not guilt-ridden, legalistic, shirt-collar-grabbing arm-twisters, but testifiers of the mighty deeds of God. We will give the witness of a satisfied customer—one who is experiencing God and genuinely wants others to share in that blessing. To get to that place requires two realities. First, we must be indwelt with and empowered by the Holy Spirit. Second, we must have the Spirit-given priorities that the first century believers lived out.

Have you invited Christ into your life, allowing His Spirit to take up residence in your heart?

As we look at the Holy Spirit in our lives, it is important to understand the difference between a "relationship" with God and "fellowship" with God. That distinction may be a new concept for you. It is important to be able to separate these two in our minds. Once God comes into your life through salvation, you have His promise that He will *"never leave you nor forsake you"* (Hebrews 13:5). That relationship is permanent. But our fellowship with Him—our enjoying all the benefits of that relationship—can be affected by sin.

As we consider our fellowship with God, we know that obedience is important. We need to be willing to do what God says and avoid doing what He says not to do. But we rest in the knowledge that He will help us keep His commands. He gives us the power to do what He asks us to do. In fact, He lives within us. By His Spirit, He takes up residence in our hearts. We have a relationship with Him through His Son, and fellowship with Him through His Spirit. We see in Scripture that there are three aspects that affect our fellowship with God woven in to how we relate to His Spirit in us. We grieve Him when we do what He says not to do (Ephesians 4:30). These are *sins of commission.* We quench Him when we do not do what He is calling us to do (1 Thessalonians 5:19). These are *sins of omission.* We resist Him when we become stubborn and insensitive to Him (see Acts 7:51). These are *sins of submission.* But how do we know if we are guilty of any of these sins? We may have a general sense that there is a problem in our abiding if we recognize that fruit is lacking. We may sense a lack of love or joy. Peace may be missing in our hearts. But how do we know what it is that is getting in the way of our abiding?

 DOCTRINE
Our Relationship to the Holy Spirit

- we can grieve the Spirit (Ephesians 4:30)

- we can quench the Spirit (1 Thessalonians 5:19)

- we can resist the Spirit (Acts 7:51)

The good news is that God loves us. He wants us to walk in fellowship with Him even more than we desire that. He is ready, willing, and able to show us if there is a problem in our relationship. We don't have to go looking for sin, as that would be introspection. Since the Spirit of God indwells us, we can trust that if we sincerely ask Him to, He will quickly reveal anything that needs to be dealt with.

Take a moment to pray through the areas listed below and ask God to bring to mind anything that is getting in the way of your experiencing the Spirit's power in your life.

Sins of commission: Is the Lord convicting you of anything you are doing that you shouldn't be doing?

_____

_____

_____

Sins of omission: Is there anything you are not doing that you sense the Lord is asking you to do by His prompting and His Word?

_____

_____

_____

Sins of submission: Is there any stubbornness and lack of sensitivity toward God in your heart that is keeping you from being submitted to Him?

_____

_____

_____

An Important Distinction: It is important when dealing with sin that we recognize the difference between the Holy Spirit's conviction and Satan's condemnation. *Conviction* is always very specific ("This is what you did wrong") and has repentance and restoration in view. *Condemnation* on the other hand, is always general ("You are a bad person") and has as its goal to keep you down and miserable. *Conviction* looks to the future (repentance and restoration). *Condemnation* looks to the past (guilty emotions, feelings of failure, and worthlessness). The apostle Paul explains what our attitude should be: *"Brethren, I do not regard myself as having laid hold of it yet [spiritual maturity], but this one thing I do, forgetting what lies behind and reaching forward to what lies ahead, I press on toward the goal for the prize of the upward call of God in Christ Jesus"* (Philippians 3:13–14). You don't have to live in past failures.

To be filled with the Spirit is a command in Ephesians 5:18, so we know it is God's will. If we sincerely ask God to fill us with His Spirit, and we confess any hinderances we are aware of to Him, then we can trust with confidence that He will answer that prayer, regardless of whether or not we have some emotional experience. By faith, we can know that He fills us, for 1 John 5:14–15 tells us, *"This is the confidence we have before Him, that, if we ask anything according to His will, He hears us. And if we know that He hears us in whatever we ask, we know that we have the requests which we have asked from Him."*

Once we are sure we are Spirit-filled, we need to honestly look at our lives and ask, "Are we continually devoting ourselves to the right priorities?" Consider the four priorities of the first century church and evaluate your life in that light.

The Apostle's Teaching—Scripture

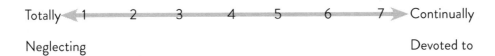

Totally Neglecting 1 — 2 — 3 — 4 — 5 — 6 — 7 Continually Devoted to

Fellowship

Totally Neglecting 1 — 2 — 3 — 4 — 5 — 6 — 7 Continually Devoted to

The Breaking of the Bread—true worship in our heart

Totally Neglecting 1 — 2 — 3 — 4 — 5 — 6 — 7 Continually Devoted to

Prayer

Totally Neglecting 1 — 2 — 3 — 4 — 5 — 6 — 7 Continually Devoted to

What application points do you need to make to get your priorities where they should be?

_____

_____

_____

_____

Why not take some time in writing to express your heart to the Lord? Tell Him what you desire in your relationship with Him. Thank Him for all He has done for you and is doing. Ask Him for the things of which you want to trust Him. Use the space below and write out your prayer to Him.

_____

_____

_____

_____

_____

LESSON 3

THE POWER OF JESUS' NAME
ACTS 3:1—4:4

What's in a name? I have always been intrigued by unique names. My own last name—Rasnake—is pretty unusual. Most who see it can't say it correctly, and those who hear it usually can't spell it. The ancestral derivation of my name is Prussian. Ethnically, the Rasnakes were apparently Jewish and lived in a region of modern Poland until the time of the Revolutionary War. Jacob Rasnake was pressed into service as a mercenary Hessian and came to America to fight alongside the British. He was eventually captured by the Americans, and at the end of the war, he accepted General George Washington's offer of amnesty and began a new life in the Shenandoah Valley of Virginia. I remember the surprise with my first book that was translated into Russian when I learned that in that language my name means "butcher." Maybe that is what an ancestor did for a living. There is no family history to go with my first name—my mother just liked it. I would guess that is the case for most of us today. My wife has a middle name—Marie that is shared with her mother, Dickie Marie, her grandmother, Marie, her great-grandmother, Grace Marie, and our daughter, Lauren Marie. When it came to naming our first son, we wanted a family connection, but weren't grabbed by my father's name—Fred Edgar. My father-in law is someone we think highly of, but Winfred Hillary just doesn't role off the lips the way it did in his generation. We settled on Blake, and named our first son after my Grandfather, a very significant person in my life. But for the rest of our sons, their names were given to them just because we liked the sound of them.

"Jesus" is the Greek transliteration of the Hebrew name "Joshua."
It literally means, "Jehovah saves."

Naming people was done a little differently in biblical times. A name was not chosen because of how it sounded, but because of what it communicated. Usually a name told a story about the person or communicated something of their character. For example, Moses' name comes from a word that reflects the fact that he was drawn out of the water. Abram's name was even changed to Abraham because He became the father of a multitude. Isaac means "he laughs" because Sarah laughed when God revealed she would become pregnant at age ninety. In Scripture, a name is more than just a means of identification. A name is an expression of one's character, reputation, and authority. It might surprise you to know that Scripture records over five hundred names and titles for God—each one reflecting something different about who He is. When God became flesh and dwelt among us, He took a name for Himself that communicated His mission. "Jesus" is the Greek transliteration of the Hebrew name "Joshua." It literally means, "Jehovah saves" (Matthew 1:1, 16, 21).

The name, Jesus, is not just a name of meaning or significance, but it is also a name of power. In His name, lives are changed, wounds are healed, captives are released. Oh, I don't mean that the letters have some mystic energy, or the word itself performs some supernatural action through being spoken. The name of Jesus—like all Biblical names—is an extension of His identity and character. When we say "there is power in the name of Jesus" what we really mean is there is power in Jesus Himself. The name of Jesus is of special significance in the third and fourth chapters of Acts. That phrase or idea is mentioned eight times in these two chapters of Scripture (3:6, 16; 4:7, 10, 12, 17–18, 30). We find in these verses a particular emphasis on the power of the name of Jesus. The apostle Peter is very careful to deflect any attention or glory sent his way, and to emphasize that it is the name of Jesus that should be noticed, not his. This is right and appropriate, for even though Jesus humbled Himself to take on the trappings of humanity, *"God highly exalted Him, and bestowed on Him the name which is above every name, so that at the name of Jesus every knee will bow, of those who are in heaven and on earth and under the earth, and that every tongue will confess that Jesus Christ is Lord, to the glory of God the Father"* (Philippians 2:9b-11).

DAY 1

THE DOING OF JESUS' MIRACLE (ACTS 3:1–11)

I am not a miracle worker—not by any stretch. But I have seen God do miracles in my life and in those around me. My own salvation was quite a miracle. Overnight I went from an amoral, rebellious, atheistic drug dealer to a radically transformed follower of Jesus. It didn't take years of therapy or drug treatment programs. It just took Jesus coming into my life. I have seen miraculous provision of finances for great need. I have seen healed relationships and disasters averted. Perhaps the greatest manifestation of God I have ever witnessed was the inexplicable miracle of God healing my wife from cancer when chemotherapy didn't produce a remission. In 1992, she was diagnosed with a very rare and aggressive form of T-cell Lymphoma, with some twenty tumors scattered in her bones, lymph system, and liver. High doses of chemotherapy left her bald and dangerously immune-suppressed, but gallium scans revealed they did not leave her cancer-free. Yet just before she was to undergo a bone-marrow transplant, God healed her. I'll never forget the conversation I had when the specialist from Vanderbilt University Hospital looked me in the eye and said, "I don't know how to explain it, but I can't find any cancer." That cancer never came back. There is no doubt in our minds that God did a miracle—just like the miracle He performs at the hands of Peter here in Acts chapter 3.

📖 Take a look at Acts 3:1–3 and answer the questions below.

Think about when Peter and John encounter the lame man. What stands out to you from these circumstances?

_____

_____

_____

_____

Why do you suppose the lame man is begging where he is?

_____

_____

DID YOU KNOW?
The hour of prayer

We are told here that the "ninth hour" is an hour of prayer. This would be about three o'clock in the afternoon, as Jews counted time from sunrise (about 6 AM). Traditionally there are three different prayer hours during the day (see Psalm 55:17; Daniel 6:10; Acts 10:30): morning, noon, and the ninth hour or 3:00 PM, which is the most attended of the three since it coincides with the offering of the evening sacrifices.

Peter and John are on their way to the temple to pray. At this stage of early church history, believers are all converted (or completed) Jews who still participate in temple activities associated with the worship of Jehovah God. As these disciples make their way to the time of prayer, they encounter the lame beggar, who apparently spends every day here seeking charity from the crowds. One would think that this is a good place to beg. Not only are there crowds to be found at the temple, but these crowds can be expected to be of a charitable nature. Whether they are motivated by divine piety or personal pride, people tend to make notice of the indigent when they are at the temple. This beggar asks alms of Peter, likely not realizing that God is about to bless Him with something far greater than money—physical and spiritual healing.

📖 Read over Acts 3:4–7.

What does the beggar expect to receive from Peter and John?

_____

_____

_____

What does he end up getting?

_____

_____

God draws the attention of Peter and John to this needy man lying by the Beautiful Gate at the Temple. Doubtless there are other beggars in the vicinity, but God singles this one out. When he asks the disciples for money, he instead receives something far greater. Like this beggar, often we come to God not knowing what we really need. We ask for little and expect little. Yet God is not bound by our feeble and frail supplications. He not only knows what we ask, but what we really need. He can and does give us more. This beggar wants enough resources to continue his meager existence. Instead of his next meal, God blesses him with a new life. An important point to note here is that the lame beggar's healing is immediate and complete.

 DID YOU KNOW?
The Beautiful Gate

Most scholars believe the "Beautiful Gate" is the Eastern Gate that leads to the Court of Women. Like most gates at the Temple, this one is large and ornate. It is made of Corinthian Bronze which is polished to a beautiful gold color. The Jewish historian Josephus tells us that this gate is so large it takes twenty men to close it.

📖 Reflect on Acts 3:8–11.

What is the beggar's response to his healing?

_____

_____

_____

Who does the beggar credit for the miracle?

_____

_____

_____

What is the response of the crowds?

_____

_____

_____

We are not the least surprised by the beggar's joy at being healed. We see him leaping up and down and praising God. This last part is important to note. Peter makes it clear in Acts 3:6 that it is in Jesus' name that he has been healed. This is not Peter's work but God's. Apparently, the beggar understands this, for God is the object of his praise. While there is gratitude to Peter (verse 11 tells us he is clinging to Peter and John), the glory and praise are reserved for God as is fitting. It is a grievous thing when men usurp God's glory and try to take credit for what He does. Peter makes it clear to the crowds that this healing is not by his "power or piety." Sadly, not all who minister in the name of Christ exhibit such fitting humility.

When this beggar who is apparently familiar to the temple crowd, is seen walking, many gather in amazement to witness this miracle. They are *"filled with wonder"* to see this man who has been lame from birth dramatically healed. As we will see, part of God's purpose in this healing is not just to benefit the lame man, but to do good to all those gathered who are suffering from their own malady—the spiritual lameness of sin.

DOCTRINE
Is Physical Healing Guaranteed?

While God can and does heal physically, He is not bound to do so at our bequest. Scripture records at least four different reasons for physical sickness. Some sickness is a result of sin (see 1 Corinthians 11:30), sickness that will not be healed until there is repentance. Some sickness serves as a trial to grow our faith (see Job 2). It will not be healed until God's purpose is accomplished. Some sickness is for God to be glorified in its healing (see John 9:2–3). Fourth, some sickness is *"to end in death"* (see John 11:3) or God's tool to call us home. This is the ultimate healing, for it takes us to that realm where there is no more death, pain, tears, or illness. I don't want to be healed from my passage to glory

God is able to heal. He who created the human body is fully capable of recreating it. Though we tend to be more impressed with the one who is restored physically, we must recognize that these legs which have been mended will still die one day. God, who always works from and for eternity, realizes that physical healing is nothing without the healing of the soul. That is why God uses the opportunity of the gathering crowd to work a greater healing. But we must always remember that it is God who heals, not a person. It is in the name of Jesus, not in the name of Peter, that this lame beggar is able to rise and walk. When I compare what we experienced in my wife's healing from cancer with much of the modern faith healing and miracle working movements, I must confess I feel somewhat abnormal. You see, we know it isn't our great faith that healed my wife. Ours is not a testimony of an unshakable faith, but of a very shaky faith placed in an unshakable God. Our immediate response was not a giddy confidence but rather, an overwhelming humility. Many in the "faith healing" community today seem to come across with an arrogance that I don't understand. We are incredibly grateful for God's healing work, but we also feel so undeserving. We want to fall on our faces before the Lord. You see, we have known plenty of people in similar trials that the Lord didn't choose to heal—or perhaps I should say, He chose to heal them by taking them to heaven. We still find ourselves asking, "Why us?" and "Why not them?" We aren't somehow more worthy. We have to accept it as God's sovereign purpose. Like Peter, we also can take none of the credit for ourselves. I wish I saw more of that attitude in the preachers who fill the cable channels on television.

DAY 2

THE DELIVERY OF JESUS' MESSAGE (ACTS 3:12-16)

Where does the power to work a miracle come from? Before you give a knee-jerk, Sunday School answer and say "Jesus," think about it. In Acts 3, God uses Peter to instantly restore a lame man to complete health. While we know God is involved in this instance, we face the same dilemma as the crowd who witnessed the miracle. If we are not careful, we too can attempt to give too much credit to Peter. Today there are many who claim to have "the gift of healing." While this statement has a biblical ring to it, it is not entirely accurate. When Paul addresses spiritual gifts in 1 Corinthians 12 and speaks of healing in verse 9, what he actually is saying is God has given to some *"gifts of healing."* Even this translation is a bit misleading, for if you translate the phrase literally from Greek to English, it reads *"gifts of healings."* It is not that God bestows on an individual the ability to heal others at will. Instead, each healing is a gift in itself. Peter heals, as does Paul, but that is not their main spiritual gift. In fact, the healings they participate in are usually byproducts of ministry, not their main focus. While the healing of Acts 3 is a great miracle, the main point of the story is not the miracle but the message that follows. Physical healing without spiritual rebirth benefits no one from the vantage point of eternity. What a tragedy it would be to be healed in this life, and still spend eternity apart from the Lord. The primary focus of Peter is fulfilling Jesus' statement in Acts 1:8—*"You will be my witnesses..."* This is the ultimate proof of the Spirit coming.

Read Acts 3:12–13a and answer the questions that follow.

What questioning is implied by Peter's response here?

_____

_____

_____

_____

What does Peter say contributes nothing to the man's healing?

_____

_____

_____

In Acts 3:11 we learn that a crowd gathers to marvel at this miracle. We also learn that the newly healed man is clinging to Peter and John. Though he is praising God, Peter's response to the crowd indicates they are giving praise to Peter. The text indicates that they are gazing at him, as if marveling at Peter. He wants to make certain they understand that it is not him but God who has healed the lame man. Peter makes it clear that neither his piety (how devout or holy he is) nor his power has anything to do with the miracle. Rather, the same God who the Jews had grown up worshiping has done this work, and Peter makes it clear that God does it to bring glory to Jesus.

> *Peter communicates to the Jews their personal guilt in the death of Christ.*
> *We must make this same recognition ourselves,*
> *for it is our sin that put Jesus on the cross.*

📖 Look over Acts 3:13-15 and summarize the points Peter makes to his Jewish audience.

_____

_____

_____

_____

_____

_____

Peter begins his witness by making it clear that he worships the same God they do—the God of their forefathers, Abraham, Isaac, and Jacob (Israel). Peter next makes it clear that the purpose of this miracle is to glorify and attest to Jesus. He then proceeds to build a case against the Jews for rejecting their Messiah, accusing them of rejecting Jesus the "holy and righteous One." He reminds them they chose a guilty murderer to be released instead (Matthew 27:17–26). Although the Romans performed the crucifixion, Peter lays the guilt of the act at the feet of the Jews. If you are not Jewish, you might wrongly be tempted to think the guilt is not yours. What Peter does is bring home the fact that each person, because of their sin, is guilty of the death of our Lord. The same is true of us, so we have no room to boast or judge.

📖 Examine Acts 3:15b. What is the significance of the resurrection in this context?

_____

_____

_____

It seems that Peter's main point in mentioning the resurrection in this context is the validation it offers of Jesus along with God's affirmation of Him. What one discovers from a thorough study of the book of Acts is that Luke records a great many evangelistic sermons in these pages, and, in almost all of them, the raising of Jesus from the dead features prominently. It is the resurrection which sets Jesus apart from every other religious figure in history. This miraculous event proves His uniqueness and affirms the hand of God the Father on Him. Only the creator of life and death has the power to conquer it. Peter speaks of the resurrection not as religious theory but as history to which he can attest as an eyewitness.

📖 What do you think the difference is between "faith in His name" at the beginning of Acts 3:16 and "the faith which comes through Him" at the end of it?

_____

_____

_____

_____

Verse 16 is a portion of the text which requires careful reflection. Its meaning is not necessarily obvious. It seems though that Peter reveals the two sides of this miracle's story. While faith is the operating force, there are two participants with Jesus in this wonder. Peter has to trust in Christ—in the power of His name. He has to exercise faith in the character and authority of Jesus. This notion seems to be wrapped in the repeated idea of His name at the beginning of the verse. But as if for clarity, Peter speaks of *"the faith which comes through Him."* Faith does not begin with us but with Jesus. Hebrews 12:2 calls Him the *"author and perfecter"* of faith. He begins it and completes it. Clearly this miracle is not initiated by Peter but by the Lord.

> *True Ministry is initiated by God, not man. Elijah prays on Mount Carmel, "O Lord, the God of Abraham, Isaac and Israel, today let it be known that You are God in Israel and that I am Your servant and I have done all these things at Your word."*

True ministry is initiated by God, not man. Consider Elijah at Mount Carmel. It is easy to read this story casually and think that the prophet comes up with a good idea and asks God to bless it. He prays and believes, and God acts on his behalf. Yet closer scrutiny reveals that the showdown with the prophets of Baal is God's idea, not Elijah's. When he prays in 1 Kings 18:36, Elijah asks that all may know that "his actions are done 'at Thy word.'" Everything Elijah does is preceded by the word of the Lord. Even his prayer for rain in 1 Kings 18:42–45, which James 5:16 offers as an example of effective prayer, is initiated by a word from the Lord that He is going to bring rain (1 Kings 18:1). Elijah's faith is expressed in taking God at His word and asking Him to do what He has already promised He will do. I think we are safe in assuming that God, by His Spirit, initiates Peter's ministry with the lame beggar at the Temple.

DAY THREE

THE DEVELOPMENT OF JESUS' MINISTRY (ACTS 3:17–26)

God works a great miracle on this day at the temple. A man who has been lame from birth is suddenly and completely healed. He not only is given new legs, but unlike an infant, he doesn't have to learn how to use them. He is a blessed man. But God's working in this man's life is not for him only. Oh, that we might understand this principle! Whatever God does for us is not for us only. Every blessing, every endowment, every miracle, every provision is not just for us, but also that others might be blessed through us. This man rejoices greatly in his physical restoration, but with him that day are thousands rejoicing, as God heals them of sin and takes up residence in their hearts. God uses the healing of this man to gather a crowd, but then His work is just beginning. He uses Peter, filled with the Holy Spirit, to preach truth to this multitude that gathers. As a result, the blessing of the one becomes the blessing of the many.

📖 Look over Acts 3:17-18.

Why do you think it is important that Peter reminds the Jews they acted in ignorance?

_____

_____

_____

> *"Father forgive them; for they do not know what they are doing"*
> *(Luke 23:34).*

How does Christ's death fulfilling prophecy fit in with the Jews' guilt?

_____

_____

_____

Although Peter builds a compelling case against the Jews in his sermon, his preaching is not without mercy. He makes it clear that he understands they acted in ignorance. The Old Testament—all the Scriptures the Jews have up to this point—drew a clear and strong distinction between sins of ignorance and willful, deliberate sin (see Leviticus chapters 4 and 5). Although ignorance of the law is no excuse, it does have a bearing on the consequences. Peter wants them to know that God understands their hearts, and in fact, is not surprised at all by their actions. All that Christ suffered had already been prophesied and is part of God's plan. In spite of their sin, God loves them, and He offers them the chance to repent. Remember, it is Jesus who said on the cross, *"Father forgive them; for they do not know what they are doing"* (Luke 23:34).

📖 Read Acts 3:19–22.

What application does Peter call for here?

_____

_____

_____

What will the results be of rightly responding to the invitation of God?

_____

_____

_____

Peter's call to the Jews is simple and straightforward—Repent and return. The only thing we can do with our guilt is repent. The Greek word, *metanoeo*, literally means "with the mind." It means a change of mind or thinking. True repentance always results in a change of action. If we make no attempt to change direction, then we really haven't changed our minds. We cannot conquer sin. But we can turn from it and "return" to the Lord. Since He lives in us, when we turn our sin over to Him, He can change what we cannot. This is true salvation, but it is also the process that we continue to live out in sanctification, one step at a time. With true repentance comes some specific results. First, sins are *"wiped away"* (3:19b). Second, *"times of refreshing"* come from the Lord (3:19c). Ultimately, this points to the millennial kingdom the Jews have long waited for. Third, the Messiah will return (3:20–21). Fourth, as we will see in the verses that follow, judgment will be averted (3:23). We should all heed the words of Peter, and as he points out, these are also the words of Moses regarding the Christ (see 3:22).

📖 Take a look at Acts 3:23. What does Peter identify as the consequences of not repenting?

Peter's message is strong and unequivocal. While repentance brings *"times of refreshing,"* failure to do so leads to destruction. Notice the personal nature of Peter's warning—he states that *"every soul"* that doesn't heed the Prophet, Jesus, is choosing his own eternal damnation.

📖 Read through Acts 3:24–26 and summarize how Peter closes out his sermon.

Peter brings this witnessing opportunity to a close by reminding them of their rich spiritual heritage. God has sent prophet after prophet to them to proclaim truth and to remind them of the covenant He had made with them. And finally, He sends them Jesus. Peter says, *"for you first, God raised up His Servant..."* Jesus came to save all mankind, but He came to the Jew first. It is important that you do not miss the Jewish flavor of what Peter preaches. In this short sermon, he mentions five different names of the Lord Jesus that all hold special significance to the Jew. Each is associated in the Old Testament with the Messiah. Peter begins and ends his message by calling Jesus God's *"Servant"* (Acts 3:13, 26). This is a common Messianic term in the Old Testament (see Isaiah 53:11). Second, Peter reminds them that His name is Jesus, "God saves." As we pointed out earlier, the name Jesus is the Greek transliteration of the Hebrew name, Joshua. Just as

Joshua led Israel into the Promised Land on earth, Jesus will lead them to the Promised Land of heaven. Third, Peter calls Him two names together—"*the Holy and Righteous One*" (see Psalm 16:10; Isaiah 53:11), both with Messianic implications. Fourth, Peter calls Him "*the Prince of life.*" How ironic it is that they put to death the ruler of life! This term has the idea of the one who governs and gives life. Since Psalm 36:9 identifies God as the "*fountain of life,*" this title associates Jesus with being deity. Finally, Peter calls Jesus God's "*Christ*"—the anointed One, or Messiah. This message is designed to reach the mind of the audience, and as we will see in our next daily section, it does exactly that.

 DID YOU KNOW?
Names of Jesus

Peter uses five different names of Jesus in his message, each one significant to his Jewish audience...

- Servant

- Jesus (Joshua)

- The Holy and Righteous One

- The Prince of life

- Christ

DAY FOUR

THE DIVISION OF JESUS' NAME (ACTS 4:1-4)

Have you ever reflected on the circumstances of the crucifixion? For example, why isn't Jesus crucified alone? The crowd that gathers is divided on the issue of His death. Some weep while others mock. The Gospels record that when our Lord hangs on a cross, He does so between two criminals (see Luke 23:33–43). They are divided in their view of Jesus also. One is seeking while the other is cynical. One hurls abuse at Him, "*saying 'Are You not the Christ? Save Yourself and us!'*" The other criminal however, has a different view. "*Jesus, remember me when You come in Your kingdom.*" The cross divides people according to their hearts. So too does the message of the cross. What we witness today in the story of the crowd gathered at Peter's miracle, we will see again and again as the gospel is preached in the book of Acts. Some eagerly respond to the truth put before them, while others emphatically reject it. The same is true today as well. We cannot know for sure the condition of the soil until the seed is sown. Then the soil is revealed by the fruit it bears. Today we want to examine the dividing work of the name of Jesus as we look at the responses to Peter's sermon.

📖 Read Acts 4:1-2.

Who is it that responds negatively to the preaching of Peter here?

Why are they *"greatly disturbed"*?

_____

_____

_____

It is an amazing thought that the people who give Peter and the rest of the disciples the greatest trouble are not the drunks, prostitutes, and pagans. Their greatest persecution comes not from the rebellious, but from the religious. It has always been so. Remember, it is the religious who are responsible for putting Jesus on the cross. Verse 2 shows us the true focus of their displeasure—it is the emphasis and content of Peter's message. He is *"proclaiming in Jesus."* In other words, he is lifting up the name of the crucified one the religious establishment has already rejected. Second, he is proclaiming the resurrection of the dead through Jesus.

DID YOU KNOW?
Sadducees

The two major rival parties in the Jewish religious scene in New Testament times are the Pharisees and the Sadducees. Although less numerous than the Pharisees, the Sadducees hold great influence since the High Priests during the time of Jesus and the disciples are all Sadducees. They are for the most part wealthy aristocracy and land owners. They are particularly incensed at Peter's words since they do not believe in any kind of resurrection from the dead, nor in angels, nor in a spirit realm (see Acts 23:8).

📖 Look at Acts 4:3. What do the religious authorities do with Peter and John?

_____

_____

_____

The Roman government officially rules Jerusalem, but they give the Jews freedom to police the temple area. The captain of the Temple Guard is the chief of the temple police force and as such is second in authority only to the High Priest. The Greek word translated *"captain"* here (*strategos*) has the idea of the leader of an army—a commander or general. He and his men arrest Peter and John and put them in jail for the night, as it is too late to resolve their case this day.

📖 Take a few moments to reflect on Acts 4:4. What stands out to you in this contrasting response to Peter's message?

_____

_____

_____

We are not provided much detail, but we are told that many (not all) of those who hear Peter's sermon *"believed."* The official head count we are given is that *"about five thou-*

sand" believe. But notice that the text specifically tells us this is the number of *the men*. The Greek word here (*aner*) does often specify men as opposed to women, but also can be used of humankind. If the former is meant instead of the latter, then perhaps the total response is twice that number. In any case, the church is growing rapidly. In a few weeks at least eight thousand new believers have been added.

The message of the cross bears fruit, but it also brings division and conflict. We cannot expect to faithfully speak truth and never offend anyone. Jesus Himself said, "*Woe to you when all men speak well of you*" (Luke 6:26). In other words, if everyone likes your message, it is probably watered-down. The name of Jesus divides. We should never be offensive in the manner we share the gospel, but we must accept the fact that to some the gospel itself is offensive.

"Woe to you when all men speak well of you" (Luke 6:26)

As we close our consideration of this passage, an important note should be added. On Pentecost, three thousand souls are saved, and this great harvest is preceded by ten days of prayer. On this day, five thousand are saved. Yet this occurs *before* they pray, not *after*. Peter and John are on their way to observe the hour of prayer when the miracle and subsequent message occurs (see Acts 3:1). Perhaps God works in this manner—greater even than Pentecost—that their faith might not rest in prayer but in God. There is always a danger of trusting in prayer instead of trusting in God. Prayer is powerful only because God is powerful.

Day Five

For Me To Follow God

What a miraculous day! As great as Pentecost is, in some ways this day is greater still. A man lame from birth is completely healed. Five thousand respond to Peter's proclamation of the gospel. The church is flourishing! The name of Jesus is being glorified and manifest. Yet persecution is beginning as well. Satan is neither silent nor passive when his kingdom is being threatened. We should not be surprised that with the great harvest also comes great opposition. It has always been so and will be until our Lord returns. But remember, it is about Him, not us. When persecution comes our way, it is only because they can't get to Jesus that they come after us. When we lift high His name, the humble of heart are drawn to Him, but the proud will resist. Of greatest importance is that we preach the right message. The good news is about Him, not us. It is His name that is to be lifted high, not ours. If people leave impressed with us, we have stolen glory from the One who deserves it. All that we say and do should be in His name, not ours. Think about it—there is no power in our names, but there is in His. The world is not at all impressed with what we do for God. But they stop and take notice at what God does. When He does what only He can do, then the world cannot explain it away. They must accept it or reject Him. Peter participates in a miracle that cannot be explained by human activity, only by Jesus.

When people look at your life, do they see you doing things for God, or do they see God doing the sort of things that only He can do?

_____

_____

_____

Do you give God the glory for the good in your life?

_____

_____

_____

_____

Peter doesn't go to the temple looking for someone to heal. He goes there to pray—to meet with God. But because God has his attention, he is sensitive to the opportunity to minister God places before him. How would you rate yourself at being sensitive to the opportunities to minister that are around you?

Very Sensitive ⟵ 1   2   3   4   5   6   7 ⟶ Insensitive

If you are not seeing chances to minister around you, perhaps it is because you are not looking, or you don't see the needs people have. Often it will be that through meeting someone's physical need, God will open a spiritual door. When people see that we care about their difficulties it earns for us the right to be heard; they will want to know what makes us care.

Do you give God the glory for the good in your life?

How many unbelievers do you think there are around you in each of the areas listed below?

At work:

_____

_____

At school:

_____

_____

In your neighborhood:

_____

_____

Among your friends:

_____

_____

Among your relatives:

_____

_____

As you close out this lesson, why not pray for God to make you sensitive to those in your circles whom He may be preparing to respond to Christ. Ask God to show you any needs He would want to meet in their lives through you.

_____

_____

_____

_____

_____

_____

_____

_____

_____

_____

_____

_____

_____

NOTES

LESSON 4

PERSECUTION IN JESUS' NAME

ACTS 4:5–31

When I first became a Christian as a young college student, someone gave me a Christian book entitled, *The Jesus Person Pocket Promise Book*. What the book did was compile Scripture promises around themes for handy reference. It was helpful for someone like me who did not yet know enough Scripture to be able to link verses to particular needs I was facing at the time. There were promises about all sorts of different topics, but conspicuously absent from all these verses was 2 Timothy 3:12, *"Indeed all who desire to live godly in Christ Jesus will be persecuted."* It is a promise, but not one believers tend to want to claim. We don't like the idea that being really serious about our faith means some people are not going to like us. And we really do not want to think about the possibility that someone might harm us because we align ourselves with Christ. Yet persecution does happen. It happens in Peter's day, and it happens in ours.

> *"Indeed all who desire to live godly in Christ Jesus will be persecuted." (2 Timothy 3:12)*

Certainly, persecution is not something we should seek out. There should be nothing in our manner that intentionally offends. The apostle Paul writes, *"If possible, so far as it depends on you, be at peace with all men"* (Romans 12:18). We should seek to get along with others where we can. But we must accept the reality that even if we try not to offend, sometimes truth affronts those who want to live contrary to it. Not everyone who knew Jesus loved or accepted Him. God in the flesh lived among people, yet the ones He created persecuted Him. How can we expect to identify with Him and escape His fate? Truth offends people because it makes demands on them. It does not leave them alone. It forces them to face the things they would like to avoid. And when it does, sometimes they react badly. *"If possible . . . be at peace,"* but recognize that it will not always be possible. We should never accept peace that requires sacrificing truth.

I remember an encounter my wife had in college with a fellow student. Somehow my name came up in conversation, and he was not aware that she was dating me. He quickly volunteered, "I hate that guy!" As she delicately probed to discern the source of his vehemence, she was surprised to learn that it had nothing to do with any conflict he and I had shared. I had never even spoken with him on a personal basis. Instead, his strong dislike of me, when chased to its origin, turned out to be rooted in the fact that in a class we shared I had taken a stand for Christ, and he didn't like it. While I hardly consider that worthy to be compared with the persecution experiences of so many others, the heart behind it was the same. Persecution comes in all shapes and sizes. It can be something as simple as someone not liking you, or as serious as a death threat. While you do not expect to hear of someone being beaten or killed for their faith here in America, there is no guarantee it will always be that way. Ancient Rome was a place of religious toleration. Many different views of God were put forward, yet it was the Christians who were burned at the stake and thrown to the lions. Today our culture preaches tolerance of every view and every vice. Everything, it seems, is to be tolerated except the intolerant views of those who believe in absolute truth. While on today's university campuses alternative lifestyles and other religions are championed under the banner of free speech, Christianity is mocked and maligned. At some point in the future the response may be much stronger.

Opposition to Christianity is quite violent in some places around the world. Recently, I received a word of thanks from a pastor in Indonesia for the spiritual encouragement he had gotten from a Bible study I wrote. I was grateful, but humbled. He faces persecution of biblical proportions. Churches in his area have been burned to the ground by militant Islamic mobs while the congregations are still inside. Pastors have been beaten and killed simply because they carry the name of Jesus. You see, that is the point—it isn't about who we are, but about Whom we follow.

DAY ONE

PETER AND JOHN'S TRIAL AND DEFENSE: ACTS 4:5-12

Communist Romania was a difficult place to be a believer. Persecution was not just a reality, it was government policy. Christians were constantly harassed. Churches were bulldozed. Church leaders were routinely arrested and tortured. Death threats were not empty intimidation. Yet with all the pressure and persistence, the communist government of Nicolae Ceaușescu did not destroy the church. Instead the church destroyed the government. The revolution came not with guns, but with prayer meetings and preaching. Hundreds of thousands of Romanians gathered in the city square in Timișoara as Baptist pastor Peter Dugulescu proclaimed over a loudspeaker, "Romania believes in God." He went on to be a member of parliament, and Ceaușescu is gone. During the days of Communist persecution, Joseph Tson was one of the pastors arrested. Police interrogators threatened him with death if he did not renounce his faith. They were masters of pressure and intimidation, but they were ill-equipped and unprepared to deal with his response. "Your greatest threat is killing me," he honestly confided, "but my greatest threat is dying." They realized he was right, so instead of killing him they kicked him out of the country. He became a powerful voice for the Romanian Church from here in America.

Persecution has been around since Cain killed Abel. Yet it has never succeeded in stamping out faith. The seeds of the gospel have often been sown with the blood of the sower, yet their willingness to die for what they believe only serves to validate that belief. The threats and actions of the persecutors only prove that they have something to fear in the people of God. The Sanhedrin has the armed strength and political influence to arrest Peter and John, but they have no ability to silence them.

"Your greatest threat is killing me, but my greatest threat is dying."

—Joseph Tson, to his Romanian persecutors

📖 Take a look at Acts 4:5–6. Write what you can find out about the participants in the trial of Peter and John.

_____

_____

_____

_____

_____

Luke identifies the prosecuting body at Peter and John's trial as *"their rulers and elders and scribes."* Together these made up what is referred to as "the Council" (see Acts 4:15) or "Sanhedrin." They are the religious governing body of the Jewish nation, operating under the ultimate authority of the Romans. There are three main parts of this group. The "rulers" refers to the representatives of the different priestly orders including present and former high priests. "Elders" are the designated heads of the tribes of Israel. "Scribes," for the most part Pharisees, are the experts in interpreting Old Testament law. Acts 4:6 gives us the names of some of these participants. Annas is identified as *"the high priest,"* though at this time he is no longer officially in this position, having been replaced by his son-in-law, Caiaphas (see Luke 3:2). We know nothing for certain about John and Alexander, though Annas does have a son named Jonathan who becomes Caiaphas' replacement as high priest. Whoever these individuals are, they are apparently well known at the time or Luke would not give their names.

📖 Reflect on Acts 4:7.

What is the gist of the prosecution's questioning?

_____

_____

_____

Why do you think they ask what they do?

_____

_____

_____

 DID YOU KNOW?
Sanhedrin

The term, *Sanhedrin* is a transliteration of the Greek word for "council" (Acts 4:15). The *Sanhedrin* or *Sanhedrim* in New Testament times is the supreme council of the Jewish nation composed of 70 members (not counting the high priest), in imitation of the seventy elders appointed by Moses (Num. 11:16ff.). The members are selected from the chief priests, former high priests, and the chief priests or heads of the twenty-four courses or divisions of the priesthood, along with elders, and scribes or lawyers. The high priest who is serving at the time acts as *ex-officio* president. A vice president sits at his right hand. The Sanhedrin deals with all important matters, both civil and religious, apparently meeting in a hall called the "Hall of Hewn Stone" not far from the temple.

The main question the Sanhedrin asks here is "Who gets the credit for this miracle?" Before we are quick to judge this court gathered against Peter and John, we should take note that the Law allows for and even calls for such an investigation after a miracle has been performed (see Deuteronomy 13:1–15). The key issue in the Law is whether this miracle is credited to God or is used to draw the people after other gods. Not all that is miraculous is of God.

📖 Read Peter's response to his accusers in Acts 4:8–12 and answer the questions that follow.

What is the significance of Peter being *"filled with the Holy Spirit"*?

How does Peter answer the specifics of his accuser's questions?

Luke tells us that Peter is *"filled with the Holy Spirit,"* and it is important we do not gloss over this important message. We will see in the chapters ahead that though the Spirit's indwelling of believers is a one-time event at Pentecost, the "filling" of the Spirit occurs many different times to these same people. In Luke's Gospel, Jesus instructs the disciples that when they are brought before the religious authorities, *"the Holy Spirit will teach you in that very hour what you ought to speak"* (Luke 12:12). Now in Acts, Luke affirms Peter and John's situation as a fulfillment of that promise. Peter answers the Sanhedrin's question by giving credit to Jesus' name, but also linking it with God the Father, who raised Jesus from the dead. Peter uses Old Testament prophesies to identify Jesus as the long-awaited Messiah and recognizes His name as the only means of salvation.

📖 Now read back over Peter's response and identify all the ways Peter turns the tables on his accusers.

By the power of the Spirit of God, Peter very quickly turns the tables on his accusers and actually puts them on trial instead. Notice what he does. First, he calls into question the fairness of the very trial itself. He reminds them that he is on trial for a good deed, not a bad one. Then after identifying Jesus as the source of the miracle, he reminds them that they are the ones who put Jesus to death, working against God who raised Him from the dead. Peter calls these leaders the "builders" prophesied in Psalm 118, who reject the very cornerstone of the building. It is amazing to realize that these men who think they are following God could miss Him so completely.

> *"The stone which the builders rejected has become the chief corner stone."*
> (Psalm 118:22)

Although we may look at this difficult circumstance Peter and John endure and focus on the injustice of it, that does not seem to be Peter's perspective at all. He recognizes that this experience has purchased for them the opportunity to share the gospel with some of the most influential Jews in Jerusalem. Instead of railing about the unfairness of the accusations, he uses the opportunity to testify of Christ and to offer salvation to these men.

DAY TWO

THE SANHEDRIN'S DEBATE (ACTS 4:13–17)

How do you know what truth is? How do you discern what is of God and what is not? You may not realize it, but the state of your heart has more to do with how you arrive at truth than the evidence itself. Jesus gives an important clue to discernment in John 7:17. He says, *"If anyone is willing to do His will, he will know of the teaching, whether it is of God."* It is our yielded heart to God that lets us discern truth; that helps us discover His will. Since truth makes demands on our lives, if we are not willing to obey God, we will defend ourselves by attacking Him. The martyr, Stephen, in his message at his stoning, accuses the Sanhedrin of being *"stiff-necked and uncircumcised in heart and ears"* and always *"resisting the Holy Spirit."* Amazing as it may seem, the leaders of God's chosen people are working against the very Lord they are supposed to serve. If our hearts are not surrendered to God's will and way, we will instead attack His will as wrong. As we will see today, instead of blessing the Lord for this miracle, the priests and leaders seek to explain it away and silence its participants.

📖 Take a look at Acts 4:13.

Why do you think Peter and John present themselves with such confidence?

What do you think it means that Peter and John are "uneducated and untrained men"?

_____

_____

_____

Why does Luke mention that they are recognized as having been with Jesus?

_____

_____

_____

_____

What a contrast between Peter at the crucifixion and Peter now. Before the resurrection he was afraid of a slave girl. Now he is confident before the leaders of Israel. Clearly this confidence is a result of the work of God's Spirit within him. The Sanhedrin views these men as "*uneducated and untrained*" because they are not part of the religious hierarchy, nor have they attended the rabbinical schools. They are not aristocracy like the Jewish leaders but are "blue collar" fishermen. However, it is not true that they are uneducated and untrained. They have "*been with Jesus.*" God's school to build leaders is not always the same as culture's. Peter is not learned in man's opinions about God. Instead, God has personally taught him about truth and righteousness. It must be quite disconcerting for the Pharisees, believing they got rid of Jesus through the cross, to discover that His ministry is continuing and expanding.

> *You could have more degrees than a thermometer, and still not make a difference in people's lives. The greatest credential of a minister is changed lives*

It seems that one of the Pharisees' complaints against the ministry of Peter and John is that they lack the proper credentials. To use a modern vernacular, they and their companions haven't been to seminary. They don't have the appropriate union card, so they are viewed with disrespect. It is interesting that the apostle Paul will address this same subject. In contrast to Peter and company, he was not a common laborer before identifying with the ministry of Jesus. He was a "*Hebrew of Hebrews,*" and a "*Pharisee*" (Philippians 3:5). He carries the credential of having been a student of Gamaliel—the "Harvard MBA" of the day. Yet he comes to recognize that such achievements really do not count in the grand scheme of things—especially when compared to knowing Christ. He may very well be in attendance here at Peter's trial. Yet once he meets Christ his perspective will change. In 2 Corinthians 3:1–3 he writes,

> *"Are we beginning to commend ourselves again? Or do we need, as some, letters of commendation to you or from you? You are our letter, written in our hearts, known and read by all men; being manifested that you are a letter of Christ, cared for by us, written not with ink but with the Spirit of the living God, not on tablets of stone but on tablets of human hearts."*

In other words, you could have more degrees than a thermometer, and still not make a difference in people's lives. The greatest credential of a minister is changed lives. If Christ has changed us—if we have *"been with Jesus."*—then we are qualified to change lives in others.

DAY THREE

THE DELIVERY OF THE VERDICT (ACTS 4:8–22)

Isn't it ironic that humans sit in judgment on the works of God? In reality, to do so is to sit in judgment of God Himself. While, as leaders, these men have a responsibility to try and discern whether or not this miracle is a work of God, such a task should be entered into with the greatest modicum of humility. With the twenty-twenty vision of hindsight, we can say with confidence that this gathering of the Sanhedrin misses God. Before we begin taking up stones to throw at them though, we should temper our judgment with the example we see in their ranks. We will see later in the book of Acts that *"a great many of the priests"* become *"obedient to the faith"* (Acts 6:7). Not all of them miss God. What leaps out from that text is the term *"a great many."* They may be slow to see God's working, but at least a good number finally do. In the meantime, the religious establishment moves into containment mode.

📖 Take a look at Acts 4:18. What is the verdict of the Sanhedrin?

> *It is impressive that, in the first century, these followers have to be instructed to keep quiet about Jesus. It is the natural tendency of many of us—myself included—to need prodding to speak up and take a stand.*

The Sanhedrin commands Peter and John not to *"speak or teach at all in the name of Jesus."* In other words, they aren't to talk about Jesus at all or give Him credit for anything. While we may focus on the term *"command,"* it is not as strong a statement in the Greek as it appears in English. The Greek verb is in the indicative mood of a statement of fact, rather than in the imperative mood of a command. The word carries the idea of a pronouncement—a giving of instructions. It is impressive that, in the first century, the followers of Jesus have to be instructed to keep quiet about Jesus. It is the natural tendency of many of us—myself included—to need prodding to speak up and take a stand.

📖 Read over the response of Peter and John in Acts 4:19–20 to the verdict and summarize the main points in your own words.

It is interesting to notice the humility blended with boldness in the disciples' response here. They do not try to sit in judgment on their accusers; they leave the judging to them. They invite the Sanhedrin to make their own decision about what is right or wrong in this circumstance, but they also make it clear they have already drawn their own conclusions. They believe they are following God in proclaiming Jesus and they will not be silenced no matter the cost. What they have *"seen and heard"* is so compelling that they cannot stop speaking about it.

📖 Look at Acts 4:21–22.

How do the Sanhedrin respond to this boldness of Peter and John?

What is the crowd's view of what has taken place?

How do you think the crowd's view affects the Sanhedrin?

Before releasing Peter and John, the Sanhedrin threatens them further, but the threats are hollow and empty. It is clear from the text that there is not much they can do to the disciples. Though the Jewish leaders don't like this preaching in the name of Jesus, Peter and John have not broken the Law. They have done a good thing, healing a man of his life-long affliction. It is clear as well that the Sanhedrin too is influenced by the opinion of the masses. Without a doubt, the crowds have drawn their own conclusion about this miracle and are giving glory to God for the man's healing. This man who has spent over forty years as an invalid has been made whole, and the majority's verdict is that it is a work of God.

DAY FOUR

THE CHURCH'S RESPONSE (ACTS 4:23-31)

How should the church of God respond to opposition? What should our perspective be? What should we do when others voice their dissent to our ministering in the name of Jesus? There is much wisdom in following the example of the early church. They do not have the political clout to make their voice heard. They have no military might to force their will on others. But they have the ear of God. There is no greater means of shaping the course of human events than to be on our knees. The immediate reaction of the church is to pray. God is pleased when we trust Him with the events of our lives. Without faith, it is impossible to please Him, and whom we trust with what happens to us is reflected in whether or not we see the need to pray.

📖 Read over Acts 4:23–26 and answer the questions that follow.

What do these verses say about how the church interprets the events of the day?

Who we trust with what happens to us is reflected in whether or not we see the need to pray

Why do you think David's prophecy identifies persecution as a *"futile"* thing?

How does the first Old Testament quote here relate to the second one?

As soon as Peter and John are released, they go straight to a gathering of believers to report what has happened. While the text doesn't tell us, undoubtedly, these are gathered to pray for Peter and John who have spent the night under arrest. It is important to recognize that they use the Word of God to evaluate and understand their circumstances. We do not interpret Scripture in light of our circumstances, but rather, the other way around. It is through Scripture—the prophecy of David in Psalm 2—that they are reminded that any stand people take against God is futile. This is where the quote from Psalm 146:6 comes in. Because God created the heavens and the earth, how foolish it is for anyone to stand against the all-powerful Creator.

📖 Examine Acts 4:27–28.

How does verse 27 relate to Acts 4:26?

_____

_____

_____

_____

What does Acts 4:28 add to our perspective on these events?

_____

_____

_____

_____

As God brings to their minds the prophecy of David in Psalm 2, they are able to recognize that every portion of that psalm was fulfilled in the crucifixion. The Roman governmental leaders were in opposition to God by allowing Jesus to be put to death. This action also had the support of the Gentiles in Jerusalem. More importantly, it is the Jews who requested Barabbas be released when Pilate offered to set Jesus free. While each of these parties listed bears responsibility before God for their individual participation, verse 28 points out, God purposed for Christ to die. It is not an either/or equation. Man chose and so did God.

WORD STUDY
Lord

The term "Lord" (*despotes*), applied to God the Father here, is rarely so used in the New Testament (only a total of six times). The Greek word is the source of our English term "despot," and conveys the idea of absolute master. In human hands, absolute power tends to lead to abuse, and the negative connotation of the English word "despot" is usually appropriate. But because ours is the God of love and grace, the thought of Him wielding absolute authority as master of all is an encouraging thought to remember in the face of persecution.

📖 Look over Acts 4:29–31 and answer what follows.

What does the church ask God to do in light of this persecution?

_____

_____

_____

What does God do for them as they finish praying?

_____

_____

It is amazing to realize that so little of God's people's prayers are focused on the persecution aimed at them. *"Take note of their threats,"* the people in Acts 4 pray, but what to do about the threats is left to God. Instead, they ask that God grant them boldness to keep doing what Christ instructed them to do. It should be noted that they do not ask that signs and wonders be done through *them*, but through the *name* of Jesus. They are careful to give Him the glory for what He does. As soon as they are finished praying, God begins to answer their prayer. Their meeting place is shaken, and suddenly they are all filled with the Spirit. Notice what the manifestation of being Spirit-filled is. They begin *"to speak the word of God with boldness,"* exactly what they asked God to work in their lives.

Day 5

For Me To Follow God

Persecution happens. There is a price to be paid for following God in a world that is at war with Him. In Philippians 3:10 the apostle Paul speaks of *"the fellowship of His sufferings,"* and in Colossians 1:24 he speaks of the church *"filling up what is lacking in Christ's afflictions."* God sometimes allows us to take the blows meant for Jesus. It is a unique fellowship with Him. Paul indicates that this *"momentary, light affliction"* produces for us an eternal weight of glory beyond comparing. Though persecution in any form is hard at the time, it is always worth it. Costly obedience is worship at the highest level. We should not seek out persecution or affliction, but when it comes, we should not shrink back. We cannot allow people to keep us from obeying the Great Commission of our Lord. We may not be arrested for speaking of Christ, but if we do it often enough, we will face opposition. Peter himself writes of this in his first epistle.

> *"To the degree that you share the sufferings of Christ, keep on rejoicing, so that also at the revelation of His glory you may rejoice with exultation. If you are reviled for the name of Christ, you are blessed, because the Spirit of glory and of God rests on you. Make sure that none of you suffers as a murderer, or thief, or evildoer, or a troublesome meddler; but if anyone suffers as a Christian, he is not to be ashamed, but is to glorify God in this name."*
> (1 Peter 4:13–16)

What is some persecution you face or have faced because of your faith?

How have you handled it?

_____

_____

_____

_____

> *"Make sure that none of you suffers as a murderer, or thief, or evildoer, or a troublesome meddler; but if anyone suffers as a Christian, he is not to be ashamed, but is to glorify God in this name." (1 Peter 4:15-16)*

Thinking of what might happen in the future as you try to take a stand for the Lord, which best expresses how you believe you will respond?

- Speak the word of God with boldness

- Speak truth with timidity

- Be silenced out of the fear of people

- Other: _____

Remember, the key to our response is not found in *us* but in *Who* lives in us. If we are filled with the Spirit—having no unconfessed sin and allowing Christ to be in control of our lives—then we have the promise of God that *"the Holy Spirit will teach you in that very hour what you ought to speak"* (Luke 12:12). Why not take a moment and affirm to the Lord that you want Him to be in control of your heart? Invite Him to convict you of any sin that is getting in the way of Him ruling and reigning in your heart. Ask Him for the boldness that comes from being filled with the Spirit.

How would you say you do at being a witness for Christ to those around you?

_____

_____

_____

_____

It is impressive that, in the first century, these followers have to be instructed to keep quiet about Jesus. It is the natural tendency of many of us—myself included—to need prodding to speak up and take a stand. It seems that a clue to their bold response can be found in the passage we have studied this week. Peter and John's response to the command of the Pharisees reveals much about who they are and why they live as they do. Their answer to the threats of the religious is *"whether it is right from God's perspective for us to obey you rather than Him, you judge, for* **we cannot stop speaking what we have seen and heard.***"*

This gutsy reply to those hindering the apostles gives many clues to their motivation and offers much help to a needy church. First and foremost, they are more concerned with pleasing God than with pleasing people. This is not true of all who know Christ in their day. John 12:42–43 states, *"many even of the rulers believed in Him, but because of the Pharisees they were not confessing Him, for fear that they would be put out of the synagogue;* **for they loved the approval of men rather than the approval of God.***"* Proverbs 29:25 says, *"The fear of man brings a snare."* If we want the faith of the apostles, we must, like them, value God's approval most.

> "We cannot stop speaking what we have seen and heard." (Acts 4:20)

Honestly, have you been silenced out of the fear of people and the love of their approval?

_____

_____

_____

If so, confess it as sin and repent of it.

A second revelation from this incident is that Peter and John cannot stop speaking of what they have seen and heard. Their encounter with the living Christ has affected them. Likewise, if we are not speaking, it may be that we are not encountering Christ. If we truly meet with Him, and He is at work in our lives, we ought to feel compelled to share that (see 2 Corinthians 5:14–15). If not, it may be that our faith is simply religious play-acting; holding to a form of godliness but denying its power. If we want to take a bold stand for Christ, then there should be something compelling in what He has done for us.

Would you say that what you have *"seen and heard"* in your relationship with the Lord is compelling enough to talk about?

_____

_____

_____

If not, then the solution is not trying to work up boldness, but in pursuing the Lord. What are some things you can do to "see and hear?"

_____

_____

What does the early church do in the face of persecution? They trust God to deal with their persecutors, and they pray for boldness. As we close out this week's lesson, why not write out a prayer to the Lord that expresses this same heart. Remember, it is He who made *"the heaven and the earth and the sea, and all that is in them."*

LESSON 5

THE FAMILY OF GOD
ACTS 4:32—5:16

We live in a selfish world. Everyone tends to look out for number one. Yet it is not so in the kingdom of God. One of the evidences that He reigns in our hearts is that we are freed from slavery to self. It is a mark of faith that we are able to trust God to meet our needs and are free to reach out to meet the needs of others. In fact, to do so is an act of great faith. The world around us is not like that. This is why Jesus says, *"By this all men will know that you are My disciples, if you have love for one another"* (John 13:35). The reason they will know is because such action is so different from the world. Paul tells us that in the last days men will be *"lovers of self"* (2 Timothy 3:2). Their hearts will have no room for others. No wonder we stand out! We are lights in a dark world. This is what we witness when we look at life in the early church. It is clear that fellow believers are viewed as family, not just as friends and acquaintances. It is said that blood is thicker than water, but what we see in the early church is that spirit is thicker still.

> *"By this all men will know that you are My disciples, if you have love for one another" (John 13:35)*

The world has rarely seen what God can do through those who lay aside the trappings of self and completely surrender to Him. It is not because of any lack of what God is able to do, but because so few are willing to get out of the way to let Him work through them. But when one makes that choice to die to self and yield to Him, it is a beautiful and authentic act of faithfulness. John the Baptist expresses well what ought to be the heart of every believer: *"He must increase, but I must decrease"* (John 3:30). What marks the first-century church is that so many are willing to decrease that Christ might increase. Yet this is not true of everyone. Unfortunately, we see the stains of sin in this holy work. While some walk in surrender, others walk in self. What we will see in Lesson 5 is alarming if one takes the time to honestly reflect on it. The actions of Ananias and Sapphira are shocking in their overt selfishness. The reaction of God is even more shocking in its severity. Yet we should not be surprised either with the action or the reaction. Sin is rampant, and yet it is serious—as is God's holiness. God deals harshly with this particular sin because the stakes are so high. The work is new and fragile, and God is not willing to allow it to be derailed by Satan's deceiving.

We will see in this week's lesson examples of humanity at its best and at its worst. The truth is that the family of God always contains humanity's best and worst. I'm not sure what is more amazing—the great works God is able to do, or the fact that He can do them in spite of the actions we humans are prone to do. That God can work through any of us is amazing indeed. Yet He does! We will see in this lesson that the work of God continues even though the stains and smudges of human selfishness are overlaid on it. We should take courage and comfort in these examples from the past, for the same problems and opportunities exist in the present.

DAY ONE

THE PRINCIPLE OF FAMILY LIFE (ACTS 4:32–37)

God is our heavenly Father. We learn this from the earliest days. Jesus teaches us to pray, "Our Father. . ." (Matthew 6:9). In the garden of Gethsemane, He prays to God as "Abba, Father" (Mark 4:36). In so doing, He uses a terminology that is foreign to the believers of His day. "Abba" is usually the first word a child would learn to speak. It is the equivalent in our culture of saying "Dada." When the apostle Paul explains what this means, he relates that "God has sent forth the Spirit of His Son into our hearts, crying 'Abba! Father!' Therefore you are no longer a slave, but a son" (Galatians 4:6–7). We are not God's slaves, but His children. We have been adopted into His family. We "have received a spirit of adoption as sons by which we cry out, 'Abba! Father!'" (Romans 8:15). I think most believers know this truth intellectually, but few really reflect on what it means practically. First, it speaks loudly of a relationship of intimacy with God. But second, it also speaks of my relationship with His other children. I am a part of His family which makes every believer my brother or sister! That family connection ought to be reflected in how I relate to other believers. I ought to want to be with them. I should be able to rejoice when they rejoice and mourn when they mourn. Their welfare becomes my concern. We are family.

📖 Read Acts 4:32–35 carefully and answer the questions that follow.

What is the attitude of the early church toward possessions (4:32)?

....

....

....

....

What is the result of this attitude (4:34a)?

....

....

....

....

How are the needs of the needy being met (4:34b-35)?

DID YOU KNOW?
Early Communism?

Some suggest that the early believers practiced a form of communism or communal living. While this appearance may hold up at a glance, it does not survive a scrutiny of the text. We see in Peter's response to Ananias that his possessions are his own and under his control. Whatever giving he does is not obligatory.

The prevailing attitude of believers at this time is that all they possess belongs to God instead of themselves. Second, they have a family mindset. They are concerned about the physical needs of their fellow believers. The early church has many diverse needs. Because many of the saved at Pentecost and thereafter are Jews from outside of Jerusalem who decide to stay to be taught by the Apostles, a temporary welfare system has to be established to care for the physical needs of those unemployed. With the advent of persecution, other needs are created as some lose their jobs because of the faith. People take their surplus (unneeded houses or land) and sell it, giving the proceeds to the church to distribute. The result is that there is *"not a needy person among them."* When the church functions in such a loving way, the difference our faith makes is put on display.

📖 Look at 4:36–37. What do you learn about Barnabas, who is given as a positive example of this practice?

First, we learn that his real name is Joseph, and he is of the tribe of Levi. This tells us that he is somewhat educated—a "white collar" worker if you will. As a Levite, he would be responsible for temple duties. He is from the Isle of Cyprus. We know from Scripture and historical writings that he is a bachelor. He seems to be a man of poise and integrity. Perhaps more telling about him than anything else in this passage, is that his life is so characterized by encouragement that the apostles begin calling him "Barnabas" which means "Son of Encouragement." This nickname sticks, and from this point on in the New Testament, he is never called Joseph again, always "Barnabas."

📖 Looking at the actions of this passage, why do you suppose the apostles give this man Joseph the nickname, Barnabas? What is it about him that is so associated with encouragement?

When God brings His people up out of Egypt, He sets aside the tribe of Levi for His service. The Levites are to devote themselves as students of the Law and servants of the people. The people are to support them by their offerings. The tribe includes the priests, the scribes, and all other supporting roles in public worship. Acts 6:7 tells us that many of the priests become obedient to the Christian faith. As a Levite, obviously Barnabas is among them.

First, we need to appreciate the fact that Galilee is looked down upon in Jerusalem. In fact, it is said of Nazareth, a town in Galilee, *"Can anything good come out of Nazareth?"* And yet, the apostles are mostly from Galilee. Barnabas, the sophisticated Levite, who owns a tract of land, sells it and brings the money and lays it at the feet of these Galilean peasants. This is an act of deference and honor. This must be a great *encouragement* to them. In fact, one must logically ask, "Why is Barnabas singled out if many people are selling property and donating the money?" We move into conjecture at this point, but it may very well be that Barnabas is the first believer to do so. This is not a mandated practice—we see nowhere in Scripture that it is commanded or even suggested. It may be that the example of Barnabas is the impetus for the whole practice. In any case, of all who participate in this practice, Scripture singles out Barnabas as the best positive example. His is a stewardship view of life. He sees all that he has as belonging to God and views himself as merely the steward of it. People are always encouraged when they see someone who isn't worried about whose position is higher. He sets a good example for the rest of the family.

DAY 2

THE PROBLEMS IN FAMILY LIFE (ACTS 5:1–4)

There is no such thing as a perfect family. Everybody can testify to that. If your family is like mine, the herd may have more black sheep than white ones. Each closet has its share of skeletons. The reason is simple—families are populated with fallen people. God's family is no exception. I once heard a wise man advise, "If you find a perfect church, by all means don't join it, for you'll mess it up!" Unfortunately, though we know that people are imperfect, we tend to be shocked when we see their imperfections. Yet this is one of the reasons that the Bible is so practical. It doesn't try to gloss over the failings and frailty of God's people. It presents their portraits with no airbrushing out the imperfections. In this lesson, we will get to see "up close and personal" some of the flaws of fallen people. Yet we will also see the hand of God moving in spite of those flaws and failures.

📖 Read through Acts 5:1–2, and summarize in your own words what takes place.

_____

_____

_____

As this practice of selling possessions and giving the proceeds to the church begins to take root, a certain couple named Ananias and Sapphira decide to participate. They sell a piece of property they own and then donate part of the proceeds to the church. Apparently, they misrepresent the sale price as being less than it actually is and pocket the difference.

📖 Now reflect on Acts 5:1–2 again. What is significant about Sapphira's participation in this?

_____

_____

_____

Luke mentions twice that Sapphira is an equal partner in the deception. In verse 1, Luke tells us that Ananias' actions are carried out *"with his wife."* In verse 2, the writer of Acts clarifies that the withholding of some of the funds is done *"with his wife's full knowledge."* Even though it is Ananias who actually tells the lie and performs the deception, Sapphira shares equally in the guilt.

DOCTRINE
The Holy Spirit

In Acts 5:3, Peter identifies that Ananias has *"lie[d] to the Holy Spirit."* In Acts 5:4, Peter accuses him of lying *"to God."* It is a subtle statement but a significant one, for Peter equates the two. He is stating emphatically that to lie to the Spirit is to lie to God—making it clear to all that the Holy Spirit is God.

📖 Look over Acts 5:3–4.

What do you think it means that Satan fills Ananias' heart?

_____

_____

_____

How does Peter interpret what is wrong in what happens?

_____

_____

_____

_____

Peter uses some interesting terminology in this passage. He credits the sin and deceit to Satan having *"filled"* Ananias' heart. It stands as what would seem to be an intentional contrast to the congregation being *"filled"* with the Holy Spirit in Acts 4:31. This does not mean that Ananias is demon-possessed, but rather that his lie is birthed in his heart and aligns him with the *"father of lies"* (John 8:44). The practice of selling possessions and donating the proceeds is not something that is mandatory in the early church. It is a voluntary practice, strictly at the discretion of the owners. Ananias and Sapphira do not sin in selling their property, nor is it wrong for them to keep part of the proceeds. Peter identifies their sin as lying to the Holy Spirit. They could have simply told the apostles that they are only giving part of the profit from the sale. Instead, they lie. Apparently, they want the glory of men for their deed even though their true heart is revealed not in what they give but in what they keep.

In 1 Corinthians 4:5, we gain some important insight into how God will judge the believer. Here, Paul tells us that God will *"bring to light the things hidden in the darkness and disclose the motives of men's hearts."* When God judges, He does so with complete fairness because He sees those things that no one else sees. God sees the hidden details in the sales transaction of Ananias' and Sapphira's property. More importantly, God sees their heart. He recognizes the motive. Ananias and Sapphira aren't really motivated by a desire to minister to the brethren and to help those in need. Their real motivation is the glory they want to receive from people for their act of charity. As amazing as it may seem, the right action can still be wrong if the motive is wrong. God is concerned with the heart, not just the deed.

DAY THREE

THE PURGING OF THE PROBLEM (ACTS 5:5–11)

Have you ever wondered why God deals with certain sins or certain people more harshly than others? Sodom and Gomorrah were destroyed because of rampant immorality, yet not all cities with such sin have been destroyed. Korah was swallowed alive for grumbling against the leadership of Moses and Aaron. Miriam, on the other hand, did much the same thing, yet her consequence is leprosy which God eventually heals. If your church is like mine, I would guess that grumbling against spiritual leaders takes place there as well, yet we don't see God dealing with it the same way. Part of the reason may lie in the motive of the heart, but also there is something in the timing of God's judging. When God is doing something new, He often makes an example of sin for the benefit of future generations. Two perspectives are essential to hold when trying to understand God's dealings. First, God is not partial. He shows no favoritism, nor does He "go soft" on sin after a while. Sin will still be judged even if judgment is delayed. Second, God sometimes uses temporal consequences as a tutor for others, but that is not the same thing as God's ultimate judgment. Korah may have been swallowed alive by the earth, but this was physical judgment. The text does not tell us he goes to hell for eternity. *As we seek to understand God's harsh dealings with Ananias and Sapphira, we must be careful not to read more into the story than Scripture tells us.*

📖 Look over Acts 5:5–6, and summarize what happened after Peter confronted Ananias.

_____

_____

_____

_____

> *When God is doing something new, He often makes an example of*
> *sin for the benefit of future generations.*

As soon as Peter voiced the indictment of Ananias, God's judgment fell. Ananias died where he stood. Peter did not lay hands on him nor speak his judgment. God acted. God judged him immediately and severely. It should be noted that the revelation of his sin came to Peter supernaturally—Peter knew what Ananias did as soon as the offering was made. In like kind, Peter dealt with the sin in supernatural fashion.

📖 Now read over Acts 5:7–10.

How does Peter deal with Sapphira?

_____

_____

_____

What is similar in this situation to that of Ananias?

_____

_____

_____

What is different?

_____

_____

_____

About three hours after God has dealt with Ananias, his wife comes into the church. Unlike her husband, she does not speak first, but when Peter inquires of her, she lies as well. It would seem that in Peter's question there is an opportunity for her to repent, but it is not acted upon. She is killed in like fashion to her husband, and before the day ends, she is buried beside him.

📖 Examine Acts 5:11. What is the result of how God deals with Ananias and Sapphira?

_____

_____

_____

In Acts 5:11 we are told, *"And great fear came upon the whole church, and upon all who heard of these things."* Since we are among those who have heard of these things, we too should bring from them a holy reverence for God.

📖 Read Leviticus 10:1–11, and compare it to Acts 5.

What is the sin of Nadab and Abihu, and how does God deal with it?

_____

_____

_____

What, according to verse 3 is the reason God deals so seriously with this sin?

_____

_____

_____

WORD STUDY
Strong Drink

One of the admonitions that flows out of Nadab and Abihu's encounter with God is the command for the priests not to drink wine nor strong drink (from the Hebrew root word *shakar*, which means to make drunk). The command of Leviticus 10:9 not to drink suggests that part of the reason for Nadab and Abihu's foolish choice is that they may be drunk, though this is not stated with certainty.

Nadab and Abihu apparently use coals of fire that are not taken from the brazen altar as prescribed by the Lord (Leviticus 16:12). The fact that it is not God's fire underscores that He cannot accept human improvisation. We must worship <u>His</u> way. Nadab and Abihu do not take the worship of God seriously and do not worship God His way. The consequence of this sin is dramatic, immediate death. It is a supernatural death, as fire comes from the cloud of glory that rests over the mercy seat, killing them but not burning up their clothes or bodies (verse 5).

God's explanation to Moses for the harsh dealing with Nadab and Abihu is *"By those who come near to Me I will be treated as holy, and before all the people I will be honored."* True worship must respect God's holiness. This is why there are not "many roads to God" as a religious pluralism emphasis often suggests. True worship also involves "honoring" the Lord.

What does this teach us about our own worship? We must make certain we respect God's holiness (which requires dealing with sin), and we must be sure that our worship honors Him. There can be no flippancy or irreverence in our worship. This narrative must be kept in the context of the whole Bible to be fully understood. It does not reflect a God who is unjust or harsh in dealing with a simple mistake. What God does is a necessary example to the ages that because He is holy, He must be treated as such. In a biology lab, sterile equipment must be handled as such, or it will be stained by unsterile hands. This serves as a good physical picture of holiness.

> *God wants to walk in relationship with people, but He will not allow people to profane His holiness with worship that does not take Him seriously*

The sin of Ananias and Sapphira is not unlike the sin of Nadab and Abihu. Both are in the context of a new method of worshiping God. Nadab and Abihu's sin comes at the very beginning of the establishment of worship with the Old Testament Tabernacle. The judgment of Ananias and Sapphira occurs at the beginning of the new method of worship in the context of the church.

God wants to walk in relationship with people, but He will not allow people to profane His holiness with worship that does not take Him seriously. These examples of wrong worship send a clear statement from the Lord that He is to be treated with reverence. If we are to worship Him, we must appreciate how important it is not to be careless or flippant in our devotion. It need not always be a somber thing to come into God's presence but is always a serious one. God is saying something about the nature of true worship through how He deals with Nadab and Abihu and with Ananias and Sapphira.

DAY FOUR

THE PROSPERING OF THE FAMILY OF GOD (ACTS 5:12–16)

Church growth experts tell us that healthy growth—the kind you can keep up with and manage—is from 5–12% a year. Anything more than that and it is quite hard to develop and deploy leaders fast enough to keep pace. The early church blows those statistics away. Their growth is off the charts. Three thousand are added one day, and five thousand another. With that rapid growth we can be sure there are problems. Yet that doesn't mean the first century congregation is unhealthy. What is a healthy church? Is it one with no problems? I don't think so. Rather, I think health is seen not just in the absence of problems, but also when the problems that emerge are being dealt with the right way. The early church faces many challenges. It has to deal with persecution almost from its very beginning. Yet as we see this week, some of the challenges are not external. Some come from within the church itself. Even then, we see God's faithfulness in dealing with these problems. As Peter faithfully confronts sin, the result is that the whole church benefits. Everyone begins to take God (and sin) more seriously. As a result, the whole church prospers.

📖 What healthy results do you see in Acts 5:12 from God's working in the early church?

The early church is marked by the supernatural. We are told that "*many signs and wonders*" are taking place among the people. While we may tend to focus on the literal here, there is a principle which must be recognized as well. God is always able to do signs and wonders, but those are not the only manifestations that God is at work. A mark of a healthy church is that prayer is being answered. People are able to recognize that God is doing the things that only He can do. Another evidence of the health of this early stage of the church is that there is a pervasive unity. Not only do they want to be together, but their gathering has a spiritual tone. They meet at the temple. True unity always has God at its center, and when God is central unity is always the result.

DID YOU KNOW?
Solomon's Portico

Solomon's portico (or porch) was situated on the eastern side of the temple toward the court of the Gentiles. It was a popular gathering place for those having business at the temple, and quickly became a favorite gathering place for believers. Apparently, they meet there regularly for prayer and worship.

Why doesn't God do more signs and wonders? We tend to think that if we have signs and wonders like the early church, more people will believe. Yet even with these miracles, many do not believe. At one point in Jesus' ministry, the Pharisees seek a sign from Jesus, and He refuses to give one. He rebukes them saying, "*an evil and adulterous generation craves for a sign*" (Matthew 12:39). The point is, our flesh loves the dramatic and miraculous, but that is not what true faith rests upon. The need for spectacular proof of God's power reflects a weak faith, not a strong one.

📖 Take a look at Acts 5:13–16. What do you think is meant by the contrast in responses we see in these verses?

It seems that there are at least three different responses to be observed in these verses. First, we see that some refuse to associate with the early Christians. The phrase, "*none of the rest,*" seems to reference Jews worshiping at the temple who have not yet embraced

Christianity. This does not imply rejection, for we are told that the people hold them in *"high esteem."* It more likely indicates that many look on them favorably but are not ready to commit. The second response is that though some aren't ready to join the followers of Jesus, many others do. But there is a third group to be observed here as well. Whether they are willing to give their lives to the Lord or not, many hope to get something from the early church. They want to be blessed physically—to have their temporal needs met. While many believe, we are told that many others seek out the apostles for healing. As we will see next week, there is yet a fourth response to be seen in this context—some respond with active opposition.

📖 Look again at Acts 5:15. Why do you suppose people think that being touched by Peter's shadow might work to their benefit?

_____

_____

_____

_____

While some respond to the early church by seeking to understand, and others have a spiritual reaction, some it would seem are superstitious. Some are seeing God in what is happening, while others are seeing Peter. This latter group, though decidedly selfish in their seeking, are still ministered to. A great number experience healing.

The most prevalent sense one gets of the early church is that the fingerprints of God are everywhere. Everywhere one looks, the working of God is evident. That should be true of us today as well. The world is not at all impressed with what we do for God. Many other religions work hard for their deity (some work to far greater excess than we do). Religious devotion does not set Christianity apart. What causes the world to stop and take notice is not what we do for God, but what they see God do for and through us. When God does what only He can do, the uninitiated see Him instead of us.

DAY FIVE

FOR ME TO FOLLOW GOD

The family of God is not yet perfected. It holds both good and bad examples. Yet for all of its imperfections, it is a glorious entity. In this lesson we have been given a glimpse into its inner workings. We see how God is able to use it to remake society, to meet needs, and to carve out a place where love for your neighbor can flourish. So, what is the main application from this week's lesson? Is it to sell all our possessions and give the money to the church? While it is possible God could call you to do that, the main application is something much more fundamental. God is more concerned with what you do with your person, than He is with what you do with your possessions. If you do right with your heart, your possessions will take care of themselves.

*God is more concerned with what you do with your **person**,*
than He is with what you do with your possessions.
If you do right with your heart, your possessions will take care of
themselves.

Luke paints us a portrait of the family of God, but he does not airbrush out the flaws. In fact, he seems to set up an intentional contrast between the positive example of Barnabas and the negative one of Ananias and Sapphira. He shows us the highest ideals alongside the lowest debasement. As we seek to apply the passage to our own lives, we must be willing to acknowledge that we are capable of either extreme. Filled with the Holy Spirit, we have the potential to live as Jesus—or better said, He is able to live through us. But filled with self, we face the prospect of manifesting all the ugliness of fallen human nature at its worst. You see, this is what spiritual battle is all about. Will we yield our lives to the Spirit's control, or will we remain in control and be susceptible to being swayed by the temptations of the god of this world?

As you reflect on the past week, which would you say is more characteristic of your experience: being filled with the Spirit, or filled with flesh?

....

....

....

What do you want next week to look like?

....

....

....

While either is possible, we must be reminded of the truth of 1 John 4:4, *"greater is He who is in you than he who is in the world."* It reminds us of two important truths about spiritual battle. First, it tells us the locale of each participant in the battle. God works from within. He has taken up residence in our lives. Satan may still influence us through his tempting of our lusts and through the fallen world system he manipulates, but he is in the world, not in us. Second, the One in us is greater than the one against us. While our stumblings may be temporary, our victory is permanent.

> *"This is the confidence which we have before Him, that, if we ask*
> *anything according to His will, He hears us. And if we know that*
> *He hears us in whatever we ask, we know that we have the requests*
> *which we have asked from Him." (1 John 5:14)*

Why not take a moment to affirm your desire to be filled with the Holy Spirit? If you have no unconfessed sin or area you are withholding from the Lord, you can pray for Him to fill you with His Spirit and by faith be confident He will. We know it is God's will that we be spirit-filled, for it is commanded in Ephesians 5:18—*"Do not get drunk with wine,* for that is dissipation, but be filled with the Spirit." We know from 1 John 5:14, "This is the confidence which we have before Him, that, if we ask anything according to His will, He hears us. And if we know that He hears us in whatever we ask, we know that we have the requests which we have asked from Him." It really is that simple. We know it is God's will that we be filled with His Spirit. We know that when we pray according to His will, we have what we ask of Him. Faith means taking Him at His Word that He will do what He promises.

WHAT CAN WE LEARN FROM BARNABAS?

As we progress through the book of Acts, we see many different evidences of the Holy Spirit's work. We see that He can manifest Himself through bold proclamation of truth. He can be manifest in the healing of disease or the working of miracles. Yet another indication is seen this week in the example of the early church. The Spirit is perceptible when we place meeting the needs of others above our own selfish desires. That is what Barnabas does.

Reflect on your possessions. Are there surplus items that you need to offer to the Lord? Ask Him to reveal worthwhile objects that you really aren't putting to use.

_____

_____

_____

_____

_____

Now, go through those items and offer them to the Lord in prayer—You don't have to do anything else. Just trust Him to show you His plan for you to use those possessions to meet needs. Trust that He will show you an opportunity, or else convict you of a place to entrust them. Remember, it is trusting God to continue to meet our needs that frees us to be generous with what we have.

WHAT CAN WE LEARN FROM ANANIAS?

It is important, as we seek to apply the Word of God to our lives, that we recognize we can learn as much from a bad example as we can from a good one. The sin of Ananias and his wife is recorded in Scripture not as part of their punishment, but to instruct us. This is what happens when we put self above God. You and I are just as capable of doing this as they are. We probably already have erred in many similar ways both big and small. We should never be surprised at what shows up in our behavior when self rules the heart instead of Christ. Even our good deeds cease to be good.

By which of the following do you find yourself being tempted?

- Wanting to be applauded by people for my good deeds

- Being dishonest to appear better than I am

- Being greedy with the surplus of what God provides

- Ignoring that God sees my hidden actions and motives

- Other_____

> *We cannot produce unity. It is a work of the Spirit of God. But it is*
> *our job to preserve that unity.*

One of the hidden problems revealed in the story of Ananias is that self gets in the way of church unity. In Ephesians 4:3 we are instructed to *"Be diligent to preserve the unity of the Spirit."* We cannot produce unity. Only God's Spirit can. Unity in the family of God is automatic if the Spirit is in control of each heart, as God will never war with Himself. Our job is not to produce unity, but to preserve it by maintaining the Spirit's control and not reclaiming the throne in our hearts. If we do find that we are in control instead of God, we must be quick to yield back to Him.

Can you think of any ways where lately you have been responsible for disrupting the unity of the Spirit in the family of God?

As you close out this week's lesson, why not write out a prayer of confession and sur-render to the Lord?

LESSON 6

THE FOOLISHNESS OF FIGHTING GOD
ACTS 5:17–42

In 1991, when Iraqi dictator Saddam Hussein made the decision not to disarm at the threat of George W. Bush, he apparently believed he could defend Baghdad. Military intelligence since the Iraq War shows that the Iraqi military planned three rings of defense around the city and felt confident they could repel an American invasion. Of course, in hindsight we know that this belief was foolish and flawed. As the war played out, the world watched events unfold on television. One of the most memorable images was a split-screen report in which one screen showed the Iraqi Information Minister emphatically denying there were any Americans in Baghdad, while the other screen showed American tanks driving through the city unopposed. The Iraqi regime of Hussein clearly ended up being no match for the superior technology, training, and strategy of the American and British military. Few countries in the world would be. In fact, one would have to say that to provoke a war with the United States is a very foolish and futile endeavor.

> *It is foolishness to fight against God,*
> *but people still do every single day.*

While I have a great respect for American military might, its power is nothing compared to the power of God, the Almighty. If it is foolish to fight America, how much more so is it to fight God. You can't outthink Him, because He is omniscient—He knows everything. He knows what you are going to do before you do it and plans accordingly. Ask Satan—he thinks he is really going to win by putting Jesus to death on the cross. You can't outrun Him, because He is omnipresent—everywhere at once. Every time you run from Him, you run back into Him. Ask Jonah how smart it is to try and outrun God. And you can't overpower Him, because He is omnipotent—all powerful. He has all authority in heaven and on earth. No purpose of His can be thwarted. It is foolishness to fight against God, but people still do every single day.

How do people find themselves in the position of fighting against God? I doubt for most it is a conscious choice. Few intentionally try to make enemies of those with infinitely greater power. To slip into such a mistake often involves one or two critical errors in judgment. First, one vastly overestimates their own power, and second, greatly underestimates their opponent. When I look at the organized opposition to the early church in

Acts, I do not think the Sanhedrin makes either of these mistakes. But there is another way to find yourself in folly. We can unintentionally make ourselves the enemy of someone with greater power when we have too much confidence in our own opinion and understanding. Pride in ourselves can set us up for a fall. We can think we are fighting for God, when we are actually fighting against Him. Pride can cause us to lose touch with His will and way and result in our resisting the will of the One we claim to follow. When this happens, God is faithful to send truth our way, but we must be humble enough to hear and to receive it. This week we want to study how the religious establishment winds up trapped in the foolishness of fighting God.

DAY ONE

THE WORK OF GOD ATTACKED (ACTS 5:17–28)

Danish philosopher Søren Kierkegaard is credited with saying, "The trouble with Christians today is that no one wants to kill them anymore." Quite an interesting idea! One point he is making is that persecution has never been effective at stamping out Christianity, but rather, has served to further its spread. He also seems to imply that when Christians enjoy prosperity and freedom to the point of self-centeredness, we tend toward complacency and conformity that renders us ineffective at impacting our culture. I believe both ideas are true. The former Archbishop of Canterbury, in a humble response to being compared to the apostle Paul on one occasion replies, "Everywhere the Apostle Paul went there was either a riot or a revival. Everywhere I go they want to serve tea." Perhaps the most effective weapon against the Christian faith is not persecution but bureaucracy. Obviously, the bureaucratic religious establishment of the first century hasn't figured that one out yet. As we will see today, they really believe they can shut Christianity down by force.

Read over Acts 5:17–18.

Who is behind the persecution of the disciples?

_____

_____

> "Everywhere the Apostle Paul went there was either a riot or a revival. Everywhere I go they want to serve tea."
>
> —A former Archbishop of Canterbury

What motivates their opposition?

_____

_____

_____

Who all are included in the arrest?

_____

_____

_____

It is interesting to note that the real impetus of persecution against Christianity within the Sanhedrin is among the Sadducees. They are the minority group, but the ones who hold power through the office of the High Priest. They have several reasons to want to arrest the apostles (this time apparently all twelve are arrested). First, these men are opposing them doctrinally. Remember, Sadducees are the ones who do not believe in a resurrection or in angels. The early Christian teaching confronts these wrong views the Sadducees hold. Second, clearly Peter and John and the others have not obeyed the mandated silence of their recent arrest. Finally, the text tells us that jealousy is the main motive of their opposition. The Sadducees, and the Sanhedrin members in general, are envious of the church's huge following that has so rapidly developed.

📖   Look over Acts 5:19–21a.

How does God deal with the apostles' difficult circumstances?

_____

_____

_____

What are they instructed to do?

_____

_____

Why do you think they aren't fearful to go back to the temple?

_____

_____

_____

I love the way God deals with the persecution coming from the Sadducees. He sends an angel—that heavenly type of being the Sadducees don't believe exists. What confidence this must give the apostles. When we know God is for us, we don't fear others being against us. The angel releases them from the public jail and instructs them to return to the temple and teach the "*whole message*" (Literally "all the words") of the Christian life. The apostles are obedient without fear, for they had seen that the power of God will protect them from the Sanhedrin.

📖 Reflect on Acts 5:21b–25 and summarize in your own words what you learn from these verses.

_____

_____

_____

_____

It is a rude awakening for the Sanhedrin when they gather to decide what to do with their prisoners. It must be a shock when they discover their prisoners are nowhere to be found. Then imagine their dismay when they learn that the apostles are back at the temple—teaching again! Perhaps the most amazing aspect of all, though, is what this passage does not say. There is no acknowledgement on the part of the religious leaders that another miracle has occurred. These men they wrongly imprisoned have been divinely released, yet still they do not recognize the hand of God in their midst.

🛈 DID YOU KNOW?
Public Jail

In Acts 5, Luke makes a point of stating that the apostles are incarcerated in a public jail (the "Custodia Publica"). This is a different and more severe form of imprisonment than was applied to Peter and John in Acts 4. Peter and John were merely in the custody of the Temple Guard and most likely held in one of the chambers of the Temple.

📖 Read over Acts 5:26–28.

Why do you think the religious leaders handle the situation the way they do?

_____

_____

What do you think their fears are?

_____

_____

The Sanhedrin is now between the proverbial rock and a hard place. If they do nothing, the apostles will keep teaching of Jesus and exposing their guilt. If they deal too harshly with them, they will have the people to contend with, for clearly public sentiment is with the apostles. The guards are obviously instructed to handle the apostles with care, but thanks to the apostles' cooperation they are able to bring them before the leaders. It has now become quite obvious that the followers of Jesus are not going to keep silent.

What does it take to silence us today? What tactic of the enemy will keep us from speaking of Jesus? What impresses most as we study the posture of the early church is that nothing is successful in silencing them, in spite of how much effort is aimed at that goal. What I find tragic is how little it takes to silence us today.

DAY TWO

THE WORK OF GOD AFFIRMED (ACTS 5:29–32)

Is it wrong to obey people? The Bible devotes quite a bit of space making the point clear that it is right to obey the human authorities in your life. Children are to obey parents (Ephesians 6:1–4). Slaves are to obey masters (Colossians 3:22). Citizens are to obey kings and governing authorities (Titus 3:1). Saints are to obey spiritual leaders (Hebrews 13:17). So, in light of our discussion of Acts, why is it that Peter and the apostles so stead-fastly refuse to obey the Jewish leaders? Because they have loyalty to a higher authority. Our highest allegiance should always be to God. As we will see today, Peter and his fellow apostles state emphatically to the Sanhedrin that we are obligated to *"obey God rather than men."* This does not dismiss us from our responsibility to obey people in authority, but it makes the point that we cannot allow people to move us to disobey God. Rarely will the requirements of human authority come into conflict with the commands of God, but when they do, we must side with the higher authority. We must side with truth. What the apostles do is affirm the message they preach as truth, confirmed by God Himself.

> *We do not disobey human authority simply because we disagree, but only when obedience would constitute direct disobedience to God.*

📖 Examine Acts 5:29. Quite often Peter's words here, as well as his words we looked at in Acts 4, are used as spiritual justification for civil disobedience. How do we balance obedience to human authority with our higher loyalty to God?

_____

_____

_____

The most obvious point here is that when the direction of human authority conflicts with the dictates of divine authority, we must take our side with God instead of government. We must be cautious when considering disobeying human dictates. We do not disobey human authority simply because we disagree, but only when obedience to them would constitute direct disobedience to God. The Old Testament prophet, Daniel, comes to mind when examining the challenges the apostles are facing. An important item to note though is that in both cases a respect for human authority is maintained and displayed. We see no rudeness or words of disrespect. When the temple guards come to arrest the apostles, they do not resist or resort to violence (see 5:26). They obey the requirement to come again before the Sanhedrin, for this does not violate the command of God. In fact, it affords them yet another opportunity to obey what God instructs through the angel—keep speaking *"the whole message of this life"* (v. 20).

The book of Daniel shows us the important balance a believer must keep between human authority and divine. Daniel spends most of his life in faithful service to pagan kings, while steadfastly maintaining his devotion to God. When the dietary demands of his king run contrary to God, he is not rebellious, but instead negotiates a creative alternative to please both God and his king (Daniel 1). When the outlawing of prayer makes obedience to Jehovah illegal (Daniel 6), Daniel shows his respect and submission to human authority by willingly accepting the consequences of his disobedience. He makes no protest and shows no anger when thrown into the lion's den for continuing to pray to his God. It is interesting to note that the next morning when King Darius comes to check on Daniel and finds him still alive, the first words to pass Daniel's lips are of respect and deference. He exclaims from the lion's den, *"O king, live forever"* (Daniel 6:21). Though obedience to God may sometimes result in civil disobedience, it can never excuse civil disrespect. Sometimes we demonstrate our submission to human authority by willingly accepting their consequences for our obedience to God while still respecting their position and their right to punish. We see this in Daniel, and we see it in the apostles.

📖 Read Acts 5:30–31 and answer the questions below.

How do these words reveal the guilt of the religious leaders?

_____

_____

_____

How does this balance with the apostles' respect for authority?

_____

_____

_____

 WORD STUDY
Prince

The Greek word translated "Prince" here (*archegos*) denotes not just a leader, but also carries the idea of a "founder." It is the same Greek word that is used in Hebrews 12:2, where Jesus is called the "Author" of our faith. In this case, Jesus is presented as the founder and leader of salvation for Israel.

Everything in the apostles' manner communicates their respect for human authority. There are no demonstrations of resistance nor words of anger. Yet their words do not shy away from truth. They honestly point out that these religious leaders are responsible for placing Jesus on the cross, even though God sent Him, and God affirmed Him by raising Him from the dead and taking Him to heaven. The apostles balance their allegiance to God with respect for human authority by leaving it to God to judge and deal with the members of the Sanhedrin. When we truly trust God, we leave vengeance and justice in His hands.

📖 Take a look at Acts 5:32.

What do the apostles mean that they are *"witnesses of these things"*?

_____

_____

_____

What do you think it means that the Holy Spirit is given *"to those who obey Him"*?

_____

_____

_____

While it is clear that the apostles are eyewitnesses of both the crucifixion and the resurrection, the term goes deeper than that. It appears they are also presenting themselves as witnesses *against* the Sanhedrin for their role in crucifying Jesus. It is interesting that in that same breath the apostles mention that the Holy Spirit is also a witness. The implied point is that the Spirit is working to convict them of their wrong and of the "rightness" of the gospel message. This is at the core of what is meant by the need to "obey" the Spirit. This same term "obey" is used often in Scripture in reference to the gospel message. It appears the apostles are inviting such a response from the Sanhedrin.

DAY THREE

THE WORK OF THE GOD AVOIDED (ACTS 5:33–39)

Can you imagine an elephant sitting in your office and you not noticing? Sounds preposterous doesn't it? What about if a meteor lands in your backyard? Does it catch your attention, or do you just try to mow around it and hope the smell of smoke goes away eventually? It is amazing to think of God showing up and anyone missing it, but that is exactly what happens with the Sadducees. God is moving in their midst. Miracles abound. The Messiah comes, and they put Him to death. God raises Him from the dead, and they try to make people stop talking about it. Signs and wonders are everywhere they look. The lame walk. The sick and the afflicted with unclean spirits are all being healed (Acts 5:16). Yet instead of acknowledging the working of God, these religious leaders try their best to avoid the evidence of God's work in favor of trying to maintain *status quo*. While this reality may bewilder us, we must not be quick to judge. Honest evaluation requires we admit to the same guilt. Often when God is working in our lives, we don't recognize it. We entertain His messengers and are unaware (Hebrews 13:2). Like Paul, we *"kick against the goads"* of God's guidance and work in our lives. The root problem for the Sanhedrin and for us is that we tend not to recognize God when He does not dress the way we expect or in the manner our agenda dictates.

We tend not to recognize God when He doesn't dress the way we
expect or in the manner our agenda dictates.

📖 Reflect on Acts 5:33. Why do you think these men respond to truth in such a violent way?

We confront an interesting reality when we are convicted of wrongdoing. Either we soften and turn from it, or we harden and try to defend it. The Sanhedrin are in a difficult spot. If they acknowledge the working of God, they have to also admit their own guilt. The apostles' words cut them to the quick, but instead of responding in humility to this conviction, they want to get rid of it. They actually desire to put these men to death. If we cannot admit our guilt, we cannot draw on God's grace. Instead, we will adopt blaming others as a means of coping.

📖 Read Acts 5:34. What do you learn about Gamaliel in this verse?

Gamaliel is mentioned only here and in Acts 22:3, where we are told that the apostle Paul had been one of his students. We learn here that Gamaliel is a Pharisee and a teacher of the Law. We are also told that people respect him. Apparently, he carries some measure of authority, for he is able to give orders in the midst of the Sanhedrin. We know from other historical sources that he is one of the leading rabbis of the day.

📖 Look over Acts 5:35–39 and answer the questions that follow.

Gamaliel shares two historical examples. What do each of these examples have in common?

What does Gamaliel propose the Sanhedrin do with the apostles?

How does his counsel change the direction of the meeting?

_____

_____

_____

It is clear, even from a casual glance, that Gamaliel is a voice of reason and caution in the midst of a very volatile situation. He cautions them to take care how they respond, and his advice may very well prevent a rash and emotional response. He shares two histori-cal examples of similar situations where a leader gathers a following but the movement quickly dies when the leader is no longer around. It is interesting to recognize what trust Gamaliel places in God's sovereignty over such circumstances. His basic instruction is to do nothing—to take a "wait and see" approach. His prudent advice completely changes the direction of the gathering. The Sanhedrin lays aside its murderous passion and decides to take his counsel.

DID YOU KNOW?
Revolts of Theudas and Judas

We know nothing of the revolt of Theudas, but the second revolt led by Judas (not Iscariot) occurs in A.D. 6 and is described by the historian, Josephus. His followers come to be known as the "Zealots." Josephus also refers to "innumerable tumults and insurrections that arose in Judea following the death of Herod the Great (4 B.C.)." Possibly Theudas is among the two thousand who are crucified during that period.

Perhaps the most interesting aspect of Gamaliel's advice comes through his warning that they might actually wind up fighting against God. James, the half-brother of Jesus, writing in the epistle which bears his name, warns that "_the anger of man does not achieve the righteousness of God_" (James 1:20). In other words, when we respond out of passion instead of prudence, we often run contrary to what God calls righteousness. The idea that passion and prejudice still influence the Sanhedrin more than seeking God is evidenced by the fact that even now, they fail to repent and recognize Jesus as the Messiah. But at least for the time being, they are redirected from an even more unrighteous course of murder. The words of Gamaliel seem almost prophetic. Though these men did not yet recognize it, they are in fact "_fighting against God._"

DAY FOUR

THE WORK OF GOD ADVANCED (ACTS 5:40–42)

Luke begins his narrative of the early church with a simple prophecy of the Lord Jesus before His ascension: "_...you will receive power when the Holy Spirit has come upon you; and you shall be My witnesses both in Jerusalem, and in all Judea and Samaria, and even to the remotest part of the earth._" As each chapter in the narrative unfolds, we see evidence of the prophecy's fulfillment. The timid, cowardly group who hide from view after the crucifixion, are transformed by the Spirit's advent. They are changed from fearfully running from their own shadow, to boldly proclaiming the gospel in the face of ever-increasing opposition. What a difference it makes when the Spirit of God is in control of our lives! These men cannot be silenced. Even at this early stage of the church, the Pharisees say of them that they have already *"filled Jerusalem"* with their teaching. As we will see in the lessons to come, the Spirit-filled disciples will indeed take the gospel to the *"remotest part of the earth."*

📖 Take a close look at Acts 5:40, and write down all you learn about the actions taken by the Sanhedrin.

....

....

....

....

Obviously, the Sanhedrin is persuaded by the wisdom of Gamaliel and takes his advice to a degree. They reconsider their intent to execute the disciples, but they still try to intimidate them into silence. They have the men flogged—presumably with forty lashes "minus one" to stay just under the restrictions of the Law. They again command them to *"speak no more in the name of Jesus,"* though by now it should be apparent the apostles have no intention of obeying this command. Having no grounds to hold them under arrest, the Jewish leaders release them.

 DID YOU KNOW?
Flogged

Flogging is the common punishment for minor offenses in Jesus' day. This could be the "forty stripes minus one," as the apostle Paul speaks of in 2 Corinthians 11:24. Forty lashes is the prescribed limit according to Old Testament Law. Another variation on this type of flogging is the Makkat Mardut ("stripes of correction"). Often such beatings are performed with a "cat-o-nine-tails," a split leather thong weighted with metal and in which are attached pieces of broken pottery to maximize the pain and damage.

📖 Read Acts 5:41. What is the perspective of the apostles on what has taken place?

....

....

....

....

What an amazing statement we find here! They go their way *"rejoicing"*! One would not expect such grace from those who have been wrongfully imprisoned and beaten, but clearly the focus of these men is not on themselves. They have just been given the opportunity to speak of Jesus to the most influential religious body in Jerusalem. Instead of grumbling about their beating, they count it a bestowed honor that they suffer because of their identification with Jesus.

📖 Look at Acts 5:42, and identify the ongoing effect of Jewish attempts to silence the apostles.

_____

_____

_____

_____

What Luke communicates here tells us much of the function of the early church. There are no separate buildings where they can assemble as most churches enjoy today. Instead, the early church has their large gatherings on Solomon's Portico, the porch outside the temple. Small gatherings take place in people's homes. The main point Luke makes though is that the apostles are not silenced. Whether in public or private, they continue to get the message out that Jesus is the Messiah.

The book of Acts is an historical narrative, and Luke makes use of two methods to convey the action taking place. Sometimes he gives us a detailed, blow-by-blow report of what transpires. Other times, such as in this verse, he gives us what I call a "fast-forward summary." In this case, though only one verse is allocated (verse 42), Luke gives us a sense of what transpires over a period of time. Sometimes such verses can cover a period of months or even years. This is what characterizes the early church. Filled with the Spirit, they do everything they can to share with others the hope they have found in Jesus.

DAY FIVE

FOR ME TO FOLLOW GOD

In his Gospel, Luke records an interesting statement by the Lord. Jesus has just cast a demon out of a mute and the Pharisees are murmuring to themselves and are crediting His miracle to Satan. In a direct affront to the religious establishment who refuse to recognize the Messiah in their midst, Jesus states, *"He who is not with Me is against Me"* (Luke 11:23). How does someone fall prey to the foolishness of fighting God? It does not take active revolt. All that is required is to fail to join Him. We cannot remain neutral in the spiritual realm. We are either in submission or in rebellion. To fail to yield to God is to resist His working in our lives. God Himself walked among the Pharisees for three years, and they did not recognize Him. Instead, they resisted Him, and we see them in Acts continuing to reject Him. While fighting God truly is foolishness, it is not a mistake reserved for Pharisees only. We too can be victimized by this direct consequence of the nature of sin. When we go our own way, we fight against God. We must remind ourselves that such action will never succeed.

"He who is not with Me is against Me" (Luke 11:23)

What are some ways we can be in passive opposition to the Lord and what He wills?

_____

_____

_____

_____

Which of these do you find the easiest to slip into?

_____

_____

_____

The early church takes the full force of persecution because the truth they teach confronts and conflicts with the traditions of the religious establishment. As an aside, we must recognize that most often it is not the rebellious who persecute righteousness but the religious. I have a long-standing relationship with the Lord's work in the former Soviet republic of Belarus. Although no longer officially an atheistic country, there is great repression and persecution against evangelicals there. Sadly, it is the Russian Orthodox church taking the lead in the persecution. One faithful laborer who goes from village to village showing the "Jesus Film" has often been accosted and beaten. On one occasion his vehicle was vandalized with the windows broken and the tires slashed. A police investigation revealed that the men who did this had been bribed with bottles of vodka by the local Orthodox priest. These men who are supposed to represent God, often end up working against Him, as they end up supporting only themselves and their own agenda.

Persecution is always aimed at silencing any opposing thought. One of the reasons it is a tool of the enemy instead of a tool of the true follower of Christ is that it lacks any faith in the power of God to defend Himself. God does not need us to defend Him. He only asks us to proclaim Him. Persecution is incompatible with true Christianity, for it seeks to coerce behavior instead of convict hearts. It may cause conformity for a time, but in the end external pressure does not change internal belief but rather, solidifies opposing thought.

The religious establishment tries everything to silence the apostles and yet is ineffective at doing so. Today, however, it seems the enemy is all too effective at coercing believers to keep silent. Consider the list below and identify the factors that keep you from speaking up to others about the Lord.

___ Fear of physical harm

___ Fear of embarrassment

___ Intimidation that others aren't interested

___ Lack of confidence that you know what to say

___ Worry that someone will ask a question you cannot answer

___ Other: _____

External pressure does not change internal belief but rather, solidifies opposing thought.

What can you do to address these problems?

_____

_____

_____

_____

While not being silenced is an application we glean from the apostles' example, we must also recognize that there is much application to our lives in the example of the Sanhedrin. They completely miss what God is doing in their midst.

Can you think of any examples of this mistake in your own life?

_____

_____

_____

_____

What would have helped you avoid this problem?

_____

_____

_____

_____

We can all miss God. The key is to keep our eyes on Jesus, not our circumstances. He will be faithful to show us when we are missing what the Lord is doing. The Spirit-filled Christian has God Himself guiding him toward truth. If we are willing to be led, He will lead us. We must make certain however that we want God's will and not merely our own.

Why not close out this week's lesson by writing a prayer to the Lord expressing what you have learned personally?

_____

_____

_____

LESSON 7

A LIFE PLACED ON THE ALTAR

ACTS 6—7

What can a human give to God? King David asks just this question as he prepares for the building of the Temple in Jerusalem. He has given millions of dollars' worth of gold and silver and jewels for the building of the Temple, but in his prayer of dedication he exclaims, *"Who am I and who are my people that we should be able to offer as generously as this? For all things come from You, and from Your hand we have given You...O Lord our God, all this abundance that we have provided to build You a house for Your holy name, it is from Your hand, and all is Yours."* In other words, he is saying, "Everything I am giving You came FROM You and belongs to You anyway." Think about the logic in what David is saying. God doesn't need our gold or silver. He can create it by just speaking the word. As our Creator and Lord, everything we have comes from Him anyway. Our possessions are only a temporary stewardship. They don't really belong to us but are merely given to us for a season. So, what can a person possibly give to God? The only thing we can truly give to God is ourselves.

> *"Therefore I urge you, brethren, by the mercies of God, to present your bodies a living and holy sacrifice, acceptable to God, which is your spiritual service of worship." (Romans 12:1)*

In Romans 12:1, the apostle Paul gives this charge: *"Therefore I urge you, brethren, by the mercies of God, to present your bodies a living and holy sacrifice, acceptable to God, which is your spiritual service of worship."* His exhortation draws on Old Testament imagery and paints a powerful picture of the life to which God calls us. Just as the sacrificed animal was placed on the temple altar, God beckons us to surrender ourselves as a living sacrifice to Him. However, there is a subtle yet significant difference between a surrendered Christian life and an animal on the altar. We are not placed there by another against our will. We are only on the altar by our own exercise of choice. As a "living sacrifice" our being on the altar is not a one-time choice either. It is an ongoing choice. Someone well said, "The problem with a living sacrifice is it keeps crawling off the altar." The responsibility of the surrendered believer is to keep moving back to the center of the altar. This is our *"spiritual service of worship."*

Stephen, the first martyr of the Christian church exemplifies for all ages just such a life of surrender. In Acts 7, Stephen worships God by placing his whole life on the altar as a sacrifice. He gives up his right to self-determination and gives himself to God. Through that offering he gives himself in service to the early church—and in sacrifice to the persecution aimed at this church. It is ironic that Paul would be the one to extend such an invitation (as we find in Romans 12:1). For in Acts 7 we have our brief introduction to the apostle Paul—before his conversion—as one of those participating in Stephen's execution. This week we want to look at the brief, yet significant life of the disciple, Stephen.

DAY ONE

STEPHEN AS A SERVANT (ACTS 6:1-7)

One of the most fundamental lessons Jesus teaches the disciples is the difference between a worldly leader and a godly one. On the night of the Last Supper, Jesus washes the disciple's feet and then instructs them:

> *"The kings of the Gentiles lord it over them; and those who have*
> *authority over them are called 'Benefactors.' But it is not this way*
> *with you, but the one who is the greatest among you must become*
> *like the youngest, and the leader like the servant." (Luke 22:25–26)*

The way to be great in the kingdom of God is to become a servant. As we will see in today's lesson, Stephen is an excellent example of Jesus' view of a godly leader. He is willing to serve. In fact, that willingness distinguishes his life from those around him.

DID YOU KNOW?
Hellenistic Jews

Hellenistic Jews were Jews who have grown up outside of Jerusalem in the region of Greece. Though they believed many of the same doctrines as native Jews, they did not adhere to all the same customs and culture. They spoke Greek instead of Hebrew and used the Greek Old Testament (called the "Septuagint") instead of the Hebrew Scriptures. They were considered by many of the Palestinian Jews, especially the Pharisees, to be second-class Jews. There existed a measure of racial prejudice against them.

📖 Read Acts 6:1-4.

What challenges does the early church have to deal with?

_____

_____

Why can't the apostles take care of this situation by themselves?

What is the proposed solution to the problem?

DID YOU KNOW?
Early Deacons

Some have identified the seven men of Acts 6 as the first "deacons" in Scripture. There is some justification for this belief. These men do fulfill a function consistent with the New Testament office of deacon (see 1 Timothy 3), and in fact, the Greek word "*dia-konia*," from which the term "deacon" is derived, is used several times in this passage. It is doubtful, however, at this early stage in the development of the church, that this has become an official office. Most likely these men merely fulfilled a specific task for a season of time. It may be that their example shows the value of this specific type of leadership as the church continues to mature.

Over the past few chapters in Acts, we have seen the early church marked by rapid growth. It is also characterized by benevolent giving. Yet in the context of managing this rapid growth, the challenge of administrating their benevolence ministry becomes more and more complicated. Here we learn that an inequity develops in the church's charitable work, and a whole group of widows are being neglected. It is not surprising that the early church faces such challenges. Were the apostles to attempt the day-to-day administration of this ministry area, it would mean neglecting their primary calling. One of the first organizational acts of the early church is to place faithful men as "administrative servants" to work under the apostles so that the apostles can devote themselves fully to their specific calling: prayer and the ministry of the Word.

It is important to recognize the wisely practical nature of the apostles' proposed solution. First, though they set the standards for the type of leaders needed ("*men of good reputation, full of the Spirit and of wisdom*"), they charge the congregation with the task of identifying these men. Often the most helpful people in solving a problem are those who identify it. This does not mean that the servants will answer to the congregation, or that the apostles will be uninvolved. Notice what is to happen once the men are identified: "*whom we may put in charge of this task.*" Literally it reads, whom we may "stand down upon this one need." A clear chain of command is established along with a specific task. These men are not to do all the work, but rather to work under the authority of the apostles to see that the work is not neglected.

📖 Look over Acts 6:5.

Where does Stephen feature in the list of the seven men?

_____

_____

_____

_____

What do you learn here about his character and reputation?

_____

_____

_____

It is worth noticing that of the seven men selected, Stephen is mentioned first. Most likely he is the leader among these equals. It is easy to understand why. His life is characterized by being *"full of faith and of the Holy Spirit."* First, he is *"full of faith."* He trusts God. A successful spiritual leader is not one who trusts in himself, but one who consistently trusts God with the challenges of leadership. Second, he is full of the Spirit. We see the idea of being "Spirit-filled" mentioned frequently so far in the book of Acts, but here it is presented with a different slant. It is not just that Stephen is "Spirit-filled" at the moment, but that he *stays that way.* He has a predictable track record of walking in the power of the Spirit instead of walking in his own strength.

As you look at this list of seven, it is worth noting that all have Greek names. The specific challenge is that the "Hellenistic" or Greek Jewish widows are being overlooked. These men with Greek backgrounds will be especially sensitive to this need.

📖 What does Acts 6:6 reveal about the process of putting these men into their leadership role?

_____

_____

_____

_____

There are a few key principles worth noticing in how the apostles put these new leadership roles into place. Once the proper men are identified, they are brought before the apostles—an affirmation of their accountability to the church's main leadership. The apostles then pray for the men. Prayer is the unseen labor that determines if the seen labor makes a difference. In this act we see reflected a trust in God, not just in men, to get the needed work accomplished. Finally, the apostles lay their hands on them. They publicly affirm and identify with these new leaders as they commission them to their appointed task.

IN THEIR SHOES
Laying on of Hands

The practice of the laying on of hands is a distinct part of Jewish culture, and many examples can be seen in the Old Testament. It speaks of identification and affirmation. In the sacrificial system priests "laid hands" on an animal before sacrificing it to use the animal to identify with the sins of the people. We see in Numbers 27:18 that God instructs Moses to lay his hands on Joshua to commission him formally as the new leader of the nation. In New Testament times, the practice was often associated with appointment of leaders and seems to contain both the value of identifying with the ministry of an individual and affirming that person before others as a minister in God's work.

Examining Acts 6:7, what do you see resulting from this new leadership structure?

_____

_____

_____

It becomes immediately obvious that Luke wants to make certain we see his thesis statement of Acts 1:8 being fulfilled. He is trying to faithfully record the impact of the Spirit coming on the disciples and making them witnesses of Christ to the whole world. The challenge of the Hellenistic Jews could have become a volatile and divisive issue. Many a church has split over far less significant problems. Yet by wisely handling the problem and bringing others into the leadership structure, the work of the Word is not neglected. The church keeps growing greatly, and even priests are being won to faith in Christ.

In the midst of a problem, Stephen shines as a light. His willingness to place himself wholly on the altar makes him useable to God. To be "full of the Spirit" requires a daily choice of surrender. Because this is true of Stephen, when an opportunity arises for greater ministry, he quickly comes to people's minds. A mark of true ministry is that it is publicly affirmed. We should be wary of the self-appointed minister. But when the hand of God is upon someone, others WILL recognize this. If, like Stephen, we keep every area of our lives surrendered to the Lord, He will bring useful service our way.

DAY TWO

STEPHEN AS A WITNESS (ACTS 6:8–15)

As we saw yesterday, one of the consequences of being "full of the Holy Spirit" is that we have a heart to serve. Stephen distinguishes himself in the early church by stepping up and leading through serving. This doesn't mean that "service" is his spiritual gift. Instead, more likely he is gifted as an evangelist. In any case, as we will see today, another consequence of being filled with the Spirit is that we are witnesses. Jesus says in Acts 1:8, *"but you will receive power when the Holy Spirit has come upon you; and you shall be My witnesses."* In Stephen we find this idea personified. God manifests through him wonders and signs, but more importantly, Stephen uses these unique opportunities to present Jesus as the Messiah. The miracles aren't an end in themselves. As a man whose life is placed on the altar of God, Stephen is concerned with the things near to God's heart.

📖 Take a look at Acts 6:8 and make note of what you learn there of Stephen's ministry.

_____

_____

_____

_____

As the early church progresses and spreads in influence, Stephen's ministry moves beyond a merely administrative role. We are told that while full of grace and power, he is *"performing great wonders and signs among the people."* The Greek verb is in the imperfect tense, indicating this is an ongoing practice and not just an isolated event. These wonders and signs are not an end in themselves. The nature of a sign is that it points to something—it gives direction. God uses these wonders to allow Stephen to point others to Christ.

📖 Read Acts 6:9-10 and answer the questions that follow.

What conflict develops as Stephen ministers in Jerusalem?

_____

_____

How did Stephen handle the opposition?

_____

_____

_____

As we see in verse 8, Stephen is performing great wonders and signs *"among the people."* He is gaining the attention of the Jewish masses. No doubt, many of them are putting their trust in Christ. A certain group of Jews begin to engage him in debate. The word "argue" here (*suzeteo*) does not refer to an angry dispute, but rather, to a rational discourse of ideas. As Stephen makes his defense of the Christian faith, his opponents have no adequate response. They are *"unable to cope with the wisdom and Spirit"* with which he speaks. Since Stephen represents the side of truth, he cannot be logically refuted.

📖 Summarize in your own words what Acts 6:11–15 reveals the opponents do in an attempt to silence Stephen's witness.

ⓘ DID YOU KNOW?
Synagogues

Synagogues are the Jewish equivalent of local churches. They are assembly houses where Jews gather to worship and read Scriptures. They originate as far back as the Babylonian Captivity, when Jews had no access to the temple. The *Talmud* records that there were 480 such synagogues in Jerusalem at one time. Since Cyrenians and Alexandrians are mentioned in Acts 6:9, it suggests that some synagogues were formed along cultural lines. The "Freedmen" mentioned in this same verse were descendants of the Jewish slaves in Rome captured by Pompey in A.D. 63 and later released.

When you must attack your opposition with lies, that is a good indication you are fighting against truth instead of with it. The English martyr Hugh Latimer once said, "Whenever you see persecution, there is more than a probability that truth is on the persecuted side." When Stephen's opponents are unable to refute him, they set about to silence him by force. They have men lie about Stephen to give grounds for him to be arrested and brought before the Sanhedrin. It is worth noticing that the charges against Stephen of threats against the Temple and blasphemy are virtually the same as those brought against Jesus at His trial (see Mark 14:57–64).

📖 Looking at Acts 6:15, what do you think it means that Stephen's face is like that of an angel?

This final comment is perhaps the most striking of the entire chapter. Stephen is before the Sanhedrin accused of being a wicked blasphemer, and yet God manifests on his face the countenance of an angel. We are told repeatedly in the Scriptures that the countenance of angels is endued with light. Here we see Stephen's face glowing in like manner, also reminiscent of Moses after his mountaintop encounter with God. Perhaps God is making a point of the fact that Stephen is not truly attacking Moses as he is accused.

The only other account we have of a glowing countenance in Scripture is that of the Lord Jesus Himself on the Mount of Transfiguration. Warren Wiersbe writes, "It is as though God is saying, 'This man is not against Moses! He is like Moses—he is my faithful servant!' "[1]

Stephen, filled with the Holy Spirit, is a faithful witness just as Acts 1:8 promises. He testifies before the Jews and their leaders of the validity of the gospel and the deity of Jesus. We may never have such opportunity to preach truth to the leaders of our country or culture, but we can be confident that if we place our lives on the altar like Stephen, we will receive power to be witnesses. God Himself will give us the words to say to the audience He gives us.

DAY THREE

STEPHEN AS A PROPHET (ACTS 7:1–53)

When you hear the word "prophet" you probably think of an Old Testament hermit with a staff and a long beard who foresees the future. Actually, the job of the prophet has always been "forthtelling," not "foretelling." Predicting future events is sometimes featured in a prophet's ministry, but only as it relates to the application he is spurring them toward. His main job is always to deliver a message from God to a specific audience. "Thus says the Lord to you" defines the prophet's aim. His ministry is to convict people of what they are doing wrong and to call them to act as God wills. In a very practical sense, prophecy is what we now tend to call preaching. It incorporates presenting God's truth, confronting man's error, and calling for change. This is what we see Stephen do at his trial before the Sanhedrin. When the false charges have been presented, the High Priest asked Stephen, "*Are these things so?*" This is his invitation to defend himself. Instead, he uses the opportunity to preach a message to the unbelieving audience before him.

DOCTRINE
What is a Sermon?

In the Old Testament synagogue and in the early church, a normal service included two or three messages from speakers who vary in giftedness. The modern church usually only has one message per gathering, and normally the same speaker week after week. Whatever the preacher's dominant giftedness, that becomes the definition of "preaching" in that location. The Bible however defines up to four main kinds of messages with four different gifts. The gift of prophecy confronts wrong and calls for change. The gift of teaching instructs in systematic fashion. The gift of exhortation illustrates, motivates, and moves toward practical application. The evangelist presents the gospel and calls for response from the unbeliever.

---

1. *Be Dynamic: Acts 1–12*, (Wheaton, IL: Victor Books, 1987), p.107.

📖 Read Acts 7:1–8. What do you see as Stephen's main point in these verses?

_____

_____

_____

Stephen begins his defense with an overview of the birth of the Jewish nation. Their father is Abraham, and the land they call home was given to Abraham by God. The rite of circumcision that sets them apart was also given to Abraham by God. As Stephen reviews the descendants of Abraham, he doesn't need to remind his audience that Jacob was renamed Israel. One thing that stands out in this discourse is the fact of revelation. God spoke to Abraham. He met with him and instructed him. This idea of hearing from God has since become foreign in Israel. They live as if God has nothing else to say, and therefore they are unable to hear God speak through Jesus or through His followers.

📖 Look over Acts 7:9–16. What common ground do you see between the story of Joseph and his brothers, and what is happening in Israel?

_____

_____

_____

_____

Though the Sanhedrin probably doesn't catch it, it seems the narrative here is more than just a review of Old Testament history. Stephen seems to be making a point of the fact that Joseph's persecution came from his own brothers. In the same way, these men who are spiritual leaders in Israel ought to be brothers to Stephen instead of enemies. More importantly, they should have recognized Jesus as such.

📖 Study Acts 7:17–36. What common ground do you see between Moses's story and the present situation?

_____

_____

_____

_____

Certainly, the story of Moses is not unfamiliar to this Jewish audience. They may at some point be thinking, "Why is he telling us this?" But it must eventually hit home to them that the main thing Stephen emphasizes in this familiar narrative is that Moses's brethren rejected him even though God had sent him. Again, the parallel to the Jews' present rejection of Jesus is the obvious point.

📖 Review Acts 7:37–50 and summarize the main points Stephen makes in these verses.

_____

_____

_____

_____

"You men who are stiff-necked and uncircumcised in heart and
ears are always resisting the Holy Spirit," (Acts 7:51)

Stephen reminds his listeners that Moses (whom they accused him of being against) taught of the Messiah to come out of the Jewish people, just as he is preaching. Yet even in Moses's day the people rebelled against God and His prophet. Stephen then continues his brief history of Israel, taking his audience from Abraham to the present temple worship.

📖 Look over Acts 7:31–53. What stands out to you from how Stephen closes out his message?

_____

_____

_____

_____

As we read the Gospels, we find that Jesus begins His communication with the Pharisees with patient instruction, but as they reject Him, his dealings with them become increasingly harsh. We see much the same pattern in the early church. Stephen obviously recognizes that these men are not open to truth. No doubt, he has heard in great detail how the previous attempts of the apostles to share truth with the Sanhedrin have gone. He accuses them of *"resisting"* the Spirit. It is an incredible concept to think that people who devote their life to following God could so harden their hearts as to think they are serving Him when they are actually working against Him. Not only does Stephen indict these men for their complicity in Jesus's murder, but he also points out that they aren't keeping the very Law by which they are trying to judge him.

📖 DOCTRINE
Sins against the Holy Spirit

Scripture lists four ways we can negatively relate to the Holy Spirit. We can *"grieve"* the Spirit by sins of commission—doing things we are instructed not to do (Ephesians 4:30). We can *"quench"* the Spirit by sins of omission—not doing what He is leading us to do (1 Thessalonians 5:19–20). The last two ways are both sins of submission. We can *"insult"* the Spirit by willfully continuing in sin (Hebrews 10:26–29). Finally, we can *"resist"* the Spirit by being stubborn and stiff-necked to His instruction and leading (Acts 7:51).

The main point that stands out in Stephen's sermon is his overriding premise that there has always been persecution against those who truly follow God, and that such persecution comes not from the world, but from those who claim to follow God. The situation has not changed since Stephen's time either. Today we still find that sometimes the staunchest opposition to spiritual devotion comes not from the rebellious, but from the religious. This is what *"resisting the Spirit"* is all about. It is not a choice that is made all at once, but rather, is the inevitable consequence of pride and the enthronement of self. If the Spirit of God lives in us, He will convict us of all sin—not just moral sins, but sins of self. If we do not respond to His conviction, our hearts will become hard and we will no longer hear His convicting voice. That puts us in a place to actually fight against God and think we are doing Him a favor. The application to us is clear. We must not resist the convicting work of the Spirit of God!

Because Stephen's life is on the altar, instead of resisting the Spirit, he is responsive to His leading. He goes where the Spirit leads, says what the Spirit says, and does what the Spirit initiates. Though his words are strong, we know that the glory of God is on him. Therefore, these are the words God wants said to this hard-hearted group of self-righteous sinners. Humanly, we may be tempted to evaluate Stephen's success or failure based on converts. For Stephen, there apparently are not any right away. But in the kingdom of God, success is not based on the results we see, but on God's will being done. By that measure, Stephen's sermon is a huge success!

Day Four

Stephen as a Martyr (Acts 7:54–60)

When you hear the word "martyr" you immediately have a concept in your mind. You quickly associate the term with someone who dies for their faith. But that really isn't what the word means. I will concede that the English term carries that as a possible definition according to Webster's Dictionary, but the word isn't an English expression. "Martyr" actually is a Greek word that has been transliterated into the English language. The Greek term *marturia* simply means "to bear witness." We find forms of this word throughout the book of Acts as the gospel moves out from Jerusalem to the uttermost parts. The idiom has become associated with the idea of dying for one's beliefs, because that is the strongest possible witness—that one truly believes what they profess. One of the greatest evidences of the resurrection of Christ is that His followers would be willing to die for that belief. Many followers of Christ have sealed their testimony with their own blood, but Stephen is the first known to do so in the church age.

Examine Acts 7:54, and write all the details you learn of the Sanhedrin's response to Stephen's testimony.

When the Sanhedrin hears the words of Stephen, we are told they are "cut to the quick." In Greek, the statement literally reads, "they are cut through to the heart." Stephen's testimony pierces to the very core of their being. This could be a good thing had they responded with repentant hearts, but instead they respond with great anger. The phrase, *"gnashing their teeth at him,"* gives us a sense of how intense their anger truly is.

 WORD STUDY
Gnash the Teeth

The Greek word for "gnash" (brucho) means to grind, gnash, or crunch the teeth together, as a person in violent rage or anger. It is applied to mad dogs and lions and seems to be a word formed from the sound it makes (*onomatopoeia*), as is the case with the English word, "crunch."

📖 Read Acts 7:55–56.

Why do you think it is important for us to know that Stephen is *"full of the Holy Spirit"*?

What stands out to you from Stephen's final words?

At the risk of being redundant, I must remind us that the book of Acts begins with Jesus' prophecy that the result of the Spirit's coming will be that they receive power and be witnesses. But such power to witness does not come automatically. We have already seen that the same group of people are "filled" with the Spirit multiple times. It is by choice, not chance that the believer is filled with the Spirit. It requires the surrender of putting all the areas of one's life on the altar. Stephen does this, and he finishes strong. Perhaps most striking in these final moments is that Stephen gazes *"intently into heaven."* It is clear he is seeking God's approval and not people's. That he receives such approval from the Lord is evidenced by the fact that he sees God's glory. Equally important, he sees Christ "standing" at the right hand of God. We know from many New Testament scriptures that once Christ finished His earthly ministry, He ascended to heaven and is seated at the right hand of the Father (evidence that His work is complete). This is the only time we hear of Christ standing. It is as if He is giving a standing ovation to Stephen's faithful testimony.

📖 Look at Acts 7:57–59a and summarize the response of the angry mob.

_____

_____

_____

> *"Father, forgive them for they do not know what they do."*—Jesus
> (Luke 23:34)

The stoning of Stephen is not so much a premeditated judicial verdict as it is a passionate mob reaction. Clearly these people are driven by impulse. Though the judgment of stoning is something that the Law allows, it is to be administered as an act of justice, not passion. It is worth noting that we are introduced to the apostle Paul here (called by his Jewish name, Saul). Though he is apparently not prominent enough yet to participate actively in the stoning, his support is evident as he keeps the garments of the members of the Sanhedrin who are actually casting the stones. They keep up their murderous attack even as Stephen cries out to God.

📖 Compare Acts 7:59–60 with Luke 23:34 and 46, and record your observations.

_____

_____

_____

_____

What a powerful testimony Stephen gives before his fellow brethren, as he echoes the words and attitude of Christ on the cross! It is not that Stephen imitates Christ's death, but that he becomes like Him in death. Doubtless there are some present and participating in Stephen's stoning who also witnessed the death of Christ. With his final words, Stephen reminds them one last time of their guilt in the death of the Messiah.

By placing his own life (and death) on the altar of God, Stephen sets a standard that others will follow. As we will see in the chapters to come, many believers will seal their testimony with their very lives. A life of surrender does not necessarily mean that we will die a martyr's death, but if our life is already on the altar, it won't matter if we do.

DAY FIVE

FOR ME TO FOLLOW GOD

What would your life look like if every aspect was placed on the altar of God and given in consecration to Him? What could our world look like if every life was so lived? Do you know that the only hindrance that keeps this from being a reality is unbelief? We struggle with really believing that God's way is best. Deep within each of us resides the lie that if we really give everything over to God, He will somehow take advantage of us. We tend to wrongly believe that if we completely surrender every area of our lives, we will have to hop the next boat to Borneo and swab sores in some native hut for the rest of our lives. But we have this promise in Romans 12:2 that the will of God for our lives is always *"good and acceptable and perfect."* Surrender should not be a scary prospect. Imagine that your child comes up to you and says, "I love you so much, I want to do whatever you want me to do." Will you quickly respond, "Aha! Now I have you where I want you. Go outside and scrub every inch of the garbage can with a toothbrush!"? Of course not! Yet often in our hearts we accuse God of such treachery. The greatest enemy of surrender is a wrong view of God.

I have spoken much in this lesson of the concept of surrender—of placing our lives on the altar of God. The most important word in the Christian life is surrender. The key to godliness is not commitment but surrender. We can be very committed, and yet displeasing to God. Such is the case with the Pharisees and Sadducees. They are devout men, yet their surrender is not to God, but to their own agendas. True surrender is when we run up the white flag in our hearts; when we say to God, "Have Thine Own Way, Lord." You may be familiar with the hymn which bears this title, but you probably don't know the story behind it. This popular hymn was written by Adelaide Pollard. She had a sense of burden for world evangelization and for years was planning to serve the Lord in Africa. Adelaide penned the song when poor health was closing the door on this lifelong dream. Often the hardest things to surrender are the things we believe to be good yet are not God's will for us. The Sanhedrin thinks that they are doing good—yet clearly, they are rebelling against God. Surrender is the only way to know for sure what God's will is. Jesus instructs the crowds at the temple, *"If anyone is willing to do His will, he will know of the teaching, whether it is of God or whether I speak from Myself"* (John 7:17). In other words, to know what God's will is, we must be willing to do it. That is what surrender is all about.

Which of these issues do you find gets in the way of surrender in your life?

___ Fear of what God will ask me to do   ___ Fear of the unknown

___ Fear of not getting what I want   ___ Fear of hardship

___ Fear of inadequacy   ___ Fear of failure

___Other: _____

> *If anyone is willing to do His will, he will know of the teaching,*
> *whether it is of God or whether I speak from Myself."* (John 7:17)

What does surrender mean in Stephen's life? If you focus on the fact that it means martyrdom, you will likely miss the point and find his example a fearful one to follow. But what we see when we look closely and honestly at his life is the kind of perspective we all truly want in our heart of hearts. Before Stephen is ever pushed to the forefront of the early church, he had already settled the issue of surrender. We are introduced to him in Acts 6:5 as a man *"full of faith and of the Holy Spirit."* This doesn't happen after he becomes a leader or evangelist or martyr. It happens before. Surrender leads Stephen into service. His yieldedness to the Lord gives him the opportunity to lead in the early church—to make a difference in people's lives. It leads him to discover his own giftedness and find where he fits in life. While we may focus on how hard it would be to be martyred for our faith, by the time this challenge is presented to Stephen, it is a delight and a joy. He gladly gives his life to preach the gospel to his countrymen and prove what he believes about Jesus. Surrender gives Stephen a life that counts. While we may wish for a long life, we must view this life from the vantage point of eternity. When we look back at our brief time on earth, what will matter more, how long it is or how significant? When we stand before God, will we boast of how much is in our retirement account, or how big our stamp collection is? Those are not the sort of accomplishments that earn the praise, "Well done, Thou good and faithful servant." If we are truly honest with ourselves, what we all long for is a life of significance. Surrender guarantees that, but here is the rub. Surrender guarantees significance in light of eternity. It guarantees significance in the eyes of God. Often what gets in the way of surrender is our love of the temporal and of the approval of people. Surrender may or may not give you those, but it will leave them at God's discretion.

Let's look at your surrender from the vantage point of Stephen. Have you ever come to the place where you put all of your life (seen and unseen) on the altar of God? If you have, why not reaffirm that. If you haven't why not do it now? If you struggle with it, why not ask God to help you be willing?

After giving his life to God, Stephen offers Him his service. There is nothing glamorous about overseeing the feeding of widows, but it needs to be done. There is no indication that it is even something Stephen is particularly gifted for. Later ministry suggests that he is an evangelist, not an administrator. Yet through surrender he is able to make a difference and at the same time earn the right to be heard. Why not tell the Lord you are willing to serve wherever the need is?

It is in the context of general service that Stephen's gifts begin to surface. You won't find out what you are good at by sitting on the sidelines. Purpose in your heart to say "yes" to the next opportunity the Lord gives you to serve. It is significant that God performs signs and wonders through Stephen *after* he has served in menial ways.

Romans 12:1–2 gives us a practical, step-by-step approach to surrender. Let's look at the verse in this light: *"Therefore, I urge you, brethren, by the mercies of God, to present your bodies a living and holy sacrifice, acceptable to God, which is your spiritual service of worship. And do not be conformed to this world, but be transformed by the renewing of your mind, so that you may prove what the will of God is, that which is good and acceptable and perfect."*

DOCTRINE

The Romans 12 Process:

1. Surrender your whole self to God

2. Set aside worldly values

3. Stay in the Word of God

The first step is to present our whole selves to God as an act of worship. Have you done that?

The second step is to set aside the world's way of thinking about your life plans. What would that mean in your situation?

The third step is to search out God's way of thinking about your life plans by letting His Word give you a new perspective. Are you doing that?

Then and only then will you be able to know what God's will for your life is. As you perform these actions, your life, like Stephen's, will become proof that God's will is good and acceptable and perfect.

Why not close out this lesson by writing a prayer to the Lord about what you have learned?

LESSON 8

THE SOVEREIGN HAND OF GOD IN MINISTRY
ACTS 8

Luke, the author of Acts, records in his Gospel a training event Jesus has with His disciples and followers. Jesus sends out the seventy by twos to go ahead of Him to cities He will visit, and instructs them that *"The harvest is plentiful, but the laborers are few; therefore, beseech the Lord of the harvest to send out laborers into His harvest"* (Luke 10:2). It is interesting that Jesus instructs His laborers to pray for laborers. Certainly, He desires that their numbers will multiply, but that is not all that his invitation to supplication means. Their praying will make them more sensitive to the needs around them—needs greater than what they alone can meet. The context also suggests that Jesus wants them praying for God's direction as they go. Most of all, to pray in this way will be a reminder of who is in charge. It is His harvest, not ours, and He WILL take care of it.

> *"The harvest is plentiful, but the laborers are few; therefore beseech the Lord of the harvest to send out laborers into His harvest"*
> (Luke 10:2)

When we involve ourselves in the work of God, sometimes it is easy to lose sight of the God for whom we work. The Lord is in charge—it is His harvest. He doesn't really need our help. He wants our participation, but He can make it without our help. I am reminded of the Book of Esther. Shortly after Esther is appointed as the new queen, a threat is made against her people, the Jews. Her cousin Mordecai implores her to intercede with the king. To do so, however will risk her life. Mordecai's counsel to her is significant. *"If you remain silent at this time, relief and deliverance will arise for the Jews from another place and you and your father's house will perish"* (Esther 4:12). In other words, "if you don't join this kingdom work, God will be just fine, but you won't make out so well." He concludes by suggesting perhaps this is God's sovereign reason she is queen after all.

Think about how God's sovereignty affects ministry. If God really is all-powerful, all-knowing, and ever-present (and He is), then Job is right in saying, *"I know that You can do all things, and that no purpose of Yours can be thwarted"* (Job 42:2). His is the unseen hand working behind the scenes in the book of Acts. He uses people to accomplish His purposes, but He is always in charge. Nowhere is that reality more clearly seen than in Acts chapter 8. We see His sovereign purposes being accomplished by persecution, in spite of prejudice, in the midst of selfishness, and to the far reaches of the earth. God is in control. It is a comforting thought to realize this and a joyous thought that we get to join Him as He works around us.

Day One

Sovereignty and Circumstances (Acts 8:1–4)

God wants everyone to know about Him. He wants His people to tell all about Him to all who don't know Him. In fact, this is God's plan for Israel in the Old Testament, though they didn't do too good of a job with it. He wanted them to take the message about Him to the nations, but instead, they hoarded this truth to themselves. Just before Jesus ascends, He tells His disciples, *"You will receive power when the Holy Spirit has come upon you; and you shall be My witnesses both in Jerusalem, and in all Judea and Samaria, and even to the remotest part of the earth"* (Acts 1:8). God chooses to use the church to represent Him to all the earth. Yet, so far in the book of Acts, though the disciples have been faithful to preach the gospel all over Jerusalem, they haven't gone beyond it. This is about to change though.

DID YOU KNOW?
Stoning

Executing a person by throwing large stones at them until they are dead was the ordinary formal and legal mode of inflicting capital punishment in the earlier history of the children of Israel. It was the penalty for Achan's sin of taking the forbidden idol (Josh. 7:25), for adultery (see Lev. 20:10), for divination (Lev. 20:6, 27), for idolatry (Deut. 13:10), for dishonor to parents (Deut. 21:21), for prophesying falsely (Deut. 13:5, 10), for Sabbath breaking (Ex. 31:14; 35:2), and for blasphemy (Lev. 24:10-24). Apparently, this is the charge used against Stephen.

📖 Look at Acts 8:1. Why do you think Saul is so much in agreement with Stephen being put to death?

Saul is a zealous Pharisee, and like most devout Jews of the day, believes that if Israel isn't pure, the Messiah won't come. He probably sees the elimination of this radical sect called "the Way" as necessary for the purification of the nation of Israel. He is likely offended as well by Stephen's rebuke of the Sanhedrin. In Acts 8:1 we see Saul in *"hearty agreement"* with the killing of Stephen. The Greek word (*suneudokeo*) has the idea of being "mutually pleased" or "to think well of something together."

📖 Read Acts 8:1 again.

How does Stephen's death change how the Jewish leaders respond to the church?

_____

_____

_____

_____

What do you think God is doing through allowing this persecution?

_____

_____

_____

_____

The killing of Stephen gives the religious leaders a taste for blood. Luke offers us a summary statement and then later will fill in the details. Clearly from Luke's perspective, this is a pivotal point in the growth of the church. While no one wants to be persecuted, God is allowing it. Some positives we can see that result from this are, first of all, that it will drive believers to trust God. Second, it will give them a chance to show how important their faith is to them and how convinced they are that it is real. Most importantly, and the benefit that Luke emphasizes, the persecution scatters believers into the areas of Judea and Samaria, where Christ has already said they will be witnesses.

The message of Christ is having a polarizing effect on the nation of Israel. While some are waging violent opposition, many are embracing the message of Jesus. Luke balances the persecution coming from the Pharisees against the fact that there are others—"*some devout men*"—who bury Stephen and make "*loud lamentation over him*" (Acts 8:2).

DID YOU KNOW?
Sovereignty in Action

Although the persecution of the church that begins with Stephen is clearly a negative, it has the positive result of scattering believers all over the regions of Judea and Samaria—the very places Christ says they will be witnesses. Luke 8:4 tells us that as they are scattered to other regions, Christians take the gospel message with them and share it freely.

📖 Examine Acts 8:3 and write down all the details you observe about this wave of persecution and Saul's role in it.

_____

_____

_____

_____

Luke describes Saul's (Paul's) persecution as "ravaging" the church. The word "ravaging" is translated from a Greek word (*lumainomai*) with particularly gruesome meaning. It is used in the New Testament only in this one occurrence. It means simply to "devastate or ruin." *Lumainomai* is applied in other literature to physical injury, particularly wild beasts mangling prey that is still alive. The verb appears in the imperfect tense, picturing that the persecution is continual action. The fact that several times Acts mentions Paul's persecution as aimed at both men *and* women is significant. It indicates that he goes to extremes in his pursuit of believers, as normally the women would be left alone. We know from Paul's own testimony that he does *"many hostile things"* to Christians (Acts 26:9) and even has some put to death (Acts 22:4; 26:10).

Although the persecution of the church that begins with Stephen is clearly a negative thing, it has the positive result of scattering believers all over the regions of Judea and Samaria—the very places Christ says they will be witnesses. Luke 8:4 tells us that as they are scattered to other regions, Christians take the gospel message with them and share it freely. We see a sovereign God taking a horribly bad occurrence and causing it to work for the ultimate good.

Day Two

SOVEREIGNTY AND A NEW HARVEST FIELD (ACTS 8:5–17)

As we saw yesterday, God in His sovereignty uses persecution to scatter believers away from Jerusalem like seeds cast by a sower. As these believers leave, they take with them the message of Christ and share it freely in many new areas. Truly Jesus' prophecy of Acts 1:8 that they will be witnesses *"in all Judea and Samaria"* is about to be fulfilled. One of these scattered believers is Philip. We are first introduced to him in Acts 6 as one of those the apostles put in charge of caring for the Hellenistic widows. God uses Philip and Stephen and their co-laborers to take care of a ministry that is needed but isn't being done. This is not the last time God will use him in pioneering church ministry. Like his fellow servant Stephen, his ministry spreads from service to sharing the gospel. As we will see this week, he is probably gifted as an evangelist, and God uses him to open an entirely new harvest field among the Samaritans.

Read Acts 8:5–8 and answer the questions below.

Why do you think Philip goes to Samaria?

How does Philip earn an audience?

What is their response to him?

_____

_____

_____

It is easier to answer why Philip leaves Jerusalem, than why he goes to Samaria. Obviously, he leaves the home base of the church because of the persecution that arises. When Acts 8:4 speaks of believers being *scattered*, it is translated from the passive voice in Greek, meaning it is done *to* them, and not of their own volition. But here in Acts 8:5 we are told that Philip *"went down"* to Samaria. This verbal expression comes from the active voice in Greek, suggesting he is choosing this path. Perhaps he is putting two and two together and concludes that God has allowed this persecution for the very purpose of getting the gospel to other places. We know that Philip is characterized by being Spirit-filled (6:3) and we can trust the Spirit is leading him to Samaria. Once there, his yieldedness to God results in great miracles and signs which validate his message. That there is *"much rejoicing"* in Samaria is not just because of the miracles though. Verse 6 tells us the crowds *"with one accord" are giving attention to what is being said by Philip.*

 DID YOU KNOW?
Good Samaritan?

Jesus' parable of the good Samaritan is confrontive of the fact that there existed a great prejudice against Samaritans among the Jews. Samaritans were basically descendants of the more liberal Jews of the Northern Kingdom who intermarried with the foreigners that settled in the lands as the nation fell. They practiced a form of worship to Jehovah, but not according to the Law. Instead, they followed the worship form established by Jeroboam when the nation of Israel became divided after Solomon. It was Judaism mingled with forms of Baal worship. Their priests were not of the tribe of Levi and their place of worship was not Jerusalem (see John 4:20).

📖 Look over Acts 8:9–11 and summarize what you learn about Simon, the magician.

_____

_____

_____

_____

Apparently, Simon is a trickster who has gained quite a reputation for his magical tricks. It is doubtful that there is any supernatural basis for his reputation, for we have no indication of a demon being cast out of him. Most likely, he has learned some sleight of hand techniques and uses them to amaze crowds with simple deceptions. That he is called *"The great power of God"* is a reputation he will have to forfeit since the true power of God is now being manifest in Samaria through Philip. His greatness is self-proclaimed according to verse 9, but he will no longer be the center of attention.

📖 Examine Acts 8:12–13.

What do you learn here of the content of Philip's preaching?

....

....

....

Where does Simon fit in the responses to Philip?

....

....

....

Luke tells us here that there are two main parts to the message Philip preaches. He teaches them the good news of the kingdom of God and teaches them of the power of Jesus' name. The name "Jesus Christ" emphasizes that part of the message is Jesus as the Messiah. Simon is one of many in Samaria who respond to the gospel message Philip brings. Like the crowds, Simon too is baptized as a public identification with Jesus. We are told that Simon sticks close to Philip, as Simon is apparently enamored with the miracles as much or more than he is with the message.

IN THEIR SHOES
Mother Church

The Mother Church at Jerusalem sends an apostolic delegation out each time the gospel penetrates a new barrier or whenever something new and different happens. In Acts we see such a response several times. Peter and John are sent to investigate the first Samaritan believers (Acts 8:14). Peter is present with the first Gentile believers (Acts 10) but later reports on this to the Mother church (Acts 11:1–18). Barnabas is sent to Antioch to investigate the first fully Gentile church (Acts 11:22). Paul is likewise the one who corrects the wrong beliefs of the disciples of John the Baptist he finds in Ephesus (Acts 19:1–7) arguably in the direction of "the remotest parts of the earth" (Acts 1:8), thus fulfilling this apostolic affirmation for them.

📖 Take a look at Acts 8:14–17.

Why do you think the apostles feel they need to send Peter and John to investigate these Samaritan conversions?

....

....

....

Can you think of any reasons why the Holy Spirit does not come upon the Samaritans when they first believe and are baptized?

....

....

Why do you think Luke says they have *"simply been baptized in the name of the Lord Jesus"*?

The conversion of Samaritans is an incredibly significant milestone in the development of the early church. Up until now, only Jews have believed. Since great prejudice exists between Jews and Samaritans, that they can be saved needs to be verified and authenticated by the leaders of the church. No doubt this is why God withholds the Spirit until Peter and John get there. He wants them to witness the Spirit coming on this new type of Christian, so they can bear witness to the Mother Church in Jerusalem. When Luke tells us they have *"simply been baptized in the name of the Lord Jesus"* he is distinguishing their public profession from the baptism *"with the Holy Spirit"* Jesus speaks of (Acts 1:5).

To understand fully what has just transpired here at Samaria, we must make note that the next verse (Acts 8:18) tells us Simon *"saw"* the Spirit bestowed on these believers. Apparently, there is some physical manifestation of the Spirit coming on these who believe. Though Luke does not give us details, this statement suggests the same types of manifestations that happened at Pentecost, such as a rushing wind, tongues of fire, and perhaps speaking in tongues as well. The gospel has just penetrated a new barrier, and God lets Peter and John be witnesses to the fact that these Samaritans are now "fellow heirs" with the Jews.

DAY THREE

SOVEREIGNTY AND THE SELFISH HEART (ACTS 8:18–25)

God is sovereign over the harvest fields of the gospel. He is "Lord of the Harvest." This doesn't take anything away from the fact that He accomplishes His work through people. We call this book we are studying "The Acts of the Apostles" because although it is all the working of God, most of this work is done through His followers. God superintends the spreading of the gospel into Samaria in spite of the church's propensity to stay in Jerusalem and in spite of Jewish prejudice. His is the unseen hand behind the scenes, sovereignly using the persecuting actions of those not believing in Christ to further the spread of the message of Christ. He is moving among the nations and leaders. It is no small wonder that God who sees every detail also knows every heart. Today we want to shift focus from God's macro-involvement in the early church to an example of His micro-involvement. Even though He is intimately involved in the affairs of nations and kingdoms, He is still able to treat each person as an individual and look into each unique heart, discerning both good and evil, true believing and make-believing.

📖   Meditate on Acts 8:18–19.

Why do you think Simon is so interested in this power to bestow the Holy Spirit?

....

....

....

What wrong thinking do you see reflected in his request?

....

....

....

Simon is a man accustomed to acclaim and recognition. He has been the center of attention in Samaria for some time and is used to people being impressed with his counterfeited power. When he sees authentic power manifested in these men, he sees it through the stained eyes of his past experience. He wants to be able to use God's power selfishly. The wrong thinking behind his request is the idea that the power can be so used— that God is like a genie in a lamp who can be made to serve us. This is not a new idea. The Philistines were motivated by a similar mistaken perspective when they captured the Ark of the Covenant in hopes it would give them military success (1 Samuel 4-6), but soon learn differently. The power of God is at God's discretion and for His purposes only.

📖 Reflect on Acts 8:20–23, and write down all that Peter reveals of what is wrong with Simon's request.

....

....

....

....

 DID YOU KNOW?
The Captured Ark

First Samuel 4 through 6 relates the story of how God refuses to be manipulated. When Israel is defeated in battle, they bring the ark to the war as an afterthought. They view it as some sort of good luck charm. However, God refuses to be manipulated. Instead of blessing Israel in battle, the ark becomes a curse and they lose more warriors with it than without it. The defeat is so great that the Philistines actually capture the ark from Israel. They fare no better with it than Israel and are cursed because of its presence. God teaches both nations that He cannot be captured and made a servant of earthly whims.

The first mistake of Simon that Peter discloses is the inaccurate idea that Peter can somehow be motivated by bribery even if the bestowing of power is up to him instead of God (which it isn't). Second, Peter points out in verse 21 that Simon's heart is not right.

The intention of his heart is *"wickedness"* (8:22), and this evil intent warrants repentance. God gives Peter the discernment to pierce through to the core of the matter. Simon is jealous of others having power he doesn't have.

📖 Look over Acts 8:23–24. What do these suggest to you about the validity of Simon's conversion?

_____

_____

_____

Fortunately for us, it is God's job and not ours to determine what faith is genuine and who is truly saved. He sees what no one else sees and knows the motives of the heart (1 Corinthians 4:5). From our vantage point however, it does not appear that Simon's conversion is true saving faith. First, Peter indicates he is *"in the bondage of iniquity."* While a Christian can still choose to sin, salvation frees us from bondage to sin. Simon's response to Peter is also telling. Instead of asking God for forgiveness, he tells Peter to pray on his behalf. There is no indication of a personal relationship with the Lord.

One side note that is worth not missing in the text is the little word in verse 25, *"they."* Until Philip, no one had been going to the Samaritans with the gospel. After Peter and John witness God's working and see the validity of the Samaritan conversions, they join Philip in this fruitful ministry.

God sees all the big picture of ministry. He is able to deal with nations and kingdoms and times and epochs. He is able to foresee every possible scenario. Yet all of this big picture of His sovereign working does not detract at all from His ability to deal with each of us as individuals. He sees through to our very hearts, and that is where true spirituality (or the lack of it) is formed. In Simon, God's sovereignty is expressed in conviction, while in Peter it is seen in the discernment given him by the Spirit.

DAY FOUR

SOVEREIGNTY AND A SEEKING HEART (ACTS 8:26–40)

Second Chronicles 16:9 offers a powerful promise. It tells us, *"the eyes of the Lord move to and fro throughout the earth that He may strongly support those whose heart is completely His."* Think about that. If your heart is completely surrendered, you can count on God's strong support. His eye is ever watchful for any with a right heart toward Him. In the midst of all the activity of the early church—in the midst of all who are coming to the Lord and all that is going on— God stops and notices a heart that is turned toward Him. God sees in the Ethiopian eunuch the heart of a seeker, and as we will see today, God strongly supports him. God guides one of His choice servants to bring further truth to this open heart. What a contrast we find between the selfish heart of Simon and the seeking heart of the Ethiopian! God in His sovereignty sees both and deals justly with each.

"The eyes of the Lord move to and fro throughout the earth that
He may strongly support those whose heart is completely His"
(2 Chronicles 16:9)

📖 Read through Acts 8:26–31.

What do you learn here of the Ethiopian's heart toward God?

_____

_____

_____

_____

Make note of everything God does to bring truth to this Ethiopian.

_____

_____

_____

_____

In Luke's brief narrative here, we catch several glimpses of the heart for God in this Ethiopian court official. Even though he is not a Jew, he has traveled to Jerusalem for the purpose of worshiping Jehovah at the Temple. In his spare time, we find him reading the Scriptures trying to learn more of God. He perseveres even though he does not understand what he is reading. A final evidence of this man's seeking heart is seen in all the trouble to which God goes to bring more truth and revelation to him. God sends an angel to direct Philip to where this man is and then speaks to Philip through the Holy Spirit to single out exactly who on this busy road is open to Him.

📖 In Acts 8:32–35 we learn that the passage the Ethiopian is reading from is Isaiah 53. Read this chapter in its context and make note of all you see in it that relates to the gospel.

_____

_____

_____

_____

_____

_____

Isaiah 53 is one of the clearest Messianic passages in the Old Testament, abounding in prophecies that we see fulfilled in Jesus. First, we see in this chapter our own guilt as sinners. We see the clear message of Christ as the innocent one taking the punishment for our sins. Most of all, we see God's love demonstrated in what He is willing to do for us. It is obvious from where the eunuch is reading that God has prepared his heart for the gospel message.

📖 Take a look at Acts 8:36–39 and summarize all you learn of the Ethiopian's response.

 WORD STUDY
Eunuch

The term "eunuch" originally was used to refer to a servant who has been emasculated so he could be trusted as the keeper of an Oriental harem. Eunuchs often rose to stations of great power and trust in eastern courts so that the term apparently came to be applied to any high officer of court, even those not emasculated. (In Genesis 37:36; 39:1, the same term is used in the Septuagint, the Greek translation of the Old Testament.) This latter definition probably best fits the eunuch in Acts 8, since the man is in charge of the queen's treasure, not the king's harem.

Obviously, Philip takes the Ethiopian eunuch through all that the Scriptures teach of Jesus and even explains baptism as identification with Jesus. The eager belief of this man is evident in his wanting to immediately be baptized and in his profession that *"Jesus Christ is the Son of God."* Though we think of Jesus Christ as simply our Lord's identifying name, Christ is actually a title. It means "the Anointed One" and by calling Jesus the Christ, the Ethiopian is calling Him the Messiah. With the phrase, *"Son of God"* this man also identifies Jesus as deity. After his baptism, though he undoubtedly is amazed at Philip's miraculous disappearance, his heart is full of the joy of salvation.

Philip too must be surprised to suddenly find himself in another location. The terminology used to describe his miraculous transfer to Azotus is the same Greek word used in Hebrews 11:5 of Enoch's rapture to heaven. We see though in Acts 8:40 that Philip keeps right on doing what he has been doing. He continues preaching the gospel city by city. Though we often think of such ministry as random encounters, the story of the Ethiopian eunuch clearly communicates the sovereign hand of God guiding the evangel to those whose hearts are prepared to hear. The key is that Philip is surrendered to the Lord's purposes and to His leading. Philip doesn't just work FOR God, he walks WITH God and lets Him lead him. The sovereign hand of God will guide us in ministry if we are surrendered to Him and willing to seek Him.

DAY FIVE

FOR ME TO FOLLOW GOD

Can you imagine a construction site where workers show up whenever they feel burdened to do so, work hard on what they think needs doing, and hope the house turns out okay and the owner is satisfied? They work hard but without the benefit of a supervisor or blueprint. What kind of house do you think such a crew will build? Ironically, there are many who view ministry in this way. They think that ministry is just something we do for God, but they fail to recognize His day-to-day involvement in the process. They hope He is pleased, but the only way they have of evaluating success is how tired they feel afterward. This is not God's plan for His church. When Peter says to Jesus, *"You are the Christ, the Son of the Living God,"* Jesus responds by saying, *"upon this rock I will build My church..."* (Matthew 16:18). Notice Jesus does not say "You will build your church," nor does He say "You will build My church." It is HIS church, and HE will build it. He will involve us in the process, but He is always here in the midst of the job and always in charge.

> *"upon this rock I will build My church..."*
>
> —Jesus (Matthew 16:18)

What we have seen this week is men laboring on the building of the church, but hopefully we also see the General Contractor behind the scenes giving direction and getting things done. We see Him use intense persecution to change the landscape much in the way a contractor would use a bulldozer to prepare the land to build. We have seen God send His crew to new areas of work instead of using them all on just one room of the house. We have seen great progress. We have seen God, the Master Architect, working from His sovereign plan. Yet with all the work going on, this Contractor always has time to deal with individual workers. Truly God builds the first century church, and it is He who builds the twenty-first century church as well.

As you consider your own life and walk with God, are there any areas of great trial and difficulty for you right now?

....

....

....

How are you handling them?

....

....

....

....

Can you think of any ways God might be sovereignly using the negatives to bring about a positive result?

_____

_____

_____

_____

📖 Read Romans 8:28–30 and reflect on its message to your current situation. What are some truths you observe?

_____

_____

_____

_____

_____

Paul reminds us that God CAUSES all to work for good. This doesn't mean that all things are good, but that in His sovereignty He turns even the bad in the direction of good for those who love Him and are the called. Paul goes on to explain what this good is—that we will be conformed to the image of Jesus. God is working in your life and mine to that end. Verse 30 makes it clear that the end is not in doubt. God sees our being glorified as a done deal. It is past tense in His mind.

One of the realities we see this week is that God wants to use us to reach those different than us, not just those who are like us. What are some factors of prejudice you see in your life that get in the way of ministry?

___ Race   ___Appearance   ____ Social status

___ Wealth   ___Religious Background   ____ Sexual Orientation

___ Personality   ___Other: _____   ____ Political Alignment

Is God trying to move you past these barriers in some way?

_____

_____

_____

Another aspect of God's sovereign involvement in ministry that we see this week is His personal and individual involvement with us. As you reflect on this truth, consider the two examples Luke gives us and what application we can draw from each.

> *"And we know that God causes all things to work together for good*
> *to those who love God, to those who are called according to His*
> *purpose" (Romans 8:28)*

We observe in Simon the Magician that God sees the heart and the motives. Are there any wrong motives about ministry or your walk with God that you sense need to be dealt with?

We perceive in the Ethiopian eunuch that God not only sees the bad motives but also the good ones. The Ethiopian has a heart to seek God, and the Lord goes to great lengths to meet the needs of this seeking heart. God is looking for any whose hearts are completely His. Can you honestly say that is where your heart is right now toward Him?

If so, reaffirm that heart to Him. If not, ask Him to work in your life to bring you to where you ought to be.

Why not close this lesson by writing a prayer to the Lord that expresses where you are and where you want to be?

LESSON 9

THE LIFE-CHANGING POWER OF GOD
ACTS 9:1–31

Everyone familiar with the Christian faith has heard of the apostle Paul. He is a hard man to avoid, since he wrote about half of the New Testament and features prominently in the spread of the church to the remotest parts of the earth. Some would argue that Paul is the single most significant individual in the New Testament apart from Jesus. Yet he does not start out as a friend of the faith. When persecution against Christians boils over, Paul is leading the charge. Referred to by his Jewish name, Saul, he outpaces all his countrymen in persecuting and prosecuting the followers of Jesus. He quickly makes himself "Public Enemy Number One" to the church. We learned in chapter 8 that he "ravages" the church like a devouring lion. In a culture dominated by men, he even arrests and arranges executions of the women who identify with Jesus. He possesses a zealous hatred for all who take the name of Christ.

"Do I not destroy [my enemies] when I make them my friends?"

– Abraham Lincoln

How do you get rid of such an enemy as Saul, the persecutor? What do you do about enemies like him? Carl Sandburg, in his epic biography of Abraham Lincoln relates an incident which happens near the end of the Civil War. Lincoln, in the context of a conversation drops a few kind words about the Southern enemy. An elderly woman in the reception room flashes a question; how can he speak kindly of his enemies when he should rather destroy them. "What, madam?" he replies, "Do I not destroy them when I make them my friends?" This was a consistent philosophy and practice of Lincoln's and is one of the reasons he was needed to guide the nation through its civil crisis. In a very practical sense, Lincoln is right, of course. The best way to get rid of an enemy is to make him or her a friend.

The early church is characterized by persistent prayer, and no doubt as the persecution heats up, the Pharisee named Saul features prominently in these prayers. I doubt though that many prayed for his conversion. More likely they prayed for God to judge him and destroy him. As we look at those who are antagonistic to the faith, it is all too easy to forget the power of God to change lives. Everyone, even the most confident or controversial, needs Christ, and God is able to save even the hardest heart.

SAUL THE PERSECUTOR (ACTS 9:1–9)

Jesus Christ is a dividing line. He does not allow people the option of neutrality. If a person is not willing to accept Christ as Savior and Lord, then they will end up His enemy. The Jewish leaders have had three years to make up their minds about Jesus, and many are still rejecting Him. Peter, and later Stephen, rightly lays the guilt of Christ's death at their feet. Their unwillingness to humble themselves and set aside their own personal agendas, makes them opponents of Christ, and then of the church after His resurrection. While many of the Sanhedrin participate in the stoning of Stephen—the spark that ignites the flames of persecution —one of their younger members will end up excelling them all in zeal. We are introduced to Saul in Acts 7 as the one who keeps the robes of the ones who actually put Stephen to death. In chapter 8 we learn that Saul is both zealous and successful in the arrest of many believers in Jerusalem. Here in Acts 9 we will see that expelling Christians from Jerusalem is not enough to satisfy Saul. He decides to go after believers wherever they run.

WORD STUDY
The Way

In John 14:6 we read that on the night of His arrest, Jesus tells His disciples, "*I am the way, and the truth, and the life; no one comes to the Father but through Me.*" He uses the same Greek word for way (*hodos*) as Luke uses here to refer to the Christian faith. It has the idea of a road or a highway. Jesus is the highway to heaven. Apparently, the early church begins to identify their beliefs with this statement by Jesus and it comes to be a public means of labeling their belief system. Followers of Jesus are not yet called Christians at this point in church history.

📖 Look at Acts 9:1–2. Who initiates the intended persecution of believers in Damascus and why?

_____

_____

_____

_____

It is obvious from the text that Saul is the main initiator of expanding the persecution to other cities. He goes to the High Priest and requests letters of authority to allow him to pursue believers outside of Jerusalem. Acts 9 finds him on his way to Damascus, breathing threats and murder against the disciples of the Lord. Again, we see mention of the fact that Saul includes women in his hit list, taking persecution to unprecedented levels.

📖 Read Acts 9:3–6 and answer the questions that follow.

What does Jesus say to Saul (v. 4)?

_____

_____

What is Saul's question, and how does Jesus answer it (v.5)?

_____

_____

What instruction does Jesus give to Saul (v.6)?

_____

_____

When Jesus confronts Saul on the Damascus road, He asks, _"...why are you persecuting Me?"_ At first this may seem a strange question, but clearly Jesus sees all that Saul is doing as aimed at Him, not simply the church. Since He is the head of the church, what hurts them, hurts Him. Saul's immediate question is _"Who are You, Lord?"_ Jesus identifies Himself and instructs Saul to go to Damascus and wait for further instructions.

📖 Examine Acts 9:7–9 and summarize what you learn here.

_____

_____

_____

The divine nature of Saul's encounter with Christ is evident in the fact that everyone can hear Jesus speak, but only Saul can see Him. Imagine what must be going through Saul's mind at this point. The man he thinks is dead, and whose followers he is trying to kill, has intercepted him. Saul intends to take Damascus by storm but ends up having to be led into town by the hand. Saul obeys Jesus's instructions, making his way to Damascus, and spends three days there fasting (and we can assume praying).

_____

DAY TWO

SAUL THE PERSUADED (ACTS 9:10–19)

Saul is confronted with a great contrast. On the one hand, he is accosted by _"a light from heaven,"_ but that is followed by three days in total darkness. He has plenty of time to think about what happened, and Saul is not an ignorant man. He is well versed in the Old Testament Scriptures. Though he knows that some believe Jesus to be the Messiah, up till now he has rejected such belief. He has heard the claims of resurrection, but like Thomas, refuses to believe without eyewitness proof. Now he has it. In fact, as far as he knows his vision of Christ will be the last thing he will ever see. God's gracious way of dealing with Saul allows him time to process all the evidence, and obviously come to a different conclusion about Jesus. Saul's extreme fast— going without both food and water—is a sign of abject humility. It gives evidence that he is truly seeking God. The Lord is always willing to meet with one who comes to Him in humility and sincerity.

📖 Look over Acts 9:10–12.

What is God's instruction to Ananias?

_____

_____

_____

How does God prepare Saul for Ananias' visit?

_____

_____

_____

Three days pass, and then God speaks by way of a vision to Ananias, a Christian in Damascus, and through this vision sends him to Saul. God's instruction is very specific, even giving the street and house where Saul can be found. Again, we see that Saul is praying, and he too has a vision, God telling him who will be coming to him and giving the good news that he will regain his sight.

📖 Read Acts 9:13–14 and reflect on the questions below.

Why do you think Ananias is hesitant to act on God's instructions?

_____

_____

_____

How do you suppose he knows so much about Saul?

_____

DID YOU KNOW?
Saul's Conversion

Saul's conversion is an answer to prayer. When God speaks to Ananias about going to Saul, Ananias responds by saying, "*Lord, I have heard from many about this man, how much harm he did to Your saints at Jerusalem; and here he has authority from the chief priests to bind all who call upon Your name*" (Acts 9:13–14). Notice what good information the Damascus believers have. They know who is coming, why he is coming, and with what authority he comes. We can be sure they are praying and praying hard. Imagine their surprise when Ananias comes in and declares Saul has become a Christian. It might not be exactly what they are praying for, but God knows their hearts. Often, we pray for God to remove someone who is unkind or harsh, when we should be praying for God to change them. He can.

When God first appears to Ananias, his response is one of total submission—*"Here I am, Lord."* However, once he hears what God wants him to do, he questions. It is easy to understand why Ananias hesitates. Saul is well known. Probably there are some in the church at Damascus who have friends or family members who have been arrested in this persecution Saul has been spearheading. Believers have been killed. No doubt, there is good reason in his mind to question the validity of Saul's conversion. Perhaps Saul is setting a trap and is faking his switch to Christianity in order to identify more believers for persecution. Obviously, the church in Damascus has heard much of what is happening in Jerusalem. They even know who is coming to Damascus, for what purpose, and with what authority. They probably have already held prayer meetings to discuss this Saul who is coming. God answers their prayers but probably not as they expect.

📖 Looking at Acts 9:15–16, what does God say to convince Ananias that Saul's conversion is genuine?

_____

_____

_____

It is one thing for Saul the Persecutor to claim a conversion to Christianity, but quite another for God to communicate that in a vision. God reveals to Ananias that He has chosen Saul as a witness to Gentiles, to kings, and to the Jews. God has also chosen Saul to suffer the same persecution he has been giving to others. There must be a sense of justice in that to Ananias.

📖 Summarize what you learn of the outcome of Ananias and Saul's meeting in Acts 9:17–19.

_____

_____

> *"...he is a chosen instrument of Mine, to bear My name before the Gentiles and kings and the sons of Israel; for I will show him how much he must suffer for My name's sake."*

God clearly works in Ananias' heart and satisfies his concerns. The first words out of his mouth are to call Saul "brother." Ananias lays his hands on Saul, identifying with him in his newfound faith, and God heals his blindness. Immediately Saul is baptized, probably in obedience to instruction from Ananias. It isn't until after this that Saul breaks his fast and begins to eat.

Saul's conversion is immediate and dramatic. Though years will pass before his main ministry begins, we will see in Day Three of our study that from the very beginning of this conversion process, Saul proclaims Christ. God will give him great opportunities to testify of the One he had been denying. It will be while Saul is in prison, suffering persecution as the Lord promises, that he will write many of his epistles. Indeed, all that God prophesies to Ananias of Saul's future will come to pass.

DAY THREE

SAUL THE PREACHER (ACTS 9:20–25)

Can you imagine what the Sanhedrin thinks when word gets back to them that Saul of Tarsus is now preaching Jesus? It has been a rough year for them. First, scores of Jews were already following Jesus, the untrained Galilean, instead of them. They finally get rid of Him, and then He rises from the dead. For forty days they have to listen to reports of Him appearing here and there and everywhere. Then reports of Him appearing cease (after He ascended to heaven), and they probably hope things will quiet down. The next thing they know, His followers, who had been intimidated into silence, suddenly become incredibly bold and begin performing miracles all over town. The time finally comes for them to get rough. Just when they think they are getting things back under control and they have a zealous guy who really seems capable of running their extermination program, he converts to Christianity! We cannot comprehend the shock waves this must send throughout the Jewish establishment. What is even more shocking though is that instead of considering that they might be the wrong ones, they continue to oppose. This unbelief—from these who are supposed to be the most spiritual in all of Israel—is the most shocking reality of all. But at least now Saul believes.

📖 Look at Acts 9:19b–21.

What does Saul do once he gets his sight back?

_____

_____

Where does he do it?

_____

_____

What do the Jews think about this?

_____

_____

DID YOU KNOW?

Immediate Evangelism

How long should one be a Christian before sharing their faith? Should they reach a certain level of maturity before being a witness? Acts 9:20 tells us that *"...immediately he began to proclaim Jesus."* Saul doesn't wait until he takes a witnessing course or passes a milestone of years in the faith. All he needs is the Holy Spirit living in him.

It is obvious that Saul is a changed man. Verse 20 tells us that *"...immediately"* he begins to proclaim Jesus, acknowledging Him, saying, *"He is the Son of God."* He goes straight to the synagogues where Jews gather and begins preaching his new faith. It is not surprising that Jews are amazed, but notice what else we learn here. Saul's zeal in persecuting the church is so well known that news of it has reached the Jews in Damascus. It must have a powerful impact on them to know that one so antagonistic to the Christian message has become convinced of its validity. Remember, these are the very same synagogues where Saul had letters of authority to see if he could find any Christians and arrest them. Christianity's greatest adversary in Damascus has just become its strongest advocate!

📖 Read Acts 9:22.

What do you think it means that Saul keeps *"increasing in strength"*?

What implications do you see in this verse of the response of the Jews to whom he is preaching?

When Luke tells us that Saul keeps increasing in strength, he apparently is speaking of his spiritual growth. His faith in Jesus as Messiah, his spiritual health, and his confidence in God are continually increasing. The response of the audience is telling but predictable. Saul is "confounding" them. The Greek word has the idea, "to throw into confusion" or "to put in an uproar." Saul's message is simple: Jesus is the Christ. His pharisaical education and his thorough knowledge of the Scriptures allow him to *"prove"* his point to the degree that none can argue. This does not mean that all become believers, though some probably do. As we will see in the verses that follow, however, the message of the cross continues to be a line of demarcation, dividing hearts.

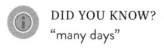

DID YOU KNOW?
"many days"

Luke begins verse 23 saying, "*...when many days had passed.*" The exact time frame is more specifically addressed in Galatians 1:17–18, where Saul writes, "*Nor did I go up to Jerusalem to those who were apostles before me; but I went away to Arabia and returned once more to Damascus. Then three years later I went up to Jerusalem to become acquainted with Cephas.*" The "*many days*" Luke speaks of are actually three years between Acts 9:22 and 9:23. It is implied that Saul spends those years learning from the Lord and meditating on Scripture.

📖 As you study Acts 9:23–25, reflect on the questions that follow.

What does verse 23 reveal about the response of some of the Jews to Saul's compelling defense of Jesus as Messiah?

....

....

....

What does verse 24 say about God's protection of Saul?

....

....

....

What is revealed in verse 25 of how the believers in Damascus view Saul?

....

....

....

Amazing as it may seem, the hardened human heart would rather murder than humble itself and admit it is wrong. After many days of ministry in Damascus, the Jews plot to kill Saul. God's protection is evident however, as He makes the plot known to Saul. We do not know how, but clearly God is watching over him. The safest place for the Christian is in the will of God, and that is where Saul has placed himself. That his new Christian friends have to sneak him out of the city by lowering him down in a large basket through an opening in the wall, speaks of their care and concern for him. Obviously, they have laid aside any reservations and have embraced him as a fellow believer in Jesus.

DAY FOUR

SAUL THE PROSELYTIZER (ACTS 9:26–31)

In a brief period of time, Saul has gone from foe to friend; from antagonist to ally. Prior to his conversion, there was probably no one the believers in Damascus feared more (and with good reason) than Saul. Yet now, his life is completely turned around. He stands as convincing testimony of the life-changing power of God. In him we find great hope for those in our lives who do not know Christ. If God can reach Saul the Persecutor, surely no one is out of the reach of His love! We must remember this when we pray for lost loved ones or for the antagonists in our lives. God can change hearts. He can reform the most reprobate life. The reason sometimes our prayers for the lost are so faithless is because we focus on the person and their rebellion instead of the power of God to save. Saul the Persecutor is now Saul the Proselytizer, Saul the converted.

WORD STUDY
Barnabas "took hold" of him

When Saul left Damascus and came to Jerusalem, he kept trying to associate with the disciples, but they feared that his conversion was just another trap. Luke tells us that Barnabas "*took hold*" of him and brought him to the apostles. The word indicates that he physically held on to him. Luke uses this same word in Luke 23:26 when he says the authorities "*seized*" Simon of Cyrene and made him carry Jesus' cross. He also uses it in Acts 16:19 saying that certain people "*seized*" Paul and Silas to arrest them, and again in Acts 18:17, when the crowd "*took hold of*" Sosthenes to beat him. It may be that by this time Saul had given up, and Barnabas was making him go meet with the disciples.

📖 Examine Acts 9:26.

What is the initial response of believers in Jerusalem to news of Saul's conversion?

_____

_____

_____

_____

Why do you think they are doubtful?

_____

_____

_____

From here, Saul goes back to Jerusalem and is "trying" to associate with the disciples. The Greek word translated "trying" is in the imperfect tense, indicating repeated attempts. He keeps trying, but it isn't working. The text says they are, "*...all afraid of him,*" not *believing that he is a disciple.* This is not difficult to understand. We must realize that Saul killed some of their friends and relatives. They would likely be hostile and bitter. Many, I'm sure, think he is faking conversion to trap more believers. Imagine how Saul is feeling. He no longer has the security of being a Pharisee. His former associates are trying to kill him (v.29), and the believers in Christ with whom he would now identify are continually rebuffing him. He must really be down, and in need of a friend characterized by *encouragement.* It is here that Barnabas, who will become a fellow-laborer and life-long friend comes on the scene.

📖 Look at verses 27 and 28 of Acts 9. What is Barnabas' role in Saul's life in Jerusalem, and what are the results of it?

_____

_____

_____

_____

We must realize that it is not Peter, the "Rock," or James, the leader of the Jerusalem church, but Barnabas, who goes to meet with Saul to see if he is genuine. He does so at the risk of his own life. It could be a trap. Notice that the apostles have such confidence in Barnabas and his spiritual discernment, that the result is Saul being completely accepted into the fellowship of believers. Barnabas believes in Saul when no one else does, when Saul needs encouragement.

DID YOU KNOW?
Tarsus

Through the help of his Christian friends, Saul fled the threats on his life and left Jerusalem for his hometown of Tarsus. It was a Greek city famous for its university, its philosophers, its harbors, and its control of the famous Cilician Gates in the Tarsus mountains. The city had been visited by the Greek philosopher Cicero and is the place where Cleopatra met Anthony. We are told that Saul was brought "down to Caesarea" (a seaport on the Mediterranean) and was "sent" to Tarsus, undoubtedly by way of boat.

📖 Compare Acts 9:29–30 with Acts 22:17–21 and record what you learn of Saul's reception from the Jews in Jerusalem and how it fits in with God's will.

_____

_____

_____

_____

_____

Here in Acts 9, we see that again there are people who want to kill Saul as he witnesses of Christ. It appears that the brethren learn of the plot to kill Saul from his own vision, recorded in Acts 22. Saul is not a coward, but by way of divine instruction, he flees for his life. Two revelations emerge from this vision. First, though logic would say a converted Pharisee is the best person to witness to Jews, Jesus makes it clear that Saul's testimony will not be received. Second, we have the clear affirmation of Saul's calling to the Gentile world. He will be faithful to that calling and will become the single most prominent figure in the gospel spreading to the known world.

📖 Read Acts 9:31.

What do you learn of the church at this point?

_____

_____

_____

Why do you think Luke links this summary statement with Saul's departure?

_____

_____

_____

Luke makes mention here of the church as being *"throughout Judea and Galilee and Samaria."* Up until the persecution, the church is only in Jerusalem, but clearly through God's sovereign plan the church has grown and spread. Two reasons, both associated with Saul, are related to the relative peace the church enjoys at this point. First, as a believer, he is no longer leading the Jewish persecution. Though they continue to oppose the believers, the Jews have lost their most passionate warrior. Second, some of the intense antagonism of late is due to the articulate ministry of Saul in debating the Jews. He becomes somewhat of a lightning rod, attracting opposition. With Saul, the converted, gone from Jerusalem, things begin to die down.

The recurring theme of Luke in the book of Acts is the continual increase of the church. His premise in chapter 1 that the disciples will witness of Jesus *"in Jerusalem, and in all Judea and Samaria, and even to the remotest part of the earth,"* is reflected over and over in his account. The church continues to spread, and one person after another gives evidence of the life-changing power of God. Our Lord has not changed, and today, you and I give evidence of that same power.

DAY FIVE

FOR ME TO FOLLOW GOD

Visit the bookshelves of any bookstore today, and you will find them filled with titles in the category called "self-help" books. While you will probably find some useful information there, the prevailing philosophy behind much in that genre is that if a person tries hard enough and long enough, they can make of themselves the kind of person they want to be. While we should endeavor to make more of ourselves and to be the best we can be, if we could truly do the job on our own we wouldn't need a Savior. The message that speaks loudly from the conversion of Saul the Persecutor is that God is the one who makes of us what we ought to be if we will allow Him to do so. He has the power to change our lives in ways we never could. None of us is beyond the reach of this power. None of those we love, or fear, are beyond it either.

As we get further into the book of Acts, we will see several examples where Luke records the specific content of Saul's witness. Each time Saul shares his testimony he relates three basic points: 1) what he is like before meeting Christ, 2) how he comes to know Christ, and 3), the changes Christ makes in his life. This serves as a good outline for all of us.

What do you think your life would be like if you had never met Christ?

What were you like before meeting Christ?

....

....

....

....

Those like me who meet the Lord later in life can easily recognize ways God has changed us. For me, I was immoral, unethical, and much of what I did was illegal. I professed atheism and practiced sin. I was a thief, a drug dealer, and a reprobate. In a word, I was rebellious. That is not the testimony of Saul, however. He isn't rebellious; he is religious. His religion professes a worship of God, but at its core is pride in self. Though he claims to follow God, his practice fails to acknowledge his need of God. Perhaps you don't have either type of testimony. Maybe you met Christ at an early age. That does not mean you fail to give evidence of a changed life. Perhaps it would be fruitful to reflect on what you would be like were it not for Christ's work in your life.

What are some evidences in you of the life-changing power of God?

....

....

....

....

It is our own changed life that gives us something to talk about as we seek to be witnesses of Christ. It is the changes He works in us that make our testifying personal. People can argue with what we say Christ can do for them, but they cannot argue with history. They cannot refute what He has already done in us. When Jesus heals the Gerasene demoniac, He performs a miraculous life-change. Here is a man who goes from violent insanity to sudden stability. Jesus' instruction to him is simple. "*Go home to your people and report to them what great things the Lord has done for you, and how He had mercy on you*" (Mark 5:19). Each of us should be prepared to testify of the life-changing power of God. Peter advises, "*but sanctify Christ as Lord in your hearts, always being ready to make a defense to everyone who asks you to give an account for the hope that is in you, yet with gentleness and reverence*" (1 Peter 3:15).

As you reflect on your own life, are there any areas where you doubt God is able to change you?

_____

_____

_____

Why do you find it difficult to believe God in this area?

_____

_____

_____

First, we must recognize that "_without faith it is impossible to please God_" (Hebrews 11:6). We must trust God to work, and Saul should serve as compelling evidence that He can. Often, we struggle with believing God can change us, not because we lack faith in God, but because we lose faith in ourselves. Perhaps we struggle with past failures that make it hard to have hope in the present. It is important to remind ourselves that our hope is in God, not in ourselves. He can change what we cannot change. The key, as we see so often in the book of Acts, is yielding ourselves to the Spirit's control. If we are in control of our lives, we will fail sooner or later. If He is in control, He never fails.

> _"And without faith it is impossible to please Him,_
> _for he who comes to God must believe that He is and that He is a rewarder of those_
> _who seek Him" (Hebrews 11:6)_

Is there anyone in your life whom you have doubted God is able to change?

_____

_____

Why have you doubted God can change that person?

_____

_____

_____

What encouragement do you find in the example of Saul?

_____

_____

_____

As you reflect on the powerful life-change we see in Saul, why not close out this week by praying for those in whose lives you would like to see change?

LESSON 10

THE GREATEST MIRACLE OF ALL

ACTS 9:32—10:48

What would you say is the greatest miracle ever performed? Think about it. Of all the extraordinary accomplishments that have ever been done, which type of event is the most miraculous? I'm sure personal opinions may vary. Some may think of the parting of the Red Sea as supreme. Others might select Jesus walking on water or calming the raging Sea of Galilee. Still others may hold Jesus' feeding of the multitudes with a few loaves and fishes as the greatest. Perhaps in the minds of a few, Creation itself would rate as the top supernatural event of all time. If you take into account what draws a crowd, you would have to place physical acts of healing near the top of the list. Maybe a number of people would rank raising the dead as the ultimate marvel. Others might think of dreams or visions from God such as those in Daniel's day as evidence of the highest form of wonder.

Each of these illustrations of the miraculous stands as a superlative example of the power of God. Each gives proof that He is not bound by the physical laws of the natural realm. But I would not place any of the items we have mentioned at the top of my list. The reason is simple. They are not eternal. God parts the Red Sea, but His people have to move on and overcome other barriers. Jesus calms the wind and the waves, but we still have to face storms sometimes. He feeds the five thousand, but each of them has need of a meal again the next day. Creation is overwhelming in significance, but not eternal, for one day God will create a new heaven and a new earth. Those who are healed physically still can get sick again. Lazarus is raised from the dead only to die again. Even though dreams and visions are miraculous visitations from God, they are not where we live every day. So, what is the greatest miracle of all?

> *"It was revealed to them that they were not serving themselves,*
> *but you, in these things which now have been announced to you*
> *through those who preached the gospel to you by the Holy Spirit*
> *sent from heaven—things into which angels long to look."*
> (1 Peter 1:12)

I believe the greatest miracle of all is the miracle of salvation—that the sinful and fallen can be redeemed. It is not something humans themselves can do. It is miraculous because it is always and only a work of God. Salvation is just about the only miracle of eternal consequence. On the Ark of the Covenant where the presence of God dwells, the cover is the mercy seat. Once a year on Yom Kippur – the Day of Atonement – blood would be sprinkled on that mercy seat as a picture of what Christ performs for us in heaven. Overshadowing that seat are two golden Cherubim, gazing ever downward. I believe they picture the truth of 1 Peter 1:12, where the gospel of our salvation is identified as *"things into which angels long to look."* Redemption is to them an incomprehensible glory. This week we will see Luke present us with many miraculous events, but with each he will come back to the theme he considers paramount: *"and many believed in the Lord"* (Acts 9:42).

DAY ONE

THE MIRACLE OF PHYSICAL HEALING (ACTS 9:32–35)

All sickness is a consequence of sin, but not necessarily individual sin. Just because we get sick does not mean we are living in sin. Illness is part of the general curse of sin on humankind. While disease can be much more than we can handle, it is never too great a challenge for God. He can heal and has healed just about every disease known. The general ability of the human body to heal itself is an amazing act of God's creative power. We cut ourselves, and a scab forms, sealing the wound and allowing the tear to be mended. But greater still are those specific acts of healing where God does what doctors can't. Today we want to look at an example of healing recorded for us by Luke from the ministry of Peter.

📖 Looking at the context of Acts 9:32, why do you think Peter is traveling through these regions?

_____

_____

_____

The regions verse 32 speak of are obviously the regions mentioned in verse 31; namely the regions of Judea, Galilee and Samaria. If you look at these regions on a Bible map you will find them west of the Jordan River from the southern point of the Dead Sea to the northern end of the Sea of Galilee. Lydda, mentioned in verse 32, is in Judea northwest of Jerusalem. Two points from verse 31 give us an idea of why Peter is traveling in these regions. First, we are told that the church in these parts is *"being built up."* Second, the church continues to increase and therefore needs apostolic leadership. No doubt, the apostle Peter is assisting in this ministry of establishing the fellowships of this region. This idea is further supported by the fact that we are told he comes specifically *"to the saints"* who live here.

📖 Read Acts 9:33–34 and answer the questions on the next page.

What do you learn here of the nature of Aeneas' problem?

_____

_____

Who does Peter say heals him?

_____

_____

What specifics stand out to you regarding his healing?

_____

_____

_____

WORD STUDY
Get up and make your bed

When Peter tells Aeneas to "*make your bed*," grammatically this is an "aorist active imperative." In New Testament Greek, an aorist imperative calls for a specific act—with a note of urgency. In other words, Peter is commanding him to take action. He is calling him to "pack up" his bed since he will no longer need it.

We know from the text that Aeneas has been paralyzed for eight years and he is bedridden. His is no small problem then, and it would be a medically impossible situation today as well. Peter makes a point of telling him that Jesus Christ is healing him. Peter wants to make certain that he does not get the credit for what can only be a work of God. One thing we notice from this situation is that with the privilege of healing comes responsibility. This man who could not care for himself before is charged to do so now that he is healed. It should be recognized that his healing is immediate, not progressive. Virtually every healing recorded in Scripture is this way. If God has the power to heal, then He has the power to do so immediately. There is no need for a waiting period.

Meditate on Acts 9:35.

What does Luke identify as the result of this miracle of healing?

_____

_____

_____

What does this tell us about the purpose of healing?

_____

_____

_____

Luke makes a point of telling us that "*all*" who live in that area *turn to the Lord*. The purpose of the healing is not as an end in itself. We tend to put too much value in physical healing and fail to recognize that from the vantage point of eternity, the act itself isn't very significant. Luke seems to be emphasizing that the healing serves as a means to an end. Its purpose is to give evidence of God's power and to gain an audience for the gospel. As for the geographical references, Lydda is the city, and Sharon is the whole area. It is a sub-district of Judea.

> *"And all who lived at Lydda and Sharon saw him, and they turned to the Lord." (Acts 9:35)*

Healing is wonderful. Ask those who experience it. Yet it is a transitory blessing. It is significant, but by no means superior to the miracle of salvation. The disease of the soul is the one most in need of healing.

DAY TWO

THE MIRACLE OF RAISING THE DEAD (ACTS 9:36–43)

It has been said that only two things are certain in life: death and taxes. While taxes may be greatly probable, death is assured. Hebrews 9:27 instructs us, "*It is appointed for men to die once and after this comes judgment.*" Death is an appointment all must keep sooner or later. While we may be tempted to view this as bad, we must remember that were it not for death we would live eternally in this present fallen state, always fighting the battles of temptation and sin. Though death is a consequence of sin, it is also an act of grace. This is the reason God kicked Adam and Eve out of the Garden of Eden, lest they eat of the tree of life and live forever in their fallen state. One day we will be freed from sins ravages for eternity. There are however, a few cases in Scripture where people die more than once. From the son of the Shunnamite raised by Elisha, to Lazarus raised from the tomb after three days, to this woman raised by Peter, Scripture shows us God can raise the dead. These miracles are noteworthy but are not actually the same as Jesus being resurrected. He is called "*the first-born from the dead*" because His resurrection is permanent. He will never again taste death. This cannot be said for the other situations we mentioned. Nevertheless, they are still glorious works of God. Today we want to examine a miraculous raising from the dead by the apostle Peter.

📖 Look at Acts 9:36–39.

What do we learn here of the woman who dies?

_____

_____

_____

How do you suppose the disciples hear that Peter is in Lydda?

_____

_____

_____

Who are the recipients of Tabitha's acts of charity?

_____

_____

_____

The central figure of Luke's narrative here is a woman named Tabitha. Her name (as well as its Greek equivalent, _Dorcas_) means "gazelle" and suggests a woman of grace. She abounds in good deeds generally but specializes in acts of charity—deeds done for the poor and destitute. The imperfect tense makes it clear that this is not a one-time service motivated by a moment's passion, but a consistent, ongoing ministry that she performs as a lifestyle. Verse 39 indicates that one of her unique ministries is to make tunics and garments and give them to the impoverished widows. That she is dead for some time is evidenced by the fact that her body is prepared for burial. Enough time passes as well to allow two men to travel the twelve miles or so from Joppa to Lydda where Peter is, and to return with him. That they know of Peter being in the area is suggestive that word of the miracle of Aeneas' healing has reached Joppa. That explains why they have hope of Peter being able to help this woman who is already dead.

DID YOU KNOW?
Preparation for Burial

It is a wide-spread custom in Peter's day to wash the body of a dead person before burial. But in this case, the second act—laying the body in an upper room—is a break from custom. Normally the body would be buried immediately (see Acts 5:6, 10). The delay indicates they hope that Peter can arrange some miraculous solution.

📖 Read Acts 9:40. How does prayer fit in with the miracle Peter performs here?

_____

_____

_____

_____

Prayer is not a ritual for Peter. It is intimate communication with the Lord. Perhaps one of the reasons Luke mentions that Peter prays is to remind us of the Lord's role in raising this woman from the dead. It is not a miracle of Peter's initiative. Prayer is not preparation for work. It is work. Peter does not raise this woman. God does. It appears that through prayer the Lord reveals His plan to Peter. Peter then has to exercise faith by speaking to the dead woman. His faith is not in himself, but in God. We know this because he prays first and then speaks. He speaks to God before he speaks to the dead girl.

📖 Take some time to digest Acts 9:41–43.

Why do you think Peter *presents* her to the saints and widows?

....

....

....

What results from this miracle other than the woman coming back to life?

....

....

....

The Greek word *"present"* has the idea of exhibiting or placing on display. Peter wants to showcase what God has done. This is not from a motive of self-glory, but apparently in the hope that God will use the event to glorify Himself and to open hearts to the gospel. Luke clearly is trying to connect these two thoughts. As a result of people hearing of the miracle, *"many" believe in the Lord.* Another result is that Peter stays on in Joppa for many days and assists the congregation of believers here.

> *"It became known all over Joppa, and many believed in the Lord"*
> (Acts 9:42)

That many believe is not included in Luke's account as an afterthought. Remember, in historical narrative such as Acts, we are not told every single event that occurs, but rather, those that the author deems important to get across. Luke wants to make sure we know that raising someone from the dead, as incredible an action as that may be, is not nearly so great a miracle as people coming to the Lord.

DAY THREE

THE MIRACLE OF DREAMS AND VISIONS (ACTS 10:1–23)

The Bible gives us many examples of God communicating through dreams or visions. Abraham hears from God that way. Joseph, son of Jacob and Joseph, father of Jesus both received them. Paul and Peter have them. Even pagan leaders like Joseph's Pharaoh and Daniel's King Nebuchadnezzar and King Belshazzar were on the receiving end of divine communication. While not every dream is a message from God, clearly there is scriptural basis for acknowledging that some are. But what is the difference between a dream and a vision? It hinges on this distinction between meaningful and meaningless dreams. A vision is a message or communication from God. Some visions happen in the daytime as the recipient falls into some sort of trance. Others appear at night while the person dreams. Job 33:15 speaks of *"a dream, a vision of the night,"* linking the two ideas as one.

Scripturally, the two ideas exist almost as synonyms with the subtle distinction of "dream visions" only coming as one sleeps. Any direct communication from God would have to be recognized as miraculous, but somehow a dream or vision stands out even more than just a heavenly voice. Here in Acts 10 we find two separate men being brought together through visions each receives. With them, Luke gives us another vantage point from which to gain perspective on the miraculous.

📖 Examine the record of Cornelius' vision in Acts 10:1–8.

What do you learn of Cornelius' faith that suggests why he receives a vision?

What instructions are given to Cornelius?

Cornelius is not a Jew, yet clearly he believes in Jehovah. He is called a *"devout"* man, indicating that he is faithful in his pursuit of God. His spiritual devotion is expressed in acts of charity as well as in his commitment to prayer. The text tells us that the vision comes at the *"ninth hour"* one of the three prescribed times of prayer each day. Undoubtedly, Cornelius is in prayer when the visitation comes. Though he does not know of Jesus yet, he is a good steward of all the spiritual enlightenment he has received up to this point, and God is honoring his seeking heart. The angel affirms Cornelius' faith and instructs him to send for Peter. Notice how specific the vision is. Cornelius is told who to send for and exactly where to find him.

📖 Read the narrative of Peter's vision in Acts 10:9–18.

Summarize the contents of Peter's vision.

Why is this vision so troubling to him?

What is significant in the timing of this vision?

_____

_____

_____

Though we talk to God in prayer, rarely do we expect Him to speak back. It is interesting that like Cornelius, Peter's vision coincides with a season of prayer. God meets with His people when we are seeking Him. Three times Peter sees the same vision of animals the Law calls unclean and wrong to eat. The message each time is the same – *"Get up, Peter, kill and eat!"* Peter's response reveals that he has never in his life violated the dietary laws. He is instructed, *"What God has cleansed, no longer consider unclean."* Imagine how hard it would be to change your thinking on something you have considered wrong your whole life. Obviously, the main point of Peter's vision is not to change his diet, though. The timing reveals that the main point is to prepare him to change his thinking about Gentiles and their place in the faith, as his vision ends just as the men from Cornelius arrive.

DOCTRINE
Unclean

The Law declares certain foods as unclean and therefore, unacceptable to those who devoutly follow God. Leviticus 20:25–26 states, *"You are therefore to make a distinction between the clean animal and the unclean, and between the unclean bird and the clean; and you shall not make yourselves detestable by animal or by bird or by anything that creeps on the ground, which I have separated for you as unclean. Thus, you are to be holy to Me, for I the Lord am holy; and I have set you apart from the peoples to be Mine."* However, there is a later rabbinical teaching that in the days of the Messiah the rules regarding unclean foods will be lifted.

Take a look at Acts 10:19–23 and answer the questions that follow.

What stands out to you from the Spirit's instruction to Peter?

_____

_____

_____

What information does the group share to represent Cornelius as worthy of Peter's visit?

_____

_____

_____

How does Peter receive their request?

_____

_____

Perhaps the most outstanding feature of Luke's record here is all that God does to reassure Peter. Think about it. Three times he receives the same vision. Then as he meditates on it, the Spirit directs that Cornelius' men are coming and that God has sent them. Peter is instructed to accompany them without misgiving. The delegation must expect resistance or doubt, for everything they say is designed to reassure. Notice the positives they point out about Cornelius. He is a centurion (a person of importance), righteous, God-fearing, well-spoken of by *"the entire nation"* of the Jews and is divinely directed to Peter. The great lengths to which God goes to reassure Peter give an indication of how strong his prejudice against Gentiles must be. He obviously overcomes his bias though, for he welcomes the group into his home and then accompanies them the next day to visit Cornelius.

There is much of a supernatural nature in Luke's record here. Cornelius experiences a divine vision. Peter has a thrice-repeated vision and a direct instruction from the Spirit. The timing of these events as well gives clear evidence of being divinely orchestrated. Yet perhaps the most important truth to recognize is that none of these supernatural actions exist as an end in themselves. The point of dreams and visions is not to edify, but to instruct. All that God does here relates to what is about to happen in Cornelius' life. The point of these visions is the salvation of a man seeking God.

DAY FOUR

THE MIRACLE OF SALVATION (ACTS 10:24–48)

Up to this point we see some significant miracles occur in the book of Acts. We learn of Jesus' miraculous ascension (Acts 1). We see the Spirit come at Pentecost with rushing wind and tongues of fire (Acts 2). We discover a lame beggar healed in Jerusalem (Acts 3). We witness Ananias and Sapphira struck dead (Acts 5). We observe the sick, afflicted and demon-possessed being healed (Acts 5:16). We view the apostles released from jail by an angel (Acts 5). We watch Stephen perform *"great signs and wonders"* (Acts 6:8), as well as Philip (Acts 8:6). We behold the Spirit supernaturally lead Phillip to the Ethiopian eunuch and then translate him to another place instantly (Acts 8). We witness God speak to Saul in a blinding light (Acts 9). In this week's lesson we have seen Peter heal Aeneas and raise Tabitha from the dead. We observe both he and Cornelius being led by visions.

But none of these are the main point for Luke. The priority for Luke thus far (and so throughout the book of Acts as well) has been to tell us of the spread of the Gospel and of the miracle of people coming to the Lord. Luke spends far more time recording the evangelistic fruit than anything else. The reason is simple. Ours is a miracle-working God, but the greatest miracle of all is when He saves a soul. That is why Luke devotes most of his time in the book of Acts recording salvations or the events leading up to them. Acts 10 is especially significant in that it marks the first time Gentiles are converted. Let's see what we can learn from the miracle of Gentiles getting saved.

EXTRA MILE
Miracles in Acts 1–11

In the first eleven chapters of Acts Luke makes mention of more events of salvations than all other miraculous events combined. Luke records salvations in the following verses in Acts 1-11...

2:41

2:47

4:3

5:14

6:1

6:7

8:12

8:13

8:37

9:18

9:31

9:35

9:42

10:44

📖 Read Acts 10:24–29 and answer the questions that follow.

Who gathers to meet Peter and why?

_____

_____

Why do you think Cornelius falls at Peter's feet?

_____

_____

What does Peter's statement reveal of what he learned from his vision?

_____

_____

It says a lot about Cornelius that once it is revealed to him that God is going to send him a divine message, he wants all his friends and family (see v.24) to share in this blessing. All we know of these gathered is that there are many of them (see v.27). Cornelius prostrates himself before Peter in a manner of worship. He is acting as if the message Peter brings originates with Peter. The apostle makes it clear that he is merely a man entrusted to deliver the message from God. The one to be worshiped is God from whom the message originates. Even today we see this same problem manifested where people are tempted to worship the one who delivers a message from God instead of just worshiping the God who sends the message. Righteous preachers will always point the attention away from themselves and back to God where it belongs.

Peter's explanation in verse 28 of why he comes makes it obvious he connects the vision regarding the unclean animals with the coming of the delegation from Cornelius. He realizes that the point is not just that it is alright to eat something formerly unclean, but that all the rules concerning what is clean are now changed. His visit would be something he would avoid before, but God clearly gives him this new freedom to consort with Gentiles.

 DID YOU KNOW?
Ceremonial Uncleanness

Not all interaction between Jews and Gentiles is forbidden by the Law. Only certain types of interaction would render a Jew ceremonially unclean and thus affect his ability to worship. This would include entering a Gentile house or handling articles belonging to Gentiles. This is why it takes a divine vision for Peter to feel free to visit Cornelius at his house.

📖 Compare Acts 10:30–33 with Acts 10:1–6 and make note of what else you learn about Cornelius' vision.

_____

_____

_____

_____

_____

_____

What Cornelius communicates to Peter mirrors the record we have at the beginning of chapter ten. The only addition we find here is that clearly Cornelius understands that Peter has a message from God for him. The wording here is interesting. Cornelius states in verse 33 that the people assembled are *present before God* and that they are gathered to hear all that Peter has been commanded by the Lord. Although Cornelius may not completely understand what he is asking, he is requesting that Peter share the gospel with him and his friends.

📖 Look over Acts 10:34–43.

Why is Peter's message of verses 34–35 important to this particular audience?

_____

_____

_____

Of the points Peter makes, which would you consider central to what one needs to know to be saved?

_____

_____

_____

Humanly speaking, at this point in church history, the apostle Peter is the single most important person. When he pronounces that "God is not one to show partiality," and that people of "every nation" are welcome to the Lord, he is establishing a new precedent for all the church. The gospel message Peter preaches to Cornelius is identical in content to the message he preaches to the Jews at Pentecost. As you walk through these verses you find the same essentials. Peter reminds them that the miraculous and God-anointed life of Jesus is followed by His death on the cross, and His resurrection by God. Peter presents Jesus as Lord of all (v.36), Messiah ("the One"—v.42), and judge (v.42) and explains that "everyone who believes in Him receives forgiveness of sins" (v.43).

DOCTRINE
Belief and Baptism

When the gospel crosses into the new territory of Samaritans believing, God withholds the Holy Spirit coming on them until Peter can be there to witness it. In this case, they believe and then receive the Spirit later. Here, as in the rest of the book of Acts, it is clear that the Holy Spirit does not enter a person after believing but concurrent with belief. In this case, water baptism is the only action that happens later (affirming that it is not essential to salvation).

Reflect on Acts 10:44–48 and answer the questions that follow.

What evidence do you see of the Gentiles' positive response to the gospel?

_____

_____

_____

What do the Jews who accompany Peter witness?

_____

_____

_____

Why is their witness important?

_____

_____

_____

That Cornelius and his Gentile friends truly believe is evident from the fact that the Holy Spirit comes upon them in the same way as with the Jews at Pentecost. These Gentiles speak in tongues; apparently in recognizable languages, since Luke is able to affirm the content of what they say as "*exalting God.*" We can see the hand of God all over this situation. It is providential that Peter brings along six other Jews from Joppa so that there can be seven witnesses (a number the Jews associate with completion or perfection) of the Holy Spirit indwelling Gentiles. It is providential as well that Cornelius invites so many Gentile friends to his house so that none will think of Cornelius as just an exception who finds God's favor. It is obvious to all that God has opened the door of faith to the Gentiles. This is perhaps the most significant cultural barrier the gospel crosses in the entire book of Acts—more noteworthy even than belief among the Samaritans.

Luke records for us many miracles in this passage, but the most amazing of all is the salvation of these Gentiles. It is the only event in this passage where Luke points out the audience's amazement (see 10:45). God's working can be seen in many different ways, but nothing gives greater testimony of His power than when He changes a life. It is a work which touches eternity when anyone is "*rescued...from the domain of darkness, and transferred...to the kingdom of His beloved Son*" (Colossians 1:13).

DAY FIVE

FOR ME TO FOLLOW GOD

As a small child, I would love it when my grandfather would take me to the county fair. A fair is a wonderful place for a kid, filled with rides and games and exhibits. My grandfather, as a retired farmer, liked to look at the livestock exhibits, which would bore me to death. I couldn't tell any difference between the prize-winning cow and those who earned no ribbons. I was far more impressed with the two-headed calf at the sideshow than with the prize-winning bull at the farmer's ring. The reason is simple—a kid didn't get to see a two-headed calf every day.

Now that I am grown up, I can understand more the value of a prize bull over a deformed calf. Novelty has given way to a more reasoned appreciation of value. It took some maturing to get to that point though. Perhaps this is one of the reasons Christians tend to be enamored with the miraculous. It is not a measure of true value, but rather attraction to novelty that makes us more impressed with physical healing or dreams and visions than with something so commonplace as salvation. Yet there is no record in Scripture that angels rejoice over healings or visions. The value system of heaven is reflected in Jesus' statement, "*there will be more joy in heaven over one sinner who repents than over ninety-*

nine righteous persons who need no repentance" (Luke 15:7). Maturing as Christians ought to bring us to a place of having heavenly values instead of earthly ones. We should not rejoice more in a temporal healing of the body than in the eternal healing of the soul, for truly that is the greatest miracle of all.

> *". . . there will be more joy in heaven over one sinner who repents*
> *than over ninety-nine righteous persons who need no repentance"*
> (Luke 15:7)

Perhaps the best place to start this week in applying what we have studied is to make sure you think rightly about your own salvation. Have you ever taken the time to thank the Lord for what He saved you from (both what you were like before you met Christ and also what you would have been like if you hadn't met Him when you did)? If not, take some time now to do so.

_____

_____

_____

_____

_____

Another very practical application to this week's lesson is that we should make sure we don't get other miracles out of perspective. Reflect honestly on your own attitudes before studying this lesson and rank the items below where you would have placed them last week (with "1" being most significant and "4" being least significant). ____ physical healing

____ raising someone from the dead

____ dreams and visions from God

____ someone coming to salvation

Now go back through this same list and rank the items below where you would place them now (with "1" being most significant and "4" being least significant).

____ physical healing

____ raising someone from the dead

____ dreams and visions from God

____ someone coming to salvation

If indeed you conclude that the greatest miracle of all is salvation, that ought to affect your own priorities and values. Most of us will never get the chance to heal someone. I know of no one personally who has ever witnessed someone being raised from the dead, let alone participate in it happening. Dreams and visions from God are not an everyday occurrence for any I know. But everyone has the opportunity to take part in helping others get saved. All it takes is a willingness to be a messenger like Peter is. It isn't our message, but we can be privileged to carry that message to all God brings across our paths. Right now, there may be someone in our lives like Cornelius who God has already prepared to respond, and they are just waiting for the messenger to arrive. Consider some of the creative ways below to carry the message and check any that the Lord impresses you with.

____ give a neighbor a copy of the "Jesus" video

____ pass out gospel tracts with your Halloween candy

____ write out your testimony and send it to friends you haven't seen in years

____ give a coworker an apologetics book and ask their opinion.

____ ask someone you care about, "Tell me about your spiritual journey," and let the Lord take it from there...

> *Right now, there may be someone in our lives like Cornelius whom*
> *God has already prepared to respond, and they are just waiting for*
> *the messenger to arrive.*

Though the Apostle Peter is committed even at the risk of his own life to taking the gospel to his fellow Jews, it took a thrice-repeated vision from heaven for him to see Gentiles as someone to whom he should preach the gospel. I don't believe he thought the Gentiles had no need of God. Either he didn't think they could be saved or because of prejudice, didn't care enough to desire that. Are there any in your life that you do not talk to about Christ because you don't think they will ever be interested or receptive?

Why not pray for them by name, that God will work in their hearts.

After you pray for them, pray for yourself that God will make you open to opportunities to talk about Christ with them. Write out what is on your heart as a closing prayer to this week's lesson.

_____

_____

_____

_____

_____

_____

_____

_____

_____

_____

_____

LESSON 11

THE RIGHT HAND OF FELLOWSHIP

ACTS 11

The center of spiritual life for the Jew in Ancient Palestine is always the temple. It is the divinely-appointed place for God's chosen people to worship Him. Several times a year, devout Jews make their way to Jerusalem to observe the holy feasts and festivals of their faith. Gentiles—all those outside the "chosen people"—are invited to worship Jehovah, but they are not allowed to enjoy the full privileges of the natural-born Jew. The temple grounds are segregated by a great barrier called the "Dividing Wall," beyond which a Gentile is not allowed to go. Above the entry way of that wall, a plaque warns of the penalty of death for any Gentiles attempting to gain entrance. Acts 21:27–40 records false accusations made against the apostle Paul that he has been bringing Greeks into the temple and "defil[ing] this holy place." The crowds are in a turmoil. So great is the prejudice and so deep is the discord that Paul would have been beaten to death if not for the timely intervention of Roman soldiers. People cannot reconcile Jew and Gentile—the division is too great.

> *"For He Himself is our peace, who made both groups into one and broke down the barrier of the dividing wall" (Ephesians 2:14)*

Can you imagine what it feels like for a Gentile who truly loves God to stare at that wall and to know he can never be fully accepted into the faith? He can follow God, but he can never become a Jew. He will always feel like a second-class citizen in the kingdom of God. Yet this wall is not a permanent barrier erected by God to keep people from Him. Rather, it is an expression of His holiness and a reminder of what spiritual wall or barrier must be overcome to gain entry—a wall erected by human sin and removed only by the forgiveness of Christ. In Ephesians 2:14, Paul writes, *"For He Himself is our peace, who made both groups into one and broke down the barrier of the dividing wall."* Though it will take some getting used to on the part of Jewish Christians, the church is desegregated by the cross.

Recently, I saw on TV news a group of immigrants being sworn in, having completed all the requirements for U.S. citizenship. You could see the emotion in their eyes. You couldn't help but feel their joy, as they waved tiny American flags and cheered at the end. You had the sense that it is the fulfillment of a dream. For centuries, people from all over the world have come to America to find freedom and opportunity. The arms of Lady Liberty still beckon. People can come as visitors, but there is a permanent commitment in those who become citizens. There are rights and privileges that accompany this commitment. We should be able to relate with this scene. You and I have had a swearing-in ceremony of our own. As Paul speaks in Philippians 3:20–21, "*Our citizenship is in heaven, from which also we eagerly wait for a Savior, the Lord Jesus Christ; who will transform the body of our humble state into conformity with the body of His glory...*" By the work of the cross, we see in Acts that for the first time in history it is now possible for Gentiles to have full rights of citizenship in the kingdom of God. Through Christ, second-class citizens can become first-class saints.

Day One

The Environment of Prejudice (Acts 11:1–3)

Perhaps every ethnic group harbors a certain measure of prejudice against those outside their group. We have all witnessed it first-hand. I have observed it everywhere in the world I have visited. I've seen Poles who are prejudiced against Russians. I've seen Russians discriminate against Chechens, Georgians, middle-Easterners and just about everyone else. I've seen Czechs and Slovaks who hate each other. I've seen Hungarians look down on Romanians whom I've seen do the same with gypsies. I've met Serbs who think little of Albanians. In the Bahamas, I've known white Bahamians who are prejudiced against all blacks. I've seen light-skinned blacks be prejudiced against those with dark skin who in turn are prejudiced against Haitian immigrants—in their minds, the lowest of the low. In America, the form of prejudice which garners the greatest attention exists between blacks and whites. While our nation has known many other prejudices, this particular one is most pronounced because it is rooted in the evil heritage of slavery. Even though the Constitution declares that "all men are created equal," Blacks were held as slaves. Even after Abraham Lincoln's "Emancipation Proclamation" set slaves free, they were not instantly made equal. I can remember the distinction which existed during my own childhood a hundred years later in the 1960's with segregated bathrooms, buses, dining areas, and water fountains. I can vividly recall the turmoil and boiling anger of many when forced busing mixed the school populations. Though I was not taught the same prejudices as many in the south, lots of my friends and neighbors were and still are. Playing with the boy next door one day, he took me into his house and pulled out a small suitcase hidden in a closet. Inside was a white cape and hat belonging to his father—the official uniform of the Ku Klux Klan. He thought it something to be proud of, while I thought it horrible. I can still remember the shock.

In 1953, North Carolina evangelist Billy Graham came to Chattanooga, Tennessee, to preach at a crusade. He saw ropes of segregation separating the blacks and whites in the audience. When event organizers refused to remove them, he got up from the platform, walked down past the ushers, and took the ropes down himself. He had come to understand that Christ broke down the barrier of the dividing wall between Jew and Gentile and this knowledge convicted a young Billy Graham to take a stand against similar division taking place at his crusades. While it is easier to judge the prejudices others hold than it is to recognize our own, all of us possess measures of favoritism, intolerance, self-pride, and bigotry. They are woven into our fallen nature. All of us are prone to pre-judge. Whether it is rooted in race or religion or orientation or financial standing or simple cultural differences, prejudice exists with every nation, tribe, and tongue. As we will see today, it exists strongly between the Jews and Gentiles.

DID YOU KNOW?
Judea

The region of Judea is in that part of Israel that used to be identified as the southern kingdom of Judah. It incorporates Jerusalem as well as the surrounding areas. Luke gives us a sense of the spread of Christianity at this time by stating that these brethren are *"throughout Judea."* Though separated geographically, even in these days before telephones and newspapers they apparently have a pretty good communication network and are aware of this new happening of Gentiles receiving the word of God.

In Acts 11:2 Luke speaks of *those who are circumcised* (literally "those of the circumcision"). Look up the verses listed below and record what you learn of the origin and purpose of this practice.

Genesis 17:10–13

_____

_____

Deuteronomy 30:6

_____

_____

Jeremiah 9:23–25

_____

_____

The act of circumcision was given to Abraham as a physical sign and reminder of God's relationship with His followers. The resulting scars of circumcision were to be a permanent evidence of the covenant. Circumcision becomes a regular practice among the Jews from Abraham's day forward. Years later, as the Jews prepare to enter the Promised Land, Moses reminded them of the spiritual point behind the practice of circumcision: to have a sensitive heart toward God and to walk in a loving relationship with Him. In Jeremiah's day though circumcision is practiced *religiously,* the Jews were far from God. As God spoke through Jeremiah, Israel was reminded again of this purpose. Jeremiah 9:25 introduces an interesting phrase, speaking of those *"who are circumcised and yet uncircumcised."* In other words, it is possible to receive the physical action and yet miss the spiritual point. This seems to accurately reflect many of the Jews at this time of Acts.

The Jews are proud of God's covenant of circumcision with Abraham and view it as evidence that they hold a superior position of privilege. However, a point that the Jews seem to miss about this covenant is that it is connected with God's promise to make Abraham *"the father of a multitude of nations"* (Genesis 17:4). Additionally, God also promises that through Abraham *"all the nations of the earth"* will be blessed. The covenant of circumcision not only means privilege, but also responsibility. Instead, to them it becomes a source of pride and arrogance, even though they are not faithful to the purpose of the practice.

📖 Look at Acts 11:1–3.

Why do *those who are circumcised* take issue with Peter?

_____

_____

_____

_____

_____

What does this say of their attitude toward the uncircumcised?

_____

_____

_____

_____

> *All the angels of heaven rejoice when there is a soul saved, yet*
> *sadly, the same is not always true for God's people on earth.*

Some of the Jewish Christians of Jerusalem, when they hear the news of Peter's encounter with Cornelius, have a surprising response. Instead of rejoicing in the salvation of so many, including this prominent and devout friend to the Jews, they complain about Peter's actions. The implication in their statement is that Peter is wrong and displeasing to God by entering a Gentile house and eating a meal with non-Jews. Clearly, even though they have been saved from their sins and their impotent devotion to the Law, they still do not grasp God's heart for the world. They view all Gentiles, even those with seeking hearts, as someone to be avoided rather than someone to whom they should reach out.

All the angels of heaven rejoice when there is a soul saved, yet sadly, the same is not always true for all of God's people on earth. Before we jump to judgment of the Jews, we must acknowledge that the same cultural bias and penchant for personal prejudice exists in us as well.

THE EXPLANATION OF PETER (ACTS 11:4–18)

What do you think it would take for you to lay down your own bias and prejudice? For Peter it not only takes a vision from heaven, but the vision has to be repeated three times. It reminds us of the Lord Jesus asking Peter three times *"Do you love Me?"* when meeting with him after the resurrection. From what we know of Peter, he may be a little thick-headed, and may need the repetition. Once he is convinced though, Peter is able to persuade others as well. In today's study we will see that Peter is proficient in winning over the hesitant Jewish Christians.

📖 Compare Peter's explanation here in Acts 11:4–14 with the record of his vision in Acts 10:9–23 that you looked at last week and write down any additional insights.

_____

_____

_____

_____

The account of Peter's vision in Acts 11 is the same as the one in Acts 10 with only a minor amount of extra information. First, in Peter's report we gain the additional insight that the number of men accompanying him from Joppa is six brethren. This is significant in that their presence makes for seven witnesses to the Gentile conversions (seven being seen by the Jews as a number of completion). We also learn in verse 14 that Cornelius is not only told to expect a message, but specifically told that Peter will *"speak words to you by which you will be saved, you and all your household."*

IN THEIR SHOES
EXALTING GOD

Luke records that when the Gentiles receive the Holy Spirit, this is evidenced by them *"speaking with tongues and exalting God"* (10:46). Here in Acts 11:15 Peter reports that the Spirit comes upon them *"just as He did upon us at the beginning."* If we look back to Pentecost, we discover that the message spoken by the Jewish believers in all the different languages has the same content as does that of these Gentiles. Acts 2:11 indicates the spirit-filled believers at Pentecost are *"speaking of the mighty deeds of God."*

📖 What do you see implied in Peter's account of how the Spirit moves among the Gentiles in Acts 11:15?

_____

_____

_____

Peter tells the Jewish believers in Jerusalem that *"the Holy Spirit fell upon them just as He did upon us at the beginning."* We learned in Acts 10:44–47 that the Spirit coming upon these Gentile converts is evidenced by them *"speaking with tongues and exalting God."* There is no mention of the building being shaken or of a rushing wind or tongues of fire, but that may very well be the case. Regardless, the experience of Cornelius and his household mirrors that of the disciples at Pentecost. This is interesting because the last mention we have of the Spirit coming upon believers in a visible way is in Acts 8 with the record of the first believers from among the Samaritans. A pattern is beginning to emerge.

So far, the only mention (or even suggestion) of speaking in tongues we find in the book of Acts is in the context of the gospel penetrating a new frontier. We see tongues clearly demonstrated at Pentecost. We see them implied at Samaria, for we are told that Simon *"saw"* the Spirit being bestowed. We see tongues here with the first significant response to the gospel from among the Gentiles. In each of these instances we also have a witness from among the Apostles who can confirm the authenticity of what happens. When you think about it, the idea makes perfect sense. It is important for the Jews to have divine affirmation if they are to accept these into the church who are not accepted at the temple.

📖 Read Acts 11:16–17 and make note of how Peter interprets the events that transpire.

As Peter reflects on the pouring out of the Holy Spirit upon these Gentiles who have believed, God brings to his mind the words of Jesus. He had taught the disciples of the *"baptism with the Holy Spirit."* Peter determines that this evidence of salvation affirms that the Gentiles have the ability to be saved just like the Jews. Peter's final statement literally reads, *"who was I that I could prevent God."* He concludes that it is up to God to save whomever He wishes.

📖 Look at Acts 11:18 and write down what you learn of how the Jewish believers respond to Peter's report.

Luke tells us that when the Jewish believers hear Peter's report, they *quiet down*. Apparently, they have been in an uproar over the idea of Peter fellowshipping with Gentiles. They go from grilling Peter to glorifying God. Peter's explanation convinces them that indeed God has granted to those who were formerly far off the same salvation the Jews have found in Christ.

> "When they heard this, they quieted down and glorified God, saying, 'Well then, God has granted to the Gentiles also the repentance that leads to life.'" (Acts 11:18)

We read these sterile words today and cannot fully appreciate what a significant event in church history it is when Gentiles begin to join the faith. Without this paradigm shift in the thinking of the Jews, the Great Commission could never be fulfilled. Jesus promises that when the Spirit comes upon them, they will be witnesses even to the remotest parts of the earth. We are now observing a huge milestone in that journey.

DAY THREE

THE ENCOURAGEMENT OF ANTIOCH (ACTS 11:19–26)

God is not finished moving among the Gentiles. In fact, He is just beginning. The salvation of Cornelius will prove to be the first of many. From Luke's grouping of that event with the one we are going to look at today, it is clear that he recognizes a relationship between the two. God is about to break open this new harvest field of the Gentiles. If that idea does not appear significant to you, reflect on this one fact. Most believers today, and indeed throughout church history, fall into that category we call "Gentiles." You probably fit there too. Humanly speaking, were it not for God breaking down the barriers of pride and prejudice, you and I might never have heard the gospel!

📖 Look at Acts 11:19–20 and answer the questions below.

Why do you suppose the Jews are speaking to *"no one except to Jews alone"*?

What do you think motivates the men of Cyprus and Cyrene to act differently?

Verse 19 begins with the phrase, *"So then…"* It gives one the idea that the preceding information is a parenthesis of sorts, and Luke is returning to a previous theme. The mention of the persecution associated with Stephen takes us back to Acts 8:4. Sandwiched between the persecution beginning to take root and the first Gentile church are Luke's references to how the gospel makes it to the Samaritans and to the Gentiles. Since these Jews who are scattered leave before either of those events, they are probably unaware of what God is doing outside the conversion of Jews. Still, God's sovereignty is seen in His working through these men of Cyprus and Cyrene. Their location identifies them as "Hellenists," Jews who speak Greek and adopt Greek culture instead of the Hebrew-speaking Jews of Jerusalem. Since they aren't as bound to Jewish culture, it is easier for them to reach beyond the boundaries of Judaism.

📖 Now read Acts 11:21–22.

What happens when the gospel of Jesus Christ begins to be preached to the Greeks (Gentiles) in Antioch (v.21)?

What is the response of the Church in Jerusalem (v.22)?

Although the persecution of the church naturally seems to be of human origin, through the reading of the Scriptures we can clearly see the hand of God behind it. Through this persecution, the gospel comes to Antioch with tremendous results among the Greeks. News of Christ's message spreading to the Gentile regions soon reaches the church in Jerusalem. Wanting assurance that this is of God's doing, the Jerusalem believers select a man of proven discernment—Barnabas—to investigate.

 WORD STUDY
"Sent"

The Greek word for "sent" that is used of Barnabas being commissioned by the church in Jerusalem has as its root the word "*apostle*." The term portrays the idea of someone being sent out as an authoritative representative. Barnabas is the official representative of the mother church, investigating this new phenomenon of Gentiles coming to faith in Christ.

📖 Reflect on Acts 11:23–24.

What does Barnabas do when he arrives (v.23)?

How does Luke describe Barnabas here (v.24a)?

_____

_____

_____

_____

What is the result of Barnabas' ministry in Antioch (v.24b)?

_____

_____

_____

_____

What does Barnabas do when he arrives? He is convinced that God is at work among the Gentiles, and he _encourages_ the new converts in this region. Look at the words Luke uses to describe Barnabas in verse 24: "_a good man...full of the Holy Spirit and of faith._" Verse 21 tells us that a large number believe before Barnabas arrives. The statement "_considerable numbers_" indicates that even more people are converted _after_ Barnabas comes on the scene. We tend to underestimate the significance of encouragement because it is indirect ministry, but the reality is that encouragement makes everyone more effective and motivated to use his or her gifts for the Lord.

📖 Look at Acts 11:25–26.

Once Barnabas gets a handle on this new work of God and is accepted as the key leader, what does he do?

_____

_____

_____

What does this say about his character?

_____

_____

_____

Rather than setting up shop and glorying in all God is doing through him, Barnabas goes to get someone else involved. Instead of hoarding the work and credit to himself, he remembers Saul and decides he will fit in well. This is admirable of Barnabas to want to include Saul in the ministry, for throughout the ages many Christians have been too insecure to share their work with anyone. If we are truly concerned with God's glory and not our own, it shouldn't matter who does the work. All that should matter is that the work gets done and that God gets the glory. Although we recognize God's sovereignty, humanly speaking, if not for Barnabas, Saul (eventually identified as Paul) never goes into the ministry. What impact for Christ the world would have been robbed of, if not for the *encouraging* ministry of Barnabas! Because he is willing to share the work, we see that his heart is more concerned with God's glory than with who gets the credit. It is worth noting that this work of God at Antioch is so impactful that the believers are first called "Christians" here.

IN THEIR SHOES
Barnabas' Impact

Because Barnabas is more concerned with the work than with his own part in it, he is able to build a team by balancing many different gifts to maximum effectiveness. Not only are considerable numbers *"brought"* to the Lord (Acts 11:24), but we also see that considerable numbers are *"taught"* as well (Acts 11:26) over the course of the next year. The ministry not only grows in numbers but also in depth.

DAY FOUR

THE EXPRESSION OF BROTHERHOOD (ACTS 11:27–30)

We have reflected much in this lesson on the prejudice existing among the Jews toward the Gentiles. Certainly, it is significant. But what are the feelings of Gentiles toward Jews? With the shoe on the other foot, the Gentiles are just as hesitant to mix with the snobbish and culturally different Jews. The barrier of the dividing wall at the temple mirrors the cultural divide that exists between the circumcised and the uncircumcised. Yet, as we will see today, God moves in a mighty way among the Gentiles at Antioch once they become believers. One of the first evidences of changed life can be seen in the fact that right away God uses them to be a blessing to their brothers and sisters in Christ from the other side of the tracks.

> *"...and the disciples were first called Christians in Antioch"*
> (Acts 11:26)

📖 Read Acts 11:27–28 and summarize what transpires.

....

....

....

As a result of Barnabas' interceding, the mother church at Jerusalem recognizes and affirms this new church at Antioch. As this Gentile church begins to grow and develop, a natural interchange and fellowship between them and Jerusalem begins to develop. On this particular occasion, prophets from Jerusalem come for a visit and presumably to come alongside them in ministry. One of their number, a man named Agabus, prophesies that a great famine is coming. Writing from the vantage point of years later, Luke informs us that this prophecy does indeed come true.

📖 Meditate on Acts 11:29 and write down what stands out to you from the response of the believers at Antioch to Agabus' prophecy.

_____

_____

_____

_____

What would your first thought be if you were told a world-wide famine is coming? It speaks volumes of these new believers that their first reaction is to look out for the well-being of others. This compassionate response is even more significant when you recognize that the object of their benevolence is the very people who used to hold them in disdain. These Gentile converts are showing their love for the brethren in a very practical way—by meeting needs.

📖 Look over Acts 11:29–30 and make note of any principles for charitable giving that stand out to you.

_____

_____

_____

_____

"The Father loves the Son and has given all things into His hand"
(John 13:35)

Not only is the charity of the Antioch Christians an example for others to follow, but so also are the principles which undergirded their giving. The first point that stands out in how they give is that the measure of giving is *"in the proportion that any of the disciples had means."* The apostle Paul will write to the Corinthian believers years later that giving is supposed to be, *"according to what a person has, not according to what he doesn't have"* (2 Corinthians 8:12). Perhaps he gleans this principle from his days at Antioch. The second point we can observe from the giving here is that it requires forethought. They *"determine"* to contribute. The Greek word here (*horizo*) is where we get our English term, "horizon." It carries the idea of looking ahead. The third point from the passage is that gifts should be handled with accountability and integrity. A plurality of the most trusted leaders in the church are given the responsibility of delivering what is probably quite a significant amount of money.

As we reflect on the theme of this section of Acts, clearly Luke is weaving together a portrait of one of the most significant events of the early church—the inclusion of Gentiles into the family of God. Gratefully, he is able to report that once the Jewish believers are convinced that God is in these happenings they quickly extend the right hand of fellowship to their new brothers and sisters, the Gentiles. But the story is not complete without this brief but significant example of how the Gentiles do the same. Their financial provision for the impoverished saints in Judea (who are most certainly Jewish Christians) shows that they too are reaching beyond the barriers of cultural bias and prejudice to extend the hand of fellowship to all who identify with Christ.

DAY FIVE

FOR ME TO FOLLOW GOD

Years ago, I spent a summer doing mission work in Hawaii. Usually when I tell people about my experience, they react with some sarcastic statement like, "Gee, suffering for the Lord, weren't you?" But actually, while Hawaii is extremely beautiful and a wonderful place to take a vacation, the culture presents unseen challenges when you live there. For one thing, there are probably as many Mormons as Christians on the islands. The majority in the ethnic mix are Asians which also impacts the cultural environment. I shared Christ with over a hundred people that summer, and only once talked with a Baptist from the South. I was not prepared for the great prejudice which exists among the island peoples against white folks. With good reason, Hawaiians resent the fact that most of the land is under the control of a rich few and has to be leased instead of owned. While I recognized this prejudice, even I was sheltered from it somewhat because of my dark skin and black hair (I'm part Native American). One encounter however, brought home to me more clearly what it means to be prejudged because of your cultural background. I was sharing Christ with a Hawaiian teenager who was quite receptive when one of my friends, a blond haired and blue-eyed Southerner, walked up to join in the conversation. The Hawaiian refused to even acknowledge his greeting, and with disdain in his voice asked me, "Who is this 'hauli' (a very derogatory local term for someone who is a foreigner)?" Apparently, the youth didn't recognize that I too was a "hauli."

It is always tough being a minority and the normal, fleshly response of an unbeliever would be to repay evil for evil and injustice for injustice. But that ought to change when a person meets Christ. As believers we all belong to the same family. One of the spiritual realities that always amazes me as I travel around the world is how you can meet believers in Belarus or Budapest or the Bahamas and the sense of kinship is instant. The common ground of Christ makes fellowship natural and normal. Jesus says, *"By this all men will know that you are My disciples, if you have love for one another"* (John 13:35). One of the evidences of being born again is that we can extend the right hand of fellowship to all who call upon the name of Christ.

We've already talked some regarding personal prejudice we each may hold. There is still more room for application though as we consider the verses we studied this week. One question that comes to mind as I look at my own life is this: *How much is my definition of right and wrong shaped by my cultural background instead of the revelation of God?* Peter doesn't recognize how wrong he is for avoiding the Gentiles until he is confronted with divine revelation. While you and I may not have visions of falling sheets, we have something more convincing—the Word of God. On the scale below, try to honestly identify which you think holds more sway in your own thinking.

Cultural   God's

Background ←———— 1 ———— 2 ———— 3 ———— 4 ———— 5 ———— 7 ——→ Word

It may be easy to say what you believe ought to be. If the truth be known, most of the time we fail to recognize the behaviors and values which we consider biblical right and wrong that are instead the result of cultural upbringing and biases passed down for generations. Take time to ask God to reveal to you any unseen prejudice that He wants to deal with. God is quick to respond to a willing heart of surrender.

Who are some people in your life that come from different ethnic, religious or otherwise divergent backgrounds?

_____

_____

_____

Have you befriended them?

_____

_____

Who are the people in your community most unreached by the gospel because of cultural walls or societal barriers?

_____

_____

_____

What can you do to effect change?

_____

_____

_____

One of the most familiar verses in the Bible is 2 Corinthians 5:17, which states, "*Therefore if anyone is in Christ, he is a new creature; the old things passed away; behold, new things have come."* What most people fail to recognize is the context of this statement. Paul is not just talking about our lives, but about our ministries. In the verse that comes before, Paul makes it clear that we are to no longer recognize people "*according to the flesh*" or by fleshly, external criteria, but rather, we must view them according to their spiritual standing. One of the ways we are to be new creatures is in the "passing away" of our old prejudices and fleshly distinctions.

> *"Therefore if anyone is in Christ, he is a new creature; the old*
> *things passed away; behold, new things have come"*
> (2 Corinthians 5:17)

As you finish this week's lesson, take some time to pray and ask the Lord to make you a new creature in this area and to show you any places where you aren't.

LESSON 12

WHEN GOD'S PEOPLE PRAY
ACTS 12:1-25

Most Christians I meet treat prayer in much the same way gamblers treat the lottery. They practice prayer regularly—hoping against hope that they might win big with some huge request. But for the most part their expectations are small. Perhaps for those playing the lottery, there is reason for skepticism. The odds truly are never in their favor. But is prayer an "against the odds" proposition akin to playing the lottery? What happens when God's people pray? I have met a lot of Christians over the course of my years as a believer. I find that just about all of them believe in the importance of prayer. Yet having said this, I wonder how many believe their prayers make a difference. Many pray, but few expect answers. As I reflect on my own praying, honesty requires me to admit that I don't always pray expectantly either. This truth is rather ironic when you reflect on it objectively. I must ask myself, "Why is this so?"

There are two opposing extremes we can move to in our view of prayer—mysticism and fatalism. The mystic extreme tends to believe that there is intrinsic power in prayers rightly prayed. This view places undue emphasis on the proper wording as if it is an incantation instead of a supplication. Great importance is placed on what we say and how we say it. This view seems to promote the idea that the greater the fervency, the greater the effect. The other prayer extreme of fatalism places such emphasis on the sovereignty of God as to leave no room for human activity to have any effect at all. It communicates a message of "Why bother? God is going to do what He is going to do, no matter what I say." What is a true view of prayer?

I believe there is no power in prayer. Now before you start piling up the brush and bringing the torches to burn me at the stake as a heretic, let me explain what I mean. The power is not in prayer but in God. The act of praying changes nothing without the working of the One to whom we pray. Having said that, I must emphatically affirm that I believe there is power in God and prayer is our means of connecting to Him and enables us to access His power.

"...the prayer of the upright is His delight." (Proverbs 15:8)

I know God wants us to pray. Proverbs 15:8 instructs us that *"the prayer of the upright is His delight."* Not many of our activities are said to delight God, but prayer is certainly one. I know that God works through praying people. James 5:16 admonishes, *"the effective prayer of a righteous man can accomplish much."* Both of these passages make it clear that it is not just any old prayer that makes a difference. It is the lifestyle of a person that prays continually. Notice the words *"upright"* and *"righteous."* I know that when groups of people agree in prayer, it makes a difference. In 2 Corinthians 1:11, Paul speaks of *"the favor bestowed on us through the prayers of the many."* I can't say that I fully understand it or can adequately explain it, but the Bible clearly speaks of favor being bestowed *"through"* the prayers of many. As we will see in this week's lesson, it makes a difference in Peter's life when *prayer for him is "being made fervently by the church to God"* (Acts 12:5).

DAY ONE

THE UNEXPECTED TRIBULATION (ACTS 12:1–5)

Have you ever wished you could schedule your trials ahead of time, so you could adequately plan and prepare? Wouldn't it be nice if you could sit down with God holding your day planner in front of you and say, "I'm free next week. How about sending me my trial on Thursday?" But it doesn't work that way. We never know when a trial is coming our way. Neither does the first century church. Just when the work of ministry is really getting going and they are having a huge response to the gospel among the Gentiles, another wave of persecution begins. Today we want to focus on this latest challenge the early church has to face.

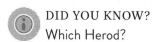 DID YOU KNOW?
Which Herod?

There are four different Herods who ruled over Palestine, all of whom are marked with wickedness. The first Herod (called "Herod the Great") tried to kill Jesus shortly after his birth by having all males under two years of age put to death (Matt.2:13–16). His son, Herod Antipas (also called "Herod the Tetrarch") was responsible for the death of John the Baptist (Matt.14:1–12) after being confronted with his sin of incest. The Herod who has James put to death (Herod Agrippa the elder) is the grandson of Herod the Great. His son (Herod Agrippa the younger) will later preside over the trial of the apostle Paul (Acts 25–26).

📖 Look at Acts 12:1. What stands out to you about the timing of this new persecution?

Luke begins this chapter with the phrase, *"Now, about that time…"* The phrase draws a corollary relationship between the explosive growth of the church into this new arena of the Gentiles and the heating up of persecution. Although King Herod is the instigator, he is probably not personally concerned about the church. Instead, he is most likely trying to curry favor among the Jews who represent the majority of his subjects. This idea is supported by the statement in verse 3 about him seeing that it pleases the Jews, but also by the particular form of the Greek word translated "mistreat" (*kakoo*). Greek words with this particular ending not only reflect that something happens, but also that it is made manifest in a visible way. Herod wants to make a show of harming the church.

📖 Read Acts 12:2–4.

What does Herod do to James?

_____

_____

_____

What motivates the arrest of Peter?

_____

_____

_____

What is implied about his plans for Peter?

_____

_____

 DID YOU KNOW?
Four Squads of Soldiers

The seriousness of Peter's arrest is reflected in how he is guarded. Assigned to him are four "quaternions"—teams of four soldiers that rotate guard duty during each of the four night watches of three hours each. Such continual guarding is usually reserved for those considered to be the most dangerous of prisoners. The Greek word **anago** (*translated "bring" as in "bring him out before the people" in 12:4) could be translated "bring up."* Most likely, *Peter was in the inner prison* or lower ward and so would be "led up," presumably for public execution.

At the hands of Herod, James becomes the first of the original disciples to meet a martyr's end. Though other Christians have already met a similar fate at the hands of the Jewish leaders, this is the first "official" execution of a follower of Jesus sanctioned by the government since the formation of the church. Death by the sword is generally reserved for those charged with a political crime. Once Herod sees that the Jews are pleased by this act, he aims for an even more prominent target—the Apostle Peter. It is apparent that Herod intends to put Peter to death as he did James.

📖 Reflect on Acts 12:4 and write your thoughts on how the Passover might fit into God's sovereign plan to protect Peter.

....

....

....

....

Herod arrests Peter at the beginning of the Jewish holiday of Passover. The timing of the arrest may be because the Jews are on Herod's mind, and he wants, in his own perverted way, to add to their festivities. However, because it is a holiday, this means the execution will be delayed until afterward. This postponement gives the church time to pray during a season when they have already gathered to seek the Lord.

📖 Look over Acts 12:5. How does the church respond to Peter's arrest?

....

....

....

When the church hears of Peter's arrest, they immediately hit their knees. We are told that *prayer for him is "being made fervently by the church to God."* The Greek word translated "fervently" has the idea both of praying intensely and continuously. The church has no judicial influence to be able to protest the injustice of the charges. They have no military might. They lack any political lobby to try and sway the authorities. But they can bend the ear of heaven, and they do. Perhaps today we trust too much in other solutions instead of praying for God to intervene in our world.

What is your catalyst to pray? What motivates you to hit your knees? Distill it down, and you will find that all supplication is rooted in an awareness of need. We pray because we know what we cannot do—and what He can do. God uses the persecutions of Herod to drive His people to prayer. When we are faced with unexpected tribulation, either we will worry and strive because of trust in ourselves, or we will pray and trust God.

DAY TWO

THE UNEXPECTED LIBERATION (ACTS 12:6–10)

Try to put yourself in Peter's shoes. One of his close friends has just been put to death. Heavily guarded under lock and key, circumstances afford him several days in jail to reflect on this reality and to acknowledge his own grim future. Before his own arrest, he probably was praying for the Lord to spare James' life and now has to adjust his thinking when that does not take place. Now he finds himself praying about his own circumstances with uncertainty of what the future will hold. Death appears to be just around the corner. Peter is not expecting an angelic visitation. In fact, as we will examine in our study today, even when the angel unlocks his chains Peter thinks it is a vision instead of reality. He has to long for God to intervene or he isn't human, but as time passes, deliverance by God seems less and less likely. Everyone would be surprised by the empty jail cell, but no one is more surprised than Peter himself.

📖 Look over Acts 12:6 and answer the questions below.

What stands out to you from the timing of God's intervention?

How secure does Peter appear to be?

God could have released Peter at any time. He could have even kept him from being arrested. Yet He waits until the last possible moment to deliver His servant. God's delay is not from lack of care, but indicates He takes the route that gives Him the greatest glory. This is underscored by Luke's report on how securely Peter is guarded. We know that Peter has teams of four soldiers working three-hour shifts guarding him at any given moment. Verse six gives us a sense of how that functions. A guard sleeps on each side of him, even as he is secured with two chains. The other two soldiers are apparently guarding the door. Humanly speaking, it would seem that every precaution is being taken to ensure the prisoner is kept secure. But soldiers are no match for God.

📖 Read Acts 12:7–10.

What do you imagine is going through Peter's mind as he is awakened by the angel?

 WORD STUDY
The Importance of a Word

There is a subtle but significant difference between Acts 12:7 in the King James version and in the New American Standard version. The KJV reads, "*the angel of the Lord...*" while the NASB reads, "*an angel of the Lord.*" The phrase, "*the angel of the Lord*" is often used in the Old Testament to speak of pre-incarnate appearances of the Lord Jesus, so a correct interpretation here has significant ramifications. The Greek wording should have a definite article to be translated "*the angel*" but in this case the definite article is not there. Therefore, it should be translated "*an angel,*" referring to one of many.

Why do you suppose the guards are unaware of his preparations to leave?

_____

_____

_____

_____

What does verse 9 reveal of Peter's expectations?

_____

_____

_____

_____

_____

_____

One would guess that Peter is groggy, being awakened from sleep, and would have difficulty absorbing all that is happening. He would notice his chains falling off, and perhaps would be surprised that this does not arouse the guards. Since they would not be asleep, being only assigned a three-hour watch, Peter must be amazed that they do not recognize his escape as he makes preparations to leave. Peter is not looking for release. Rather, his expectation is most likely that he will die.

📖 Go back over Acts 12:7–10 and identify all the supernatural happenings that would contribute to Peter's belief that this is a vision instead of reality.

_____

_____

_____

_____

_____

_____

Certainly, there are many aspects of the situation which defy logic. An angel suddenly appears, filling the cell with a divine light. After several days of putting up with the noise and discomfort of the iron chains, suddenly they fall off by themselves. Somehow the guards are supernaturally unaware of all that is transpiring. Peter walks right past them and even the iron gate opens by itself. Anyone who has ever heard an iron gate swing open can imagine the noise. No wonder Peter has difficulty determining if this is real or a dream.

The Scriptures are filled with examples of the hand of God going unrecognized because it is unexpected. No doubt we would struggle with the same dilemma were we in Peter's shoes. It makes me wonder how many times God's actions around us today remain unnoticed by us. God is always at work, but we don't always see or acknowledge what He does.

THE UNEXPECTED VISITATION (ACTS 12:11–19)

> *"Don't worry about anything. Instead, pray about everything and don't forget to thank Him for the answers." (Philippians 4:6, The Living Bible)*

One winter in college I experienced a particularly amazing adventure in prayer. I was attending a college ministry gathering at our church, and while we were inside, several inches of snow fell. When the meeting let out, most of us participate in a lengthy and heated snowball fight in the parking lot. Near the end of our escapade, one of my best friends (and my ride back to campus) reported that somewhere in the process of packing powder and hurling spherical ice, his car keys had fallen out of his coat pocket. In unison we all groaned as we realized that someplace on these two acres of asphalt now buried in inches of snow are his car keys. We divided up and began trying to search the area, but the task seemed impossible. After about a half an hour of fruitless wandering, it suddenly occurred to me to pray. I'm not proud of the fact that it took so long to dawn on me to take my concern to God. When it did however, I stopped in my tracks in the middle of the parking area and bowed my head. I acknowledged that God knew exactly where the keys were and confessed that our finding them would be impossible without His help. As I closed out my prayer, I had a sense of peace that the problem was now in God's capable hands and no longer in mine. I opened my eyes with my head still bowed and discovered the missing keys lying between my feet! I have experienced lots of answered prayers over the years, but this is one of the most memorable of my early Christian life. It drives home to me the need to do as Paul instructs—*"Don't worry about anything. Instead, pray about everything and don't forget to thank Him for the answers"* (Philippians 4:6, The Living Bible).

The early church knows the importance of prayer. It is their habit to talk to God about everything. Yet even they are surprised at finding God's answer in the midst of their prayer meeting. God doesn't have to answer our prayers in such dramatic fashion, but we need to never lose confidence that He can.

📖 Look at Acts 12:11–12 and reflect on Peter's response to his release.

What does Peter conclude once the angel disappears?

_____

_____

_____

How do you suppose Peter knows the church will be gathered at Mary's house?

_____

_____

We have here in Acts 12 our introduction to Mark, the writer of one of the four gospels and properly known as John Mark. He is a Jew, probably a native of Jerusalem where his mother Mary resides. Mark is probably converted through Peter, who calls him his "son" (1 Peter 5:13). He travels as a servant with Paul and Barnabas, his uncle (Col. 4:10), on their first missionary journey, but leaves them at Perga (Acts 13:13). Later he appears as a companion of Paul in Rome (Colossians 4:10; Philemon 1:24). He is with Peter when the apostle writes his first epistle (1 Peter 5:13), but is at Ephesus with Timothy, probably at a later date (2 Timothy 4:11)

It isn't until the angel vanishes that Peter fully understands what is happening to him. The idea of the phrase literally reads, "When Peter came to be in himself." In other words, when he comes to his senses, he pieces together the details of his circumstances and recognizes that God has not only rescued him from jail but has also delivered him from imminent death at the hands of Herod and the Jews. Peter immediately makes his way to Mary's house to find the brethren. The fact that Peter knows where to go says something of the prayer structure of the early church. Obviously, it is their custom to gather here for prayer. Peter was probably among them here days earlier as the church fervently prayed for James. When God releases Peter, he knows where to find his friends, and he can't wait to tell them their prayers are answered.

Study Acts 12:13–16.

What is implied in the servant girl's reaction to finding Peter at the gate (vs. 13-14)?

What do verses 15–16 reveal of the expectations of these at the prayer meeting?

The scene that greets Peter when he arrives at the gathering is both humorous and touching. The servant girl is so shocked and excited to discover Peter alive that she completely forgets her manners as she runs to tell everyone of Peter's release. When the prayer meeting hears her report, they first think she has lost her mind. Their second response is equally inaccurate. Once she convinces them that indeed she has seen Peter, they still don't believe he is physically present. Instead, they conclude it must be his ghost. This shows us that even though they are praying fervently, they expect Peter will die. The Greek word translated "amazed" in verse 16 (*existemi* – *from ex, out of, and histemi, to stand*) has the idea of being beside oneself or out of one's mind. They are in a state of shock. When Peter comes to his senses, the rest of the church loses theirs!

📖 Examine Acts 12:17, reflecting on why Peter wants them to give a report to James and why Peter immediately leaves the gathering.

_____

_____

_____

_____

James (a different James than the one mentioned as being executed earlier in Acts 12) has by this time become the main leader of the Jerusalem church. Though originally Peter seems to have filled that role, his ministry has expanded far beyond Jerusalem, and perhaps his being singled out by Herod is part of bringing his ministry here to an end. The "brethren" probably refers to the other apostles who make up the main leadership of the church. The fact that Peter asks the gathering to bring a report instead of doing so himself, coupled with his immediate departure, indicates that he knows Herod will search for him and that his life is still in danger.

📖 What does the response to Peter's escape in Acts 12:18–19 reveal about what would probably happen to him if he is found?

_____

_____

_____

_____

One can only imagine what goes through the minds of the guards when they discover Peter missing. It would be quite frustrating trying to come up with a natural explanation for this supernatural event. Herod no doubt concludes that Peter's escape is due either to some laxity or conspirator involvement on the part of the guards. Either way, he blames them and has them executed. There can be no doubt that the same fate would await Peter were he to be found in Jerusalem. He is no longer safe there as long as Herod is alive.

> _Like the early church, we must learn to trust God with the when and how of answered prayer._

As we reflect on the church's surprise at God's answer to their prayers through Peter's miraculous deliverance, we must be careful not to judge too harshly. We probably would have had the same response if we were in their shoes. Remember, they most likely held the same prayer meetings when James is arrested. Yet even when that situation doesn't turn out as they hope, they continue to pray and to trust God's sovereign answers. We know God hears our prayers. We don't know how He will choose to answer them. Like the early church, we must learn to trust God with the when and how of answered prayer.

Day Four

The Unexpected Vindication (Acts 12:20–25)

In 1 Peter 5:7, the apostle Peter writes of *"casting all your anxiety on Him, because He cares for you."* This is most certainly the practice of the early church. We know that they pray fervently when they learn of Peter's arrest. We can suppose that they also pray much about King Herod. Exactly what they pray we can only guess. They have to be concerned when he begins arresting and mistreating those belonging to the church. Their concern turns to alarm when he executes John's brother, James. Their alarm is compounded when the beloved Peter is arrested. What do they pray when Herod shows up in their supplications? I doubt anyone would imagine a scenario like the one God had planned for this wicked king. Their prayer is likely a simple request for God to take note of him and do what is best.

📖 Reflect on Acts 12:19–20 and then answer the questions that follow.

What sort of mood do you suppose Herod is in when he goes to Caesarea?

_____

_____

_____

What do you learn in verse 20 about how the people are treating Herod here and why?

_____

_____

_____

_____

 DID YOU KNOW?
Down to Caesarea

As we look at a Bible map, the phrase *"down from Judea to Caesarea"* in Acts 12:19 may appear odd, since Caesarea is *north* and not south of Judea. In Palestine, however, this would be the common way of referring to a trip from the mountainous region to the coast regardless of the direction according to the compass. It means *"down"* in the sense of elevation. The cities of Tyre and Sidon lie even further to the north in the region of Phoenicia.

A man with the power and authority of Herod is not accustomed to having his plans frustrated. No doubt he is quite upset with his guards and assumes they have somehow let his prize prisoner escape. For this reason, he is already in a bad mood when he makes his way to Caesarea. We are not told why, but apparently Herod is also upset with the people of Tyre and Sidon. Though the local inhabitants would normally have honored Herod because of his position, no doubt his disfavor and their dependence on his good graces motivates them to take their public devotion to excess. They desperately need the grain they get from the region of Galilee.

📖 Read Acts 12:21–22 and summarize what you learn here of Herod's address and the people's response to it.

_____

_____

_____

DID YOU KNOW?
Herod

The Jewish historian, Josephus, writes extensively of the reign and death of Herod Agrippa. He records that this occasion of Herod's public appearance was a festival in honor of the emperor. It was possibly on the first of August (his birthday) or in October of A.D. 43, at the Caesarean Games to honor the emperor. According to Josephus, Herod's robe was made of silver which glittered in the sun as he entered the theater at daybreak. The historian tells us that in addition to calling Herod a god, the people go on to flatter him by saying, "May you be propitious to us, and if we have hitherto feared you as a man, yet henceforth we agree that you are more than mortal in your being." Josephus adds, "the king did not rebuke them nor did he reject their flattery as impious." For the life and death of Herod Agrippa I, see _Josephus, Antiquities 18:126–309; 19:1–227, 292–366._

On a day of particular importance, Herod makes a formal public appearance at the local area provided for such occasions. The term translated "rostrum" here (bema) literally means "judgment seat" and is a raised platform with a judicial throne where disputes are resolved by one in authority, much like a courtroom functions today. Herod dresses in all his royal regalia and delivers "an address" to the people which is received with unusual favor. Whether the people are sincere or simply flattering, it is clear that Herod takes their adulation to heart as they liken him to a god.

📖 What happens to Herod in Acts 12:23 and why?

_____

_____

_____

Herod is struck dead instantaneously as an act of judgment by God through one of His angels. The explanation we are given for his demise is not in retribution for his killing of James or for his attempt to do the same to Peter. The reason for his untimely passing is his failure to give God the glory due His name. When the people cry, "the voice of a god and not a man," Herod keeps for himself praise that is only deserved by the one true God. It is uncertain how long it takes for him to be eaten by worms, but the implication is that this too is rapid and supernatural.

📖 Look at Acts 12:24–25 in its context and answer the following questions.

How is the church affected by Herod's death?

_____

_____

_____

_____

Why does Luke say "the word of the Lord" continues to grow?

_____

_____

_____

How does verse 25 fit with this context?

_____

_____

_____

With the death of King Herod, a potentially huge obstacle is removed from the early church. They continue on the course Christ has set for them, and Herod's evil intent is unable to deter them at all. It is interesting to note how Luke words verse 24. He does not say, *"the church continues to grow and to be multiplied"* though certainly that is the idea he conveys. His phrasing emphasizes not the structure of the church but its mission. The church growing bigger is of no consequence unless the reach of God's Word is expanded. While verse 25 at a casual glance may appear to be disjointed from the context, it is instead a very strong bridge between verse 24 and chapter 13. Luke is getting ready to introduce the next significant step in the advance of the church—the missionary journeys. The chapters that follow will show exactly how *"the word of the Lord"* continues to grow.

God's people pray. They fervently seek the Lord about the difficulties they are encountering. They do not know how He will answer, but they trust that He will. The story of King Herod gives powerful testimony to the fact that God is able to deal with our enemies, and He will at the proper time. He can handle the challenges that we cannot. We must remind ourselves that whatever is over our heads is still under His feet. That is why perhaps the single most important action of the church is prayer. Satan may mock our labors and laugh at our trials, but he trembles when he sees the weakest saint on his knees.

FOR ME TO FOLLOW GOD

*"The Lord will rescue me from every evil deed, and will bring me
safely to His heavenly kingdom." (2 Timothy 4:18)*

Life is filled with unexpected events. We never know where our next trial or challenge is coming from. We know that *"in this world [we] have tribulation"* (John 16:33), but we take courage in the knowledge that Christ has overcome the world. The means of our deliverance may be unexpected, but the fact of it is sure. The apostle Paul writes from his final imprisonment in the Mamertine dungeons of Rome, *"The Lord will rescue me from every evil deed, and will bring me safely to His heavenly kingdom"* (2 Timothy 4:18). It is a sure promise on which we can bank. If something is evil, God WILL deliver us. If He does not deliver us, then it can only be that He has determined that ultimately it is not evil. Psalm 84:11 promises, *"No good thing does He withhold from those who walk uprightly."* If something is good, God will NOT withhold it. If He holds something back that we perceive as good, then we can know that at least for the time being, it isn't good for us. These two truths serve as faithful bookends on each of the trials in our lives. God rescues us from every evil deed, and He does not withhold any good thing. God always uses the trials He allows into our lives. If they are not useful to Him, He doesn't allow them to reach us. If He allows them to come our way, then we can know that He finds purpose in them. Even the wicked acts of pagan rulers God is able to use for His own glory and the advance of the church. The same holds true in our lives as well.

Are there any unexpected tribulations in your life right now?

Have you shared them with others who can join you in prayer?

"No good thing does He withhold from those who walk uprightly."
(Psalm 84:11)

If we do not pray about the tribulations in our lives, it expresses one of several wrong beliefs. One direction of our misbelief is toward trusting in ourselves. We incorrectly believe that we can handle all the difficulties of life on our own. Certainly, we are expected to do that which is in our ability to address the trials which come our way, but we must also recognize that God wants us to cast our cares on Him because He cares for us (1 Peter 5:7). Another direction of our misbelief can be toward God. A wrong view of Him can certainly affect our prayers. Though few Christians would ever voice a doubt in

God's power, their lack of praying belies an inaccurate view that God is unable to help in their unique situation. They doubt His power. Others, by the absence of their supplication, express the mistaken conviction that God doesn't really care. We will not "cast our cares" on Him if we do not believe that He cares for us. Honestly reflect on these reasons people don't pray and check any that you sense hinder you.

___ Too much faith in self to handle problems

___ Doubt in God's ability to help

___ Doubt in God's willingness to help

___ Other:_____

Any of these three wrong beliefs can wreak havoc on our prayer life. If you sense a problem in any of these areas, take time to confess this to the Lord and ask His aid in addressing the problem.

The obvious application of this lesson flows in the direction of prayer, but its message is not simply the need to pray as individuals. What we see modeled here and elsewhere in the book of Acts is the importance of *corporate prayer*. God wants His children to join in prayer. The small embers of our own supplications can become a bonfire when joined with the flames of others. What marks the first century church is not simply prayer but praying together in one accord.

Are you aware of any corporate opportunities for prayer your church may offer?

_____

_____

_____

When and where do such meetings take place?

_____

_____

How are prayer requests shared at your church?

_____

_____

Every local church is different. The prayer ministry of your church may be obvious and easily visible, or it may be somewhat hidden. It may be a live gathering or electronically sharing requests through email or group texts. If you are not aware of opportunities in your church to pray for others or share prayer requests, do not assume that they don't exist. Ask your pastor or other leaders. Even if no such corporate gatherings are organized on a regular basis, or no formal system exists to share churchwide requests, this does not mean that your church lacks people with a passion to pray. Perhaps God wants you to take the initiative to organize other believers to prayer for each other.

There is a third area of application I would like you to consider as you reflect on the message of this week's study. As I study this passage, it convinces me of my own deficiencies in this area. Though I believe in the importance of prayer and am faithful to pray for others, I am convicted that I do not share my own needs with others who will pray as I should. As I look into my own heart, I find several reasons for this. One cause is rooted in lifetime habits from my upbringing. I was taught the importance of carrying my own weight and not complaining about it to others. But it is not complaining to vulnerably share the challenges we face. The church is called to *"bear one another's burdens and thereby fulfill the law of Christ"* (Galatians 6:2). An offshoot of "carrying my own weight," I have sometimes viewed sharing my prayer needs as a sign of weakness. Another reason I don't always share prayer needs is the wrong belief that others will not care about the concerns that trouble me. This misconception doubts the family nature of the body of Christ. With a mixture of motives to blame, I am convicted that I need to be more willing to share my prayer needs with others. There are times in each of our lives when we need *"prayer for [us]* **being made fervently by the church to God"** (Acts 12:5).

Check any reasons that apply to you for not sharing your prayer needs with others...

___ Don't want to complain

___ Don't want to appear weak

___ Think others won't care

___ Haven't recognized that the church is supposed to pray corporately

___ Other:_____

> *"...bear one another's burdens and thereby fulfill the law of Christ."*
> *(Galatians 6:2)*

Having learned in this study the importance of prayer, why not close out this lesson by writing your own prayer to the Lord?

NOTES

LEADER'S GUIDE

TABLE OF CONTENTS

The best way to become a better discussion leader is to regularly evaluate your group discussion sessions. The most effective leaders are those who consistently look for ways to improve.

But before you start preparing for your first group session, you need to know the problem areas that will most likely weaken the effectiveness of your study group. Commit now to have the best Bible study group that you can possibly have. Ask the Lord to motivate you as a group leader and to steer you away from bad habits.

How to Guarantee a Poor Discussion Group:

1. Prepare inadequately.

2. Show improper attitude toward people in the group (lack of acceptance).

3. Fail to create an atmosphere of freedom and ease.

4. Allow the discussion to wander aimlessly.

5. Dominate the discussion yourself.

6. Let a small minority dominate the discussion.

7. Leave the discussion "in the air," so to speak, without presenting any concluding statements or some type of closure.

8. Ask too many "telling" or "trying" questions. (Don't ask individuals in your group pointed or threatening questions that might bring embarrassment to them or make them feel uncomfortable.)

9. End the discussion without adequate application points.

10. Do the same thing every time.

11. Become resentful and angry when people disagree with you. After all, you did prepare. You are the leader!

12. End the discussion with an argument.

13. Never spend any time with the members of your group other than the designated discussion meeting time.

Helpful Hints

One of the best ways to learn to be an effective Bible discussion leader is to sit under a good model. If you have had the chance to be in a group with an effective facilitator, think about the things that made him or her effective.

Though you can learn much and shape many convictions from those good models, you can also glean some valuable lessons on what not to do from those who didn't do such a good job. Bill Donahue has done a good job of categorizing the leader's role in facilitating dynamic discussion into four key actions. They are easy to remember as he links them to the acrostic ACTS:

*A leader ACTS to facilitate discussions by:

- Acknowledging everyone who speaks during a discussion.

- Clarifying what is being said and felt.

- Taking it to the group as a means of generating discussion.

- Summarizing what has been said.

*Taken from *Leading Life-Changing Small Groups* ©1996 by the Willow Creek Association. Used by permission of ZondervanPublishing House.

Make a point to give each group member ample opportunity to speak. Pay close attention to any nonverbal communication (i.e. facial expressions, body language, etc.) that group members may use, showing their desire to speak. The four actions in Bill Donahue's acrostic will guarantee to increase your effectiveness, which will translate into your group getting more out of the Bible study. After all, isn't that your biggest goal?

Dealing with Talkative Timothy
Throughout your experiences of leading small Bible study groups, you will learn that there will be several stereotypes who will follow you wherever you go. One of them is "Talkative Timothy." He will show up in virtually every small group you will ever lead. (Sometimes this stereotype group member shows up as "Talkative Tammy.") "Talkative Timothy" talks too much, dominates the discussion time, and gives less opportunity for others to share. What do you do with a group member who talks too much? Below you will find some helpfulideas on managing the "Talkative Timothy's" in your group.

The best defense is a good offense. To deal with "Talkative Timothy" before he becomes a problem, one thing you can do is establish as a ground rule that no one can talk twice until everyone who wants to talk has spoken at least once. Another important ground rule is "no interrupting." Still another solution is to go systematically around the group, directing questions to people by name. When all else fails, you can resort to a very practical approach of sitting beside "Talkative Timothy." When you make it harder for him (or her) to make eye contact with you, you will create less chances for him to talk.

After taking one or more of these combative measures, you may find that "Timothy" is still a problem. You may need to meet with him (or her) privately. Assure him that you value his input, but remind him that you want to hear the comments of others as well. One way to diplomatically approach "Timothy" is to privately ask him to help you draw the less talkative members into the discussion. Approaching "Timothy" in this fashion may turn your dilemma into an asset. Most importantly, remember to love "Talkative Timothy."

Silent Sally

Another person who inevitably shows up is "Silent Sally." She doesn't readily speak up. Sometimes her silence is because she doesn't yet feel comfortable enough with the group to share her thoughts. Sometimes it is simply because she fears being rejected. Often her silence is because she is too polite to interrupt and thus is headed off at the pass each time she wants to speak by more aggressive (and less sensitive) members of the group.

It is not uncommon in a mixed group to find that "Silent Sally" is married to "Talkative Timothy." (Seriously!) Don't mistakenly interpret her silence as meaning that she has nothing to contribute. Often those who are slowest to speak will offer the most meaningful contributions to the group. You can help "Silent Sally" make those significant contributions. Below are some ideas.

Make sure, first of all, that you are creating an environment that makes people comfortable. In a tactful way, direct specific questions to the less talkative in the group. Be careful though, not to put them on the spot with the more difficult or controversial questions. Become their biggest fan—make sure you cheer them on when they do share. Give them a healthy dose of affirmation. Compliment them afterward for any insightful contributions they make. You may want to sit across from them in the group so that it is easier to notice any nonverbal cues they give you when they want to speak. You should also come to their defense if another group member responds to them in a negative, stifling way. As you pray for each group member, ask that the Lord would help the quiet ones in your group to feel more at ease during the discussion time. Most of all, love "Silent Sally," and accept her as she is—even when she is silent!

Tangent Tom

We have already looked at "Talkative Timothy" and "Silent Sally." Now let's look at another of those stereotypes who always show up. Let's call this person, "Tangent Tom." He is the kind of guy who loves to talk even when he has nothing to say. "Tangent Tom" loves to chase rabbits regardless of where they go. When he gets the floor, you never know where the discussion will lead. You need to understand that not all tangents are bad, for sometimes much can be gained from discussion that is a little "off the beaten path." But diversions must be balanced against the purpose of the group. What is fruitful for one member may be fruitless for everyone else. Below are some ideas to help you deal with "Tangent Tom."

EVALUATING TANGENTS

Ask yourself, "How will this tangent affect my group's chances of finishing the lesson?" Another way to measure the value of a tangent is by asking, "Is this something that will benefit all or most of the group?" You also need to determine whether there is a practical, spiritual benefit to this tangent. Paul advised Timothy to refuse foolish and ignorant speculations, knowing that they produce quarrels. (See 2 Timothy 2:23.)

ADDRESSING TANGENTS:

1) Keep pace of your time, and use the time factor as your ally when addressing "Tangent Tom." Tactfully respond, "That is an interesting subject, but since our lesson is on _____, we'd better get back to our lesson if we are going to finish."

2) If the tangent is beneficial to one but fruitless to the rest of the group, offer to address that subject after class.

3) If the tangent is something that will benefit the group, you may want to say, "I'd like to talk about that more. Let's come back to that topic at the end of today's discussion, if we have time."

4) Be sure you understand what "Tangent Tom" is trying to say. It may be that he has a good and valid point, but has trouble expressing it or needs help in being more direct. Be careful not to quench someone whose heart is right, even if his methods aren't perfect. (See Proverbs 18:23.)

5) One suggestion for diffusing a strife-producing tangent is to point an imaginary shotgun at a spot outside the group and act like you are firing a shot. Then say, "That rabbit is dead. Now, where were we?"

6) If it is a continual problem, you may need to address it with this person privately.

7) Most of all, be patient with "Tangent Tom." God will use him in the group in ways that will surprise you!

Know–It–All Ned

The Scriptures are full of characters who struggled with the problem of pride. Unfortunately, pride isn't a problem reserved for the history books. It shows up today just as it did in the days the Scriptures were written.

Pride is sometimes the root-problem of a know-it-all group member. "Know-It-All Ned" may have shown up in your group by this point. He may be an intellectual giant, or only a legend in his own mind. He can be very prideful and argumentative. "Ned" often wants his point chosen as the choice point, and he may be intolerant of any opposing views— sometimes to the point of making his displeasure known in very inappropriate ways. A discussion point tainted with the stench of pride is uninviting—no matter how well spoken!

No one else in the group will want anything to do with this kind of attitude. How do you manage the "Know-It-All Ned's" who show up from time to time?

EVALUATION

To deal with "Know-It-All Ned," you need to understand him. Sometimes the same type of action can be rooted in very different causes. You must ask yourself, "Why does 'Ned' come across as a know-it-all?" It may be that "Ned" has a vast reservoir of knowledge but hasn't matured in how he communicates it. Or perhaps "Ned" really doesn't know it all, but he tries to come across that way to hide his insecurities and feelings of inadequacy.

Quite possibly, "Ned" is prideful and arrogant, and knows little of the Lord's ways in spite of the information and facts he has accumulated. Still another possibility is that Ned is a good man with a good heart who has a blind spot in the area of pride.

APPLICATION

"Know-It-All Ned" may be the most difficult person to deal with in your group, but God will use him in ways that will surprise you. Often it is the "Ned's" of the church that teach each of us what it means to love the unlovely in Gods strength, not our own. In 1 Thessalonians 5:14, the apostle Paul states, "And we urge you, brethren, admonish the unruly, encourage the fainthearted, help the weak, be patient with all men." In dealing with the "Ned's" you come across, start by assuming they are weak and need help until they give you reason to believe otherwise. Don't embarrass them by confronting them in public. Go to them in private if need be.

Speak the truth in love. You may need to remind them of 1 Corinthians 13, that if we have all knowledge, but have not love, we are just making noise. First Corinthians is also where we are told, "knowledge makes arrogant, but love edifies" (8:1). Obviously, there were some "Ned's" in the church at Corinth. If you sense that "Ned" is not weak or faint-hearted, but in fact is unruly, you will need to admonish him. Make sure you do so in private, but make sure you do it all the same. Proverbs 27:56 tells us, *"Better is open rebuke than love that is concealed. Faithful are the wounds of a friend, but deceitful are the kisses of an enemy."* Remember the last statement in 1 Thessalonians 5:14, *"be patient with all men."*

Agenda Alice

The last person we would like to introduce to you who will probably show up sooner or later is one we like to call "Agenda Alice." All of us from time to time can be sidetracked by our own agenda. Often the very thing we are most passionate about can be the thing that distracts us from our highest passion: Christ. Agendas often are not unbiblical, but imbalanced. At their root is usually tunnel-vision mixed with a desire for control. The small group, since it allows everyone to contribute to the discussion, affords "Agenda Alice" a platform to promote what she thinks is most important. This doesn't mean that she is wrong to avoid driving at night because opossums are being killed, but she is wrong to expect everyone to have the exact same conviction and calling that she does in the gray areas of Scripture. If not managed properly, she will either sidetrack the group from its main study objective or create a hostile environment in the group if she fails to bring people to her way of thinking. "Agenda Alice" can often be recognized by introductory catch phrases such as "Yes, but . . ." and "Well, I think. . . ." She is often critical of the group process and may become vocally critical of you. Here are some ideas on dealing with this type of person:

1) Reaffirm the group covenant.

   At the formation of your group you should have taken time to define some ground rules for the group. Once is not enough to discuss these matters of group etiquette. Periodically remind everyone of their mutual commitment to one another.

2) Remember that the best defense is a good offense.

Don't wait until it is a problem to address a mutual vision for how the group will function.

3) Refocus on the task at hand.

The clearer you explain the objective of each session, the easier it is to stick to that objective and the harder you make it for people to redirect attention toward their own agenda. Enlist the whole group in bringing the discussion back to the topic at hand. Ask questions like, "What do the rest of you think about this passage?"

4) Remind the group, "Remember, this week's lesson is about _____."

5) Reprove those who are disruptive.

Confront the person in private to see if you can reach an understanding. Suggest another arena for the issue to be addressed such as an optional meeting for those in the group who would like to discuss the issue.

Remember the words of St. Augustine: "In essentials unity, in non-essentials liberty, in all things charity."

Adding Spice and Creativity

One of the issues you will eventually have to combat in any group Bible study is the enemy of boredom. This enemy raises its ugly head from time to time, but it shouldn't. It is wrong to bore people with the Word of God! Often boredom results when leaders allow their processes to become too predictable. As small group leaders, we tend to do the same thing in the same way every single time. Yet God the Creator, who spoke everything into existence is infinitely creative! Think about it. He is the one who not only created animals in different shapes and sizes, but different colors as well. When He created food, He didn't make it all taste or feel the same. This God of creativity lives in us. We can trust Him to give us creative ideas that will keep our group times from becoming tired and mundane. Here are some ideas:

When you think of what you can change in your Bible study, think of the five senses: (sight, sound, smell, taste, and feel).

SIGHT:
One idea would be to have a theme night with decorations. Perhaps you know someone with dramatic instincts who could dress up in costume and deliver a message from the person you are studying that week.

Draw some cartoons on a marker board or handout.

SOUND:
Play some background music before your group begins. Sing a hymn together that relates to the lesson. If you know of a song that really hits the main point of the lesson, play it at the beginning or end.

SMELL:

This may be the hardest sense to involve in your Bible study, but if you think of a creative way to incorporate this sense into the lesson, you can rest assured it will be memorable for your group.

TASTE:

Some lessons will have issues that can be related to taste (e.g. unleavened bread for the Passover, etc.). What about making things less formal by having snacks while you study? Have refreshments around a theme such as "Chili Night" or "Favorite Fruits."

FEEL:

Any way you can incorporate the sense of feel into a lesson will certainly make the content more invigorating. If weather permits, add variety by moving your group outside. Whatever you do, be sure that you don't allow your Bible study to become boring!

Handling an Obviously Wrong Comment

From time to time, each of us can say stupid things. Some of us, however, are better at it than others. The apostle Peter had his share of embarrassing moments. One minute, he was on the pinnacle of success, saying, "Thou art the Christ, the Son of the Living God" (Matthew 16:16), and the next minute, he was putting his foot in his mouth, trying to talk Jesus out of going to the cross. Proverbs 10:19 states, "When there are many words, transgression is unavoidable. . . ." What do you do when someone in the group says something that is obviously wrong? First of all, remember that how you deal with a situation like this not only affects the present, but the future. Here are some ideas:

1) Let the whole group tackle it and play referee/peacemaker. Say something like, "That is an interesting thought, what do the rest of you think?"

2) Empathize. ("I've thought that before too, but the Bible says. . . .")

3) Clarify to see if what they said is what they meant. ("What I think you are saying is. . . .")

4) Ask the question again, focusing on what the Bible passage actually says.

5) Give credit for the part of the answer that is right and affirm that before dealing with what is wrong.

6) If it is a non-essential, disagree agreeably. ("I respect your opinion, but I see it differently.")

7) Let it go —some things aren't important enough to make a big deal about them.

8) Love and affirm the person, even if you reject the answer.

Transitioning to the Next Study

For those of you who have completed leading a Following God Group Bible Study, congratulations! You have successfully navigated the waters of small group discussion. You have utilized one of the most effective tools of ministry—one that was so much a priority with Jesus, He spent most of His time there with His small group of twelve. Hopefully yours has been a very positive and rewarding experience. At this stage you may be looking forward to a break. It is not too early however, to be thinking and planning for what you will do next. Hopefully you have seen God use this study and this process for growth in the lives of those who have participated with you. As God has worked in the group, members should be motivated to ask the question, "What next?" As they do, you need to be prepared to give an answer. Realize that you have built a certain amount of momentum with your present study that will make it easier to do another. You want to take advantage of that momentum. The following suggestions may be helpful as you transition your people toward further study of God's Word.

- Challenge your group members to share with others what they have learned, and to encourage them to participate next time.

- If what to study is a group choice rather than a church-wide or ministry-wide decision made by others, you will want to allow some time for input from the group members in deciding what to do next. The more they have ownership of the study, the more they will commit to it.

- It is important to have some kind of a break so that everyone doesn't become study weary. At our church, we always look for natural times to start and end a study. We take the summer off as well as Christmas, and we have found that having a break brings people back with renewed vigor. Even if you don't take a break from meeting, you might take a breather from homework—or even get together just for fellowship.

- If you are able to end this study knowing what you will study next, some of your group members may want to get a head start on the next study. Be prepared to put books in their hands early.

- Make sure you end your study with a vision for more. Take some time to remind your group of the importance of the Word of God. As D. L. Moody used to say, "The only way to keep a broken vessel full is to keep the faucet running."

Evaluation

Becoming a Better Discussion Leader

The questions listed below are tools to assist you in assessing your discussion group. From time to time in the Leader's Guide, you will be advised to read through this list of evaluation questions in order to help you decide what areas need improvement in your role as group leader. Each time you read through this list, something different may catch your attention, giving you tips on how to become the best group leader that you can possibly be.

Read through these questions with an open mind, asking the Lord to prick your heart with anything specific He would want you to apply.

1. Are the group discussion sessions beginning and ending on time?

2. Am I allowing the freedom of the Holy Spirit as I lead the group in the discussion?

3. Do I hold the group accountable for doing their homework?

4. Do we always begin our sessions with prayer?

5. Is the room arranged properly (seating in a circle or semicircle, proper ventilation, adequate teaching aids)?

6. Is each individual allowed equal opportunity in the discussion?

7. Do I successfully bridle the talkative ones?

8. Am I successfully encouraging the hesitant ones to participate in the discussion?

9. Do I redirect comments and questions to involve more people in the interaction, or do I always dominate the discussion?

10. Are the discussions flowing naturally, or do they take too many "side roads" (diversions)?

11. Do I show acceptance to those who convey ideas with which I do not agree?

12. Are my questions specific, brief and clear?

13. Do my questions provoke thought, or do they only require pat answers?

14. Does each group member feel free to contribute or question, or is there a threatening or unnecessarily tense atmosphere?

15. Am I allowing time for silence and thought without making everyone feel uneasy?

16. Am I allowing the group to correct any obviously wrong conclusions that are made by others, or by myself (either intentionally to capture the group's attention or unintentionally)?

17. Do I stifle thought and discussion by assigning a question to someone before the subject of that question has even been discussed? (It will often be productive to assign a question to a specific person, but if you call on one person before you throw out a question, everyone else takes a mental vacation!)

18. Do I summarize when brevity is of the essence?

19. Can I refrain from expressing an opinion or comment that someone else in the group could just as adequately express?

20. Do I occasionally vary in my methods of conducting the discussion?

21. Am I keeping the group properly motivated?

22. Am I occasionally rotating the leadership to help others develop leadership?

23. Am I leading the group to specifically apply the truths that are learned?

24. Do I follow through by asking the group how they have applied the truths that they have learned from previous lessons?

25. Am I praying for each group member?

26. Is there a growing openness and honesty among my group members?

27. Are the group study sessions enriching the lives of my group members?

28. Have I been adequately prepared?

29. How may I be better prepared for the next lesson's group discussion?

30. Do I reach the objective set for each discussion? If not, why not? What can I do to improve?

31. Am I allowing the discussion to bog down on one point at the expense of the rest of the lesson?

32. Are the members of the group individually reaching the conclusions that I want them to reach without my having to give them the conclusions?

33. Do I encourage the group members to share what they have learned?

34. Do I encourage them to share the applications they have discovered?

35. Do I whet their appetites for next week's lesson discussion?

Getting Started

The First Meeting of Your Bible Study Group

Main Objectives of the First Meeting: The first meeting is devoted to establishing your group and setting the course that you will follow through the study. Your primary goals for this session should be to . . .

- Establish a sense of group identity by starting to get to know one another.

- Define some ground rules to help make the group time as effective as possible.

- Get the study materials into the hands of your group members.

- Create a sense of excitement and motivation for the study.

- Give assignments for next week.

BEFORE THE SESSION

You will be most comfortable in leading this introductory session if you are prepared as much as possible for what to expect. This means becoming familiar with the place you will meet, and the content you will cover, as well as understanding any time constraints you will have.

Location—Be sure that you not only know how to find the place where you will be meeting, but also have time to examine the setup and make any adjustments to the physical arrangements. You never get a second chance to make a first impression.

Curriculum—You will want to get a copy of the study in advance of the introductory session, and it will be helpful if you do the homework for Lesson One ahead of time. This will make it easier for you to be able to explain the layout of the homework. It will also give you a contagious enthusiasm for what your group will be studying in the coming week.

You will want to have enough books on hand for the number of people you expect so that they can get started right away with the study. You may be able to make arrangements with your church or local Christian Bookstore to bring copies on consignment. We would encourage you not to buy books for your members. Years of small group experience have taught that people take a study far more seriously when they make an investment in it.

Time—The type of group you are leading will determine the time format for your study. If you are doing this study for a Sunday school class or church study course, the time constraints may already be prescribed for you. In any case, ideally you will want to allow forty-five minutes to an hour for discussion.

WHAT TO EXPECT

When you embark on the journey of leading a small group Bible study, you are stepping into the stream of the work of God. You are joining in the process of helping others move toward spiritual maturity. As a small group leader, you are positioned to be a real catalyst in the lives of your group members, helping them to grow in their relationships with God. But you must remember, first and foremost, that whenever you step up to leadership in the kingdom of God, you are stepping down to serve. Jesus made it clear that leadership in the kingdom is not like leadership in the world. In Matthew 20:25, Jesus said, "You know that the rulers of the Gentiles lord it over them, and their great men exercise authority over them." That is the world's way to lead. But in Matthew 20:26–27, He continues, "It is not so among you, but whoever wishes to become great among you shall be your servant, and whoever wishes to be first among you shall be your slave." Your job as a small group leader is not to teach the group everything you have learned, but rather, to help them learn.

If you truly are to minister to the members of your group, you must start with understanding where they are, and join that with a vision of where you want to take them. In this introductory session, your group members will be experiencing several different emotions. They will be wondering, "Who is in my group?" and deciding "Do I like my group?" They will have a sense of excitement and anticipation, but also a sense of awkwardness as they try to find their place in this group. You will want to make sure that from the very beginning your group is founded with a sense of caring and acceptance. This is crucial if your group members are to open up and share what they are learning.

DURING THE SESSION

GETTING TO KNOW ONE ANOTHER

Opening Prayer—Remember that if it took the inspiration of God for people to write Scripture, it will also take His illumination for us to understand it. Have one of your group members open your time together in prayer.

Introductions—Take time to allow the group members to introduce themselves. Along with having the group members share their names, one way to add some interest is to have them add some descriptive information such as where they live or work. Just for fun, you could have them name their favorite breakfast cereal, most (or least) favorite vegetable, favorite cartoon character, their favorite city or country other than their own, etc.

Icebreaker—Take five or ten minutes to get the people comfortable in talking with each other. Since in many cases your small group will just now be getting to know one another, it will be helpful if you take some time to break the ice with some fun, nonthreatening discussion. Below you will find a list of ideas for good icebreaker questions to get people talking.

____ What is the biggest risk you have ever taken?

____ If money were no object, where would you most like to take a vacation and why?

____ What is your favorite way to waste time?

____ If you weren't in the career you now have, what would have been your second choice for a career?

____ If you could have lived in any other time, in what era or century would you have chosen to live (besides the expected spiritual answer of the time of Jesus)?

____ If you became blind right now, what would you miss seeing the most?

____ Who is the most famous person you've known or met?

____ What do you miss most about being a kid?

____ What teacher had the biggest impact on you in school (good or bad)?

____ Of the things money can buy, what would you most like to have?

____ What is your biggest fear?

____ If you could give one miracle to someone else, what would it be (and to whom)?

____ Tell about your first job.

____ Who is the best or worst boss you ever had?

____ Who was your hero growing up and why?

DEFINING THE GROUP: 5–10 MINUTES
SETTING SOME GROUND RULES

There are several ways you can lay the tracks on which your group can run. One is simply to hand out a list of suggested commitments the members should make to the group. Another would be to hand out 3x5 cards and have the members themselves write down two or three commitments they would like to see everyone live out. You could then compile these into the five top ones to share at the following meeting. A third option is to list three (or more) commitments you are making to the group and then ask that they make three commitments back to you in return. Here are some ideas for the types of ground rules that make for a good small group:

Leader:

____ To always arrive prepared

____ To keep the group on track so you make the most of the group's time

____ To not dominate the discussion by simply teaching the lesson

____ To pray for the group members

____ To not belittle or embarrass anyone's answers

____ To bring each session to closure and end on time

Member:

____ To do my homework

____ To arrive on time

____ To participate in the discussion

____ To not cut others off as they share

____ To respect the different views of other members

____ To not dominate the discussion

It is possible that your group may not need to formalize a group covenant, but you should not be afraid to expect a commitment from your group members. They will all benefit from defining the group up front.

INTRODUCTION TO THE STUDY:
15–20 MINUTES

As you introduce the study to the group members, your goal is to begin to create a sense of excitement about the Bible characters and applications that will be discussed. The most important question for you to answer in this session is "Why should I study _____?" You need to be prepared to guide them to finding that answer. Take time to give a brief overview of each lesson.

CLOSING: 5–10 MINUTES

Give homework for next week. In addition to simply reminding the group members to do their homework, if time allows, you might give them 5–10 minutes to get started on their homework for the first lesson.

Key components for closing out your time are a) to review anything of which you feel they should be reminded, and b) to close in prayer. If time allows, you may want to encourage several to pray.

PREPARATION OF THE DISCUSSION LEADER

I. Preparation of the Leader's Heart

A. Pray. It took the inspiration of the Holy Spirit to write Scripture, and it will require His illumination to correctly understand it.

B. Complete the Bible Study Yourself

1. Prayerfully seek a fresh word from God for yourself. Your teaching should be an overflow of what God taught you.

2. Even if you have completed this study in the past, consider using a new book. You need to be seeking God for what He would teach you this time before looking at what He taught you last time.

3. Guard against focusing on how to present truths to class. Keep the focus on God teaching you.

II. Keeping the Big Picture in Sight

One value of discussion: It allows students to share what God's Word says.

A. Looking back over the homework, find the one main unifying truth. There will be a key emphasis of each day, but all will support one main truth. Keep praying and looking until you find it (even if the author didn't make it clear).

B. Begin to write questions for each day's homework. Do this as you go through the study.

1. Consider key passage(s) for the day and ask questions of the text. For example, use the 5 Ws and an H (Who, What, When, Where, Why, and How): What was Jesus' main point? What is the context here? Do you see any cultural significance to this statement? How did this person relate to... (God? His neighbor? An unbeliever? The church? etc.)

2. Don't ask, "What do you think" questions unless it's "What do you think GOD is saying...?" It's easy to slip into sharing opinions if we don't carefully guide students to consider what God says. What I think doesn't matter if it differs from what God thinks.

3. Ask application questions as well. For example, "What steals our joy?" "How are we like these Bible characters?" "How can we learn from _____'s lessons so that we don't have to learn it the hard way?" "How can I restore/protect my _____ (joy, faith, peace...)?" Consider making a list where you write answers to "So what?" questions: So, what does this mean to me? How do I put this truth into practice?

4. Include definitions, grammar notes, historical/cultural notes, cross references, and so forth, from your own study. Go back over your notes/questions and add/delete/re-write after further prayer and thought. Go through your notes again, highlighting

(underlining, color coding, whatever works for you) what you believe is MOST important. This will help when time gets cut short. It will also jog your memory before moving
to next day's homework,

III. Leading the Discussion

A. Begin with prayer

1. Consider varying the method - this will help to remind the group that we pray not as
   habit but as needy children seeking our loving Father Who teaches us by His Spirit.

2. If having a time of prayer requests, consider ways to make it time effective and to
   avoid gossip disguised as a prayer request. Time management is a way you can serve
   the group.

B. Start the Study with Review—Briefly review context of the study (or have a student
   come prepared to do it). This keeps the group together for those joining the study
   late or who've missed a week. This also serves as a reminder since it's been a week or
   so since your previous study session.

C. Go through the study questions day by day.

1. You may offer a "unifying theme" of study or ask if students can identify a theme.

2. Follow the Holy Spirit. Remember that you can't cover everything from every day. As
   you prepare, highlight any notes He leads you to consider as being most important.

3. Watch your time! When you are leading a group Bible study, you enter into a different
   dimension of the physical realm. Time moves at a completely different pace. What is
   20 minutes in normal time flies by like 5 minutes when you are in the speaking zone.

4. Manage the questions raised by students and consider their value to the whole group
   within time constraints. Turn any questions raised back to the group.

5. Whether you make application day by day (probably best) or make application at end,
   be sure to allow time for students to name ways to put knowledge into practice.

IV. Evaluation

1. After 1-2 days, evaluate how the lesson went.

2. Thank God—thank Him for using His Word in all participants' lives and ask Him to
   guard the good seed planted!

V. Begin Preparation for the Next Lesson

Lesson #1 - Waiting for God to Move – Acts 1:1–26

Memory Verse: Acts 1:8

"But you will receive power when the Holy Spirit has come upon you;
and you shall be My witnesses both in Jerusalem, and in all Judea and Samaria, and
even to the remotest part of the earth.

- Be sure you have read through the introductory material and that you are seeking to apply the principles yourself. The more impact the Word makes in your heart the more enthusiasm you will communicate.

- Spread your homework out rather than trying to cram everything into one afternoon or night. You may want to use this as your daily quiet time.

- As you study, write down any good discussion questions you think of as they come to mind.

- Be transparent before the Lord and before your group. We are all learners – that's the meaning of the word "disciple."

WHAT TO EXPECT

One of the hardest directions from the Lord to follow is "wait." Patience may be a virtue, but it is not a favorite pastime for anyone. Yet some of life's most profound lessons are learned here. As you seek to teach this week's lesson, expect that, for most, waiting will be viewed as a passive thing, and it will be a real eye-opener to begin to understand the active side of waiting. Make sure they do not miss this part of the lesson. Help them to see that waiting is a very active thing when we understand that it is a choice not to do something we could, to make sure that we are sensitive to God, and that we are not just striving in our own energy.

THE MAIN POINT

The main point to be seen in the lesson on waiting for God to move is how we must learn to be sensitive to how God is working and leading and to make sure we do not get ahead of Him in the process of His will unfolding.

DURING THE SESSION

OPENING: 5–10 MINUTES

Opening Prayer – You or one of your group members should open your time together in prayer.

Opening Illustration – Warren Wiersbe makes the observation, "The ability to calm your soul and wait before God is one of the most difficult things in the Christian life. Our old nature is restless...the world around us is frantically in a hurry. But a restless heart usually leads to a reckless life." G. Campbell Morgan makes this point, "Waiting for God is not laziness. Waiting for God is not going to sleep. Waiting for God is not the abandonment of effort. Waiting for God means, first, activity under command; second, readiness for any new command that may come; third, the ability to do nothing until the command is given." From the Ascension to Pentecost the disciples had ten days of waiting. Yet as we will see in this week's lesson, there are many practical applications to be drawn from those days of waiting for God to move.

DISCUSSION: 30 MINUTES

Main Objective in Day One: The first eleven verses of Acts could be labeled "Previews of Coming Attractions." In them we are introduced to what the disciples are waiting for and why. We also are given an overview of what will be expressed in the whole book – the spread of the gospel from Jerusalem to the remotest parts of the earth. Below are some possible discussion questions for the Day One discussion. Check which questions you will use.

___ From comparing Acts with Luke's Gospel, what did you learn about why Luke wrote his books?

___ Why do you think Jesus only stayed forty days after the resurrection?

___ What did you learn from Jesus about the Holy Spirit's effect on people?

___ What do you think was going through the disciples' minds as they watched Jesus leave?

Main Objective in Day Two: Our relationship to God often leads us to places of waiting. Day two focuses on the importance of doing what we know to do while God has us waiting. Check which discussion questions you will use for Day Two.

___ What do you think would have happened if the disciples had not obeyed Jesus' command?

___ Sometimes we are inactive because there is nothing we can do, but this is not the same as waiting on God. What would have happened if they didn't seek God while they waited?

___ What have you found that helps you when God has you waiting?

___ What is the greatest challenge while you wait on God?

Main Objective in Day Three: The focus in Day Three is the fact that prayer was the main activity for the disciples while they waited on God. Check which discussion questions for Day Three you might use.

___ Can you picture yourself spending ten days in focused prayer?

___ What do you think contributed to the disciples being "of one mind"?

___ What do you think the disciples were praying?

___ How do you interpret the verse, "Pray without ceasing"?

Main Objective in Day Four: Day Four takes a look at the importance of doing what you know to do while you are waiting on God. In addition to any discussion questions that may have come to your mind in your studying, the following suggested questions may prove beneficial to your group session:

___ Are you satisfied with the book's explanation of the different versions of Judas' death?

___ In Acts 1:20-22, how did God reveal to the disciples what they needed to do next?

___ What do you think of the method the disciples used to pick Judas' replacement?

___ Do you think casting lots is an acceptable way to make decisions today? Why or why not?

Day Five – Key Points in Application: The most important application from our study this week is to recognize there will be times of waiting in the Christian life, and to glean some practical principles on what to do when we find ourselves there. Check which discussion questions you will use for Day Five.

___ Is there some area of waiting in your life right now?

___ How are you at seeking God when He has you waiting on Him?

___ What was the main application you saw from this week about your own prayer life?

___ Do you ever struggle with missing what you are supposed to do today because you are waiting on direction for tomorrow?

CLOSING: 5–10 MINUTES

Summarize – Restate the key points highlighted in the class.

Preview – Take just a few moments to preview next week's lesson.

Encourage the group to be sure to do their homework.

Pray – Close in prayer.

TOOLS FOR GOOD DISCUSSION

Some who are reading this have led small group Bible studies many times. Here is an important word of warning: experience alone does not make you a more effective discussion leader. In fact, experience can make you less effective. You see, the more experience you have the more comfortable you will be at the task. Unfortunately, for some that means becoming increasingly comfortable in doing a bad job. Taking satisfaction with mediocrity translates into taking the task less seriously. It is easy to wrongly assert that just because one is experienced, that he or she can successfully "shoot from the hip" so to speak. If you really want your members to get the most out of this study, you need to be dissatisfied with simply doing an adequate job and make it your aim to do an excellent job. A key to excellence is to regularly evaluate yourself to see that you are still doing all that you want to be doing. We have prepared a list of over thirty evaluation questions for you to review from time to time. This list of questions can be found on page 192–93 in this Leader's Guide. The examination questions will help to jog your memory and, hopefully, will become an effective aid in improving the quality of your group discussion. Review the evaluation questions list, and jot down below two or three action points for you to begin implementing next week.

ACTION POINTS:

1.

2.

3.

Lesson #2—Power From on High – Acts 2:1-47

Memory Verse: Acts 2:38

"Repent, and each of you be baptized in the name of Jesus Christ for the forgiveness of your sins; and you will receive the gift of the Holy Spirit."

- Remember that your goal is not to teach the lesson, but to facilitate discussion.

- Make sure your own heart is right with God. Be willing to be transparent with the group about your own life experiences and mistakes. This will make it easier for them to open up.

- Don't be afraid of chasing tangents for a while if the diversions capture the interest of the group as a whole, but don't sacrifice the rest of the group to belabor the questions of one member. Trust God to lead you.

- You may want to keep a highlight pen handy as you study to mark key statements that stood out to you.

WHAT TO EXPECT

You need to recognize that great controversy exists among believers today about the applications of Pentecost. Be prepared for questions and perhaps even disagreement. Keep focused on the main point that God has given us the power we need to live the Christian life by sending His Spirit. Expect that your group not only needs to understand truths in this area of the power God has made available to us, but also needs your help in applying them. It is important that they grasp the concept that the Christian life is not me trying hard to be like Jesus, but rather, me yielding myself to Christ's control and allowing Him to live through me by His Spirit. No doubt, all in your group will have experienced their own share of failure and frustration as they tried to live the Christian life in their own efforts. They will want to share their own stories as time allows. Expect that this will be a very motivating lesson with lots of interest.

THE MAIN POINT

The main point of this week's lesson is to focus in on the impact of Pentecost and the coming of the Holy Spirit and to gain perspective on how it applies to us today.

DURING THE SESSION

OPENING: 5–10 MINUTES

Opening Prayer – You or one of your group members should open your time together in prayer.

Opening Illustration – When Hudson Taylor, the famous missionary, first went to China, it was in a sailing vessel. Very close to the shore of cannibal islands, the ship was becalmed, and it was slowly drifting shoreward unable to go about while savages onshore were eagerly anticipating a feast. The captain came to Mr. Taylor and asked him to pray for the help of God. "I will," said Taylor, "provided you set your sails to catch the breeze." The captain declined to make himself a laughing stock by unfurling in a dead calm. Taylor said, "I will not undertake to pray for the vessel unless you will prepare the sails." And it was done. While engaged in prayer, there was a knock at the door of his stateroom. "Who is there?" The captain's voice responded, "Are you still praying for wind?" "Yes." "Well," said the captain, "you'd better stop praying, for we have more wind than we can manage." A sailing vessel is a good picture of serving in the Lord's strength. It is not merely "letting go and letting God"—Him doing everything and us doing nothing. There are things we must do. We have responsibilities to trust and obey. But having done our part, our work is nothing without His work. Our job is to set the sails—His job is to bring the wind. The sails are no good by themselves. We need His empowering. But His empowering does us no good when we are sitting still. The sails cannot catch the wind of His power until they are unfurled. We have to surrender control of our lives to Him to access His power for living, and then trust and obey as He leads.

DISCUSSION: 30 MINUTES

Once your group gets talking you will find that all you need to do is keep the group directed and flowing with a question or two or a pointed observation. You are the gate-keeper of discussion. Don't be afraid to ask someone to elaborate further or to ask a quiet member of the group what they think of someone else's comments. Time will not allow you to discuss every single question in the lesson one at a time. Instead, make it your goal to cover the main ideas of each day, and help the group to personally share what they learned. You don't have to use all the discussion questions. They are there for your discretion.

Main Objective in Day One: In Day One, the central objective of the study is to introduce the historical record of Pentecost and its effect on those first century believers. Below, check any discussion questions that you might consider using in your group session.

___ Did anything new stand out to you as you reviewed verses 1–4?

___ What would you have been thinking and feeling if you were a Jew witnessing the events of Pentecost?

___ Why do you think the Lord chose this particular day to send the Holy Spirit?

___ What was the value in having the disciples speak in the different languages of all those gathered?

Main Objective in Day Two: In Day Two, we see the important principle that Peter's sermon is evidence of what Jesus said would happen when the Spirit came upon them. It also gives us a summary of the gospel message. Below, check which discussion questions you will use for Day Two.

___ What did you consider to be the main points in Peter's sermon?

___ Is there anything a person needs to know to be saved that Peter doesn't mention?

___ What questions were raised in your mind from looking at the prophecies from Joel?

___ What else did you learn from the Scriptures we looked up in Day Two?

Main Objective in Day Three: Day Three gives us a look at the response to Peter's sermon at Pentecost. Look over the discussion-starter questions below to see if any are applicable to your group.

___ What stood out to you from verse 37 about how people reacted to Peter's sermon?

___ In verse 38 do you think Peter is saying a person must be baptized to be saved?

___ Why do you think so many responded to the gospel message that day?

___ What else stood out to you in Day Three?

Main Objective in Day Four: Day Four shows us some of the practical functioning of the first century Church. Review the discussion question list below and choose any that you feel are good questions for your session.

___ What did you learn from Acts 2:42 about the priorities of the early church?

___ How do you feel your church does at each of those priorities?

___ What stood out to you from what you learned from verse 43?

___ Which of the other results of the early church priorities did you consider the most significant?

Day Five – Key Points in Application: The most important application point from our study this week is to recognize that although the Spirit is resident in our lives if we are saved, He may not be president. Some good application questions from Day Five include...

___ What is one thing new that you learned this week about your relationship with God?

___ How does what you learned this week help you in your relationship with God?

___ Which of the three types of sin do you find to be the most challenging in your own walk?

___ Which of the four priorities of the early church do you feel needs more emphasis in your church or in your life?

CLOSING: 5–10 MINUTES

Summarize—Review the main objectives for each day.

Remind them that living a victorious Christian life is not attained when we try hard to be like Jesus, but only when we surrender our lives to God and let Him work through us.

Preview—Take a few moments to preview next week's lesson. Encourage your group members to complete their homework.

Pray—Close in prayer.

TOOLS FOR GOOD DISCUSSION

Bill Donahue, in his book, The Willow Creek Guide to Leading Life-Changing Small Groups (©1996 Zondervan Publishing House), lists four primary facilitator actions that will produce dynamic discussion. These four actions are easy to remember because they are linked through the acrostic method to the word, ACTS. You will profit from taking time to review this information in the "Helpful Hints" section of How to Lead a Small Group Bible Study, which can be found on page 185 of this book.

Lesson #3—The Power of Jesus' Name - Acts 3:1—4:4

Memory Verse: Acts 3:16b

"...it is the name of Jesus which has strengthened this man whom you see and know; and the faith which comes through Him has given him this perfect health in the presence of you all."

BEFORE THE SESSION

- Pray each day for the members of your group. Pray that they spend time in the Word, grasp the message God wants to bring to their lives, and that they surrender to what God is saying.

- Thoroughly prepare for your group session—don't procrastinate!

- As you go through the study, jot down any ideas or questions you want to discuss. Those, along with the suggested questions listed throughout this Leader's Guide, can personalize the discussion to fit your group. Think of the needs of your group and look for applicable questions and discussion starters.

- Remain ever teachable. Look first for what God is saying to you.

- Be prepared to be transparent and open about what God is teaching you. Nothing is quite as contagious as the joy at discovering new treasures in the Word.

WHAT TO EXPECT

We all have a tendency to view Scripture through the eyeglasses of our own culture. In modern times little meaning is conveyed by a person's name, but such was not the case in biblical times. A name was chosen not because of how it sounded but because of the message it carried about the person and the circumstances of their birth. That is why it is profitable to study the names of God, for each reveals something of His nature and character. Realize however, that some will take this point too far and attempt to imbue mystical powers from the mere speaking of Jesus' name. Peter makes it clear that it was not the act of speaking the name, but "the faith which comes through Him" which produced healing.

THE MAIN POINT

The main point to be seen in this lesson is the power associated with Jesus and those who follow Him. When we say "there is power in the name of Jesus" what we really mean is there is power in Jesus Himself.

DURING THE SESSION

OPENING: 5–10 MINUTES

Opening Prayer—Remember the Lord is the Teacher and wants us to depend on Him as we open the Scriptures. Ask Him to teach you as you meet together.

Opening Illustration—In the mid twentieth century, author J. B. Phillips wrote a book entitled "Your God Is Too Small." The title itself is engaging. In the preface he writes, "The trouble with many people today is that they have not found a God big enough for modern needs. While their experience of life has grown in a score of directions, and their mental horizons have been expanded to the point of bewilderment by world events and by scientific discoveries, their ideas of God have remained largely static. It is obviously impossible for an adult to worship the conception of God that exists in the mind of a child of Sunday-school age, unless he is prepared to deny his own experience of life. If, by great effort of will, he does do this he will always be secretly afraid lest some new truth may expose the juvenility of his faith. And it will always be by such an effort that he either worships or serves a God who is really too small to command his adult loyalty and cooperation." No wonder many unbelievers stand away from the church at a distance. But the problem here lies not with God, but with man's limited view of God. As G. K. Chesterton put it, "Most people have not rejected Christianity per se, but a poor caricature of it." What is needed both for the unbeliever and the believer as well is a greater, more accurate view of God as He really is. That is what Peter is advocating as he explains the miracle we will see in this week's lesson.

DISCUSSION: 30 MINUTES

Keep the group directed along the main point of the power of God. You may have a pointed observation that helps sharpen the focus of the group. Encourage some to elaborate further on a key point or ask a quiet member of the group what they think of someone's comments. Watch the time, knowing you can't cover every single question in the lesson. Seek to cover the main ideas of each day and help the group to personally share what they have learned.

Main Objective in Day One: In Day One, the main objective is for you and your study group to get an overview of the miracle around which the events of this passage revolve. Check which discussion questions you will use from Day One.

___ What stood out to you from the circumstances of when Peter and John encountered the lame man?

___ Do you think the beggar really expected Peter to heal him?

___ What do you see as the role of faith in this man's healing?

___ How was God glorified in this miracle?

Main Objective in Day Two: Day Two focuses on how Peter used the opportunity the miracle afforded to preach the gospel message. The following questions may serve as excellent discussion starters for your group session:

___ What does Peter do to make sure he isn't credited for the miracle?

___ What points stood out to you in Peter's message to the crowd?

___ Why do you think Peter brings up the resurrection in this context?

___ What do you think the difference is between "faith in His name" at the beginning of Acts 3:16 and "the faith which comes through Him" at the end of it?

Main Objective in Day Three: Day Three introduces us to the need for acting on the message Peter brought. Check which discussion questions you will use from Day Three.

___ Why do you think it was important for Peter to acknowledge that the Jews acted in ignorance?

___ What application does Peter call for in his message?

___ What does Peter say will result if the people repent? ...if they don't?

___ Did anything stand out to you from how Peter closed out his message?

Main Objective in Day Four: In Day Four, we look at the contrasting responses to Peter's message and what they reveal of the hearts of the people. Check which discussion questions you will use from Day Four.

___ Why do you suppose it was the religious and not the rebellious who opposed Peter the most?

___ What do you think disturbed the religious leaders the most in what Peter was preaching?

___ What stands out to you from how the Jews handled Peter's arrest?

___ Did anything specific grab your attention when you considered the contrasting responses?

Day Five – Key Points in Application: The most important application point for this week's study is going to be reflecting on the centrality of Christ and the need for Him to be lifted up. Below, select a question or two for your Day Five discussion.

___ What is the main thing you learned from looking at this passage?

___ How do you see people getting in the way of God's glory when He works?

___ Were you challenged as you reflected on how many unbelievers you are aware of in your personal life?

___ Did anything else grab you this week?

CLOSING: 5–10 MINUTES

Summarize—Restate the key points the group shared. Review the objectives for each of the days found in these leader notes.

Remind—Using the memory verse, remind the group of the importance of a greater view of God.

Ask them to share their thoughts about the key applications from Day Five.

Preview—Take a few moments to preview next week's lesson. Encourage your group to do their homework and to space it out over the week.

Pray—Close in prayer.

TOOLS FOR GOOD DISCUSSION

One of the people who show up in every group is a person we call "Talkative Timothy." Talkative Timothy tends to talk too much and dominates the discussion time by giving less opportunity for others to share. What do you do with a group member who talks too much? In the "Helpful Hints" section of How to Lead a Small Group Bible Study (p. 185), you'll find some practical ideas on managing the "Talkative Timothy's" in your group.

Lesson #4—Persecution in Jesus' Name - Acts 4:5–31

Memory Verse: Acts 4:29

"And now, Lord, take note of their threats, and grant that Your bond-servants may speak Your word with all confidence."

BEFORE THE SESSION

- Be sure to do your own study far enough in advance so as not to be rushed. You want to allow God time to speak to you personally.

- Don't feel that you have to use all of the discussion questions listed below. You may have come up with others on your own, or you may find that time will not allow you to use them all. These questions are to serve you, not for you to serve.

- You are the gatekeeper of the discussion. Do not be afraid to "reel the group back in" if they get too far away from the subject of the lesson.

- Remember to keep a highlight pen ready as you study to mark any points you want to be sure to discuss.

- Pray each day for the members of your group—that they spend time in the Word, grasp the message God wants to bring to their lives, and that they surrender to what God is saying.

WHAT TO EXPECT

Everyone will come in with some understanding of what persecution is, but they probably have not taken the time to identify how and why it happens. This lesson has the potential to bring much practical application as we look at the cost of following Christ in a world at war with Him. Expect questions and be prepared to share honestly from your own experiences.

THE MAIN POINT

The main point to be seen in this lesson is that to abide in Christ, we must expect that there will be opposition, but God is always faithful to give us the grace to handle it.

DURING THE SESSION

OPENING: 5–10 MINUTES

Opening Prayer—Remember that if it took the inspiration of God for people to write Scripture, it will also take His illumination for us to understand it. Have one of the members of your group open your time together in prayer.

Opening Illustration—More than 160,000 Christians are killed each year because of their religious affiliation, according to figures compiled by the World Evangelization Research

Centre. The number is rising each year because of the continuing collapse of communism and the expansion of terrorism. And a recent report claims Christians are the most persecuted religious group in the world. In China, North Korea, and Laos, Christians are being arrested and tortured. In southern Sudan they are sold as slaves and become victims of the worst form of psychological and physical abuse. And in some Muslim countries people who convert to Christianity are often tortured and killed, as Islam does not tolerate apostasy. The report states that a complete picture of persecution in the world remains unattainable because in certain countries, such as China, "there is much more going on than we are allowed to find out." We do know that since 1998, approximately two million people have become victims of the Islamisation policy, particularly Christians and followers of nature religions." (information quoted in *The Catholic Weekly*, 17 November, 2002)

DISCUSSION: 30 MINUTES

Once your group gets talking, you will find that all you need to do is keep the group directed and flowing with a question or two or a pointed observation. You are the gatekeeper of discussion. Don't be afraid to ask someone to elaborate further ("Explain what you mean, Barbara?") or to ask a quiet member of the group what they think of someone else's comments ("What do you think, Dave?"). Time will not allow you to discuss every single question in the lesson one at a time. Instead, make it your goal to cover the main ideas of each day and help the group to share what they learned personally. You don't have to use all the discussion questions. They are there for your choosing and discretion.

Main Objective in Day One: Day One focuses on introducing the circumstances surrounding Peter and John's trial before the Sanhedrin. Below, check which discussion questions you will use from Day One.

___ Why do you think it was the religious who brought the strongest opposition to Christians?

___ In what way is it a good thing to investigate a miracle before crediting it to God?

___ What stood out to you from Peter's answers to his accusers?

___ Did you see any ways that Peter put his accusers on trial?

Main Objective in Day Two: Day Two studies the debate within the Sanhedrin on what to do with Peter and John. Check which discussion questions you will use from Day Two.

___ Why do you think Peter and John presented themselves with such confidence?

___ What are some ways people can tell we have "been with Jesus?"

___ Why do you suppose the religious leaders wanted to cover up the miracle instead of acknowledge it?

___ Did anything else stand out to you in Day Two?

Main Objective in Day Three: In Day Three, we focus in on the verdict the Sanhedrin delivered to Peter and John. In addition to any discussion-starter questions that you may have in mind, the following questions may also prove useful to your group time.

___ What was the verdict of the Sanhedrin?

___ What are some ways you saw Peter's confidence in the Lord expressed in his response to the authorities?

___ How did the common people view what had taken place?

___ What do you think they would have done if the Sanhedrin tried to do away with Peter and John?

Main Objective in Day Four: In Day Four, we examine how the church responded to these threats and restrictions from the Jewish authorities. Below, place a checkmark next to the questions that you feel are worthy of mention in your session. Or you may want to place ranking numbers next to each question to note your order of preference.

___ How did the church interpret the events that were taking place?

___ What stands out to you from the prophecies that are mentioned here?

___ What did the church ask God to do in light of their situation?

___ How did God answer their prayers?

Day Five—Key Points in Application: The most important application point your group can glean from the lesson on the principle of persecution is the importance of drawing on God's strength and not our own. Examine the question list below and decide if there are any that fit your group discussion for the Day Five application time.

___ What is some persecution you have faced because of your faith?

___ How do you think you would respond if you were persecuted like the early church?

___ Does the fear of man and the love of approval affect your willingness to share what you believe?

___ Would you say that what you have "seen and heard" in your relationship with the Lord is compelling enough to talk about?

___ What is the main application you saw this week?

CLOSING: 5–10 MINUTES

Summarize—Restate the key points that were highlighted in the class. You may want to briefly review the objectives for each of the days found at the beginning of these leader notes.

Focus—Using this lesson's memory verse, focus on the heart that Jesus wants us to have

Ask the members of your group to reveal their thoughts about the key applications from Day Five.

Preview—Take a few moments to preview next week's lesson.

Pray—Close in prayer.

TOOLS FOR GOOD DISCUSSION

As mentioned earlier, there are certain people who show up in every discussion group. Last week we looked at "Talkative Timothy." Another person who is likely to show up is "Silent Sally." She doesn't readily speak up. Sometimes, her silence is because she doesn't yet feel comfortable enough with the group to share her thoughts. Other times, it is simply because she fears being rejected. Often, her silence is because she is too polite to interrupt and thus is headed off at the pass each time she wants to speak by more aggressive (and less sensitive) members of the group. In the "Helpful Hints" section of How to Lead a Small Group Bible Study (p. 186), you'll find some practical ideas on managing the "Silent Sally's" in your group.

Lesson #5—The Family of God - Acts 4:32—5:16

Memory Verse: Acts 4:32

"And the congregation of those who believed were of one heart and soul;
and not one of them claimed that anything belonging to him was his own, but all things
were common property to them."

BEFORE THE SESSION

- Resist the temptation to do all your homework in one sitting or to put it off until the last minute. You will not be as prepared if you study this way.

- Make sure to mark down any discussion questions that come to mind as you study. Don't feel that you have to use all of the suggested discussion questions included in this leader's guide. Feel free to pick and choose based on your group and the time frame with which you are working.

- Remember your need to trust God with your study. The Holy Spirit is always the best teacher, so stay sensitive to Him!

WHAT TO EXPECT

Most in your group know something about the story of Ananias and Sapphira being struck dead because of lying. This is understandable since it is one of the most dramatic events in the book of Acts. This is not the main point of the lesson though. You will want to deal with the dramatic, but make sure the focus ends up on the practical application of the lesson. The members of your group need to understand that the early church was characterized by selflessness, not selfishness.

THE MAIN POINT

The main point to be seen in this lesson is that when the body of Christ functions as He intends, practical needs are met in a natural way.

DURING THE SESSION

OPENING: 5–10 MINUTES

Opening Prayer—Remember that if it took the inspiration of God for people to write Scripture, it will also take His illumination for us to understand it. Have one of the members of your group open your time together in prayer.

Opening Illustration—One day, while trying to eke out a living for his family, a poor Scottish farmer named Fleming heard a cry for help coming from a nearby bog. He dropped his tools and ran to the bog. There, mired to his waist in black muck, was a terrified boy, screaming and struggling to free himself. Farmer Fleming saved the lad from what could have been a slow and terrifying death. The next day, a fancy carriage pulled up to the Scotsman's sparse surroundings. An elegantly dressed nobleman stepped out and introduced himself as the father of the boy Farmer Fleming had saved. "I want to repay you," said the nobleman. "You saved my son's life." "No, I can't accept payment for what I did," the Scottish farmer replied, waving off the offer. At that moment, the farmer's own son came to the door of the family hovel. "Is that your son?" the nobleman asked. "Yes," the farmer replied proudly. "I'll make you a deal. Let me take him and give him a good education. If the lad is anything like his father, he'll grow to a man you can be proud of." And that he did. In time, Farmer Fleming's son graduated from St. Mary's Hospital Medical School in London, and went on to become known throughout the world as the noted Sir Alexander Fleming, the discoverer of Penicillin. Years afterward, the nobleman's son was stricken with pneumonia. What saved him? Penicillin. The name of the nobleman was Lord Randolph Churchill, and his son's name was Sir Winston Churchill. When we reach out to meet the needs of others, we set in motion a chain of events that reaches the whole family of humanity, including ourselves.

DISCUSSION: 30 MINUTES

Remember that your job is not to teach this lesson, but to facilitate discussion. Do your best to guide the group to the right answers, but don't be guilty of making a point some-one else in the group could just as easily make.

Main Objective in Day One: Day One focuses on the principle of family life illustrated in the first century practice of selling possessions in order to meet charitable needs. Below, check which discussion questions you will use from Day One.

___ What was the attitude of the early church toward member's possessions?

___ How is that attitude different in the modern church?

___ What are some practical needs that ought to be met by the church today?

___ What things stood out to you from the positive example set by Barnabas?

Main Objective in Day Two: Day Two studies the problem of Ananias and Sapphira's deception and the motives behind it. Check which discussion questions you will use from Day Two.

___ Who would like to summarize the problem we see in Acts 5:1–2?

___ What stood out to you from Sapphira's role in the deception?

___ What do you think it means that Satan "filled" Ananias' heart?

___ Did Day Two raise any questions for you?

Main Objective in Day Three: Day Three takes a look more specifically at how the early church dealt with the sin of Ananias and Sapphira. Review the questions below and see if any are suitable to your group discussion on Day Three.

___ How did God judge Ananias and Sapphira?

___ Why do you think God dealt with their sin so severely?

___ How was the church affected by God's dealings with this sin?

___ Did anything stand out to you as you compared the Acts narrative with Nadab and Abihu?

Main Objective in Day Four: In Day Four, we see that after this sin was dealt with, the church continued to prosper. Check which discussion questions you will use from Day Four.

___ What sort of things in the early church seem most attractive to you?

___ What do you think kept some who looked favorably on the church from publicly identifying with it?

___ Why do you suppose people thought being touched by Peter's shadow might work to their benefit?

___ Do you think Peter's shadow actually healed anyone?

Day Five—Key Points in Application: The important thing to see out of Day Five is the contrast between believers who are filled with the Spirit and believers who are filled with flesh. Decide on some discussion-starter topics for the application section of Day Five. The following questions are suggested questions that you may want to use for your discussion:

___ As you reflect on the past week, which would you say was more characteristic of your experience – being filled with the Spirit, or filled with flesh?

___ What lessons did you learn from the example of Barnabas?

___ What lessons did you learn from the example of Ananias?

___ Let's take a few minutes in closing to pray and make sure the Spirit is in control of our lives.

Closing: 5–10 minutes

Summarize—Go over the key points of the lesson.

Remind them that living a victorious Christian life is not attained when we try hard to be like Jesus, but only when we surrender our lives to God and let Him work through us.

Ask them what they think are the key applications from day five

Preview—Take a few moments to preview next week's lesson. Encourage them to be sure to complete their homework.

Pray—Close in prayer.

TOOLS FOR GOOD DISCUSSION

Hopefully your group is functioning smoothly at this point, but perhaps you recognize the need for improvement. In either case, you will benefit from taking the time to evaluate yourself and your group. Without evaluation, you will judge your group on subjective emotions. You may think everything is fine and miss some opportunities to improve your effectiveness. You may be discouraged by problems you are confronting when you ought to be encouraged that you are doing the right things and making progress. A healthy Bible-study group is not one without problems but is one that recognizes its problems and deals with them the right way. At this point in the course, as you and your group are nearly halfway-completed with the study, it is important to examine yourself and see if there are any mid-course corrections that you feel are necessary to implement. Review the evaluation questions list found on page 192-93 of this book, and jot down two or three action points for you to begin implementing next week. Perhaps you have made steady improvements since the first time you answered the evaluation questions at the beginning of the course. If so, your improvements should challenge you to be an even better group leader for the final seven lessons in the study.

ACTION POINTS:

1.

2.

3.

Lesson #6—The Foolishness of Fighting God - Acts 5:17–42

Memory Verses: Acts 5:38–39

"...stay away from these men and let them alone, for if this plan or action is of men, it will be overthrown; but if it is of God, you will not be able to overthrow them; or else you may even be found fighting against God."

BEFORE THE SESSION

- Remember the Boy Scout motto: BE PREPARED! The main reason a Bible study flounders is because the leader comes in unprepared and tries to "shoot from the hip."

- Make sure to jot down any discussion questions that come to mind as you study.

- Don't forget to pray for the members of your group and for your time studying together. You don't want to be satisfied with what you can do—you want to see God do what only He can do!

WHAT TO EXPECT

In studying this lesson, you should realize that it is possible even for the devoutly religious to find themselves working against God and His will instead of with it. This certainly was the case with the Sanhedrin. Remember, these were the same men who had Jesus put to death. Expect the group to view these religious leaders as the bad guys but recognize they may not at first see themselves as capable of fighting God. Guard your group from listening with their elbows and applying the principles only to others rather than to themselves.

Main Point: The main point to be seen in this lesson is that it is foolish to place our own agenda ahead of God and His will.

DURING THE SESSION

OPENING: 5–10 MINUTES

Opening Prayer—Remember to have one of your group members open your time together in prayer.

Opening Illustration—A park ranger was leading a group of hikers to a lookout tower in Yellowstone National Park. Along the way he pointed out some of the famous sites in the park. He was so intent on the stories he was telling, that he paid no attention when his two-way radio received a message. He turned it down. Later they stopped to look at some flowers and view some of the birds in nearby trees. Once again, his radio distracted the ranger, so this time he turned it off. As the group neared the lookout tower, they were met by a nearly breathless ranger who asked why the guide hadn't responded to the messages on his radio. From their viewpoint, high in the tower, some other rangers had observed a large grizzly bear stalking the group. They had been trying desperately to warn the hikers. Many times, we are so involved in personal activities and pursuits in this life, we don't pay attention to what God is revealing to us. The danger in such distraction is that if we miss what God is saying and where He is heading, the consequences can be disastrous.

DISCUSSION: 30–40 MINUTES

Remember to pace your discussion so that you will be able to bring closure to the lesson at the designated time. You are the one who must balance lively discussion with timely redirection to ensure that you don't end up finishing only part of the lesson.

Main Objective in Day One: In Day One, the main objective is to explore how the religious leaders of the day were trying to squelch the message of Jesus as Messiah. Check which discussion questions you will use from Day One.

___ Why do you think the Sanhedrin were so opposed to the message of Jesus as Messiah?

___ What stands out to you from the way God chose to release the apostles from jail?

___ Why do you think the religious leaders handled the situation the way they did?

___ Were there any questions raised by your study in Day One?

Main Objective in Day Two: In Day Two, we look at the tension between obeying human authorities and our submission to God. Choose a discussion question or two from the Day Two list below.

___ Under what circumstances would you consider it okay to disobey human authorities?

___ What stood out to you most from the example of Daniel and his relationship to authority?

___ What did the apostles do to communicate respect for human authority?

___ What do you think it means that the Holy Spirit is given "to those who obey Him"?

Main Objective in Day Three: Day Three introduces us to Gamaliel's counsel and how that impacted the outcome of the apostle's arrest. Decide on some discussion-starter questions for your session on detours. Below, are some possible discussion questions for you to consider.

___ The Sanhedrin wanted to kill the apostles. Why do you think they responded so violently?

___ What do you think of Gamaliel and his advice?

___ Is there any danger in Gamaliel's approach to solving the problem?

___ What else stood out to you in Day Three?

Main Objective in Day Four: In Day Four, we take some time to learn about the continued prospering of the church in spite of opposition. Check which discussion questions you will use from Day Four.

___ What is the main impression you come away with as you look at the Sanhedrin's verdict?

___ How does the perspective of the apostles on what happened differ from what you would expect?

___ Were the Jewish leaders effective at silencing the apostles? ...Why or why not?

Day Five—Key Points in Application: The most important application point from Day Five is that we personalize the lessons from the Sanhedrin as well as the apostles. Below, check any discussion questions that are best suited to your group for application.

___ What are some ways we can be in passive opposition to the Lord and what He wills?

___ What factors tend to keep you from speaking up to others about the Lord?

___ Can you think of any examples in your own life of missing what God is doing in a situation?

___ What other applications did you see in this week's lesson?

CLOSING: 5–10 MINUTES

Summarize—Restate the key points.

Remind those in your group that living a victorious Christian life is not attained when we try hard to be like Jesus, but only when we surrender our lives to God and let Him work through us.

Preview—Take a few moments to preview next week's lesson.

Pray—Close in prayer.

TOOLS FOR GOOD DISCUSSION

As discussed earlier, there are certain people who show up in every discussion group that you will ever lead. We have already looked at "Talkative Timothy" and "Silent Sally." This week, let's talk about another person who tends to show up. Let's call this person "Tangent Tom." He is the kind of guy who loves to talk even when he has nothing to say. Tangent Tom loves to "chase rabbits" regardless of where they go. When he gets the floor, you never know where the discussion will lead. You need to understand that not all tangents are bad. Sometimes, much can be gained from discussion "a little off the beaten path." But these diversions must be balanced against the purpose of the group. In the "Helpful Hints" section of How to Lead a Small Group (pp. 186–87), you will find some practical ideas on managing the "Tangent Toms" in your group. You will also get some helpful information on evaluating tangents as they arise.

Lesson 7—A Life Placed on the Altar – Acts 6—7

Memory Verse: Acts 6:5a

"And the statement found approval with the whole congregation; and they chose Stephen, a man full of faith and of the Holy Spirit"

BEFORE THE SESSION

- Try to get your lesson plans and homework done early this week. This gives time for you to reflect on what you have learned and process it mentally. Don't succumb to the temptation to procrastinate.

- Make sure you keep a highlight pen handy to highlight any things you intend to discuss, including any questions that you think your group may have trouble comprehending. Jot down any good discussion questions that come to your mind as you study.

- Don't think of your ministry to the members of your group as something that only takes place during your group time. Pray for your group members by name during the week that they would receive spiritual enrichment from doing their daily homework. Encourage them as you have opportunity.

WHAT TO EXPECT

Most people in your group will probably have some knowledge of Stephen as the first Christian martyr, but few will have studied the other aspects of his life and ministry revealed in Acts. Expect that some will be surprised to learn of his service ministry with waiting on tables, and even more will be unaware of his evangelizing and his being used of God to perform miracles. While each of these aspects of Stephen's life are significant, the larger importance is seen in the source behind his service. Expect that everyone in your group will find common ground with this saint and discover application from his life and death.

THE MAIN POINT

The main point to be seen in this lesson is that when we surrender our lives completely to the Lord, then He is able to work through us. This is what true ministry is all about.

DURING THE SESSION

OPENING: 5-10 MINUTES

Opening Prayer—It would be a good idea to have a different group member each week open your time together in prayer.

Opening Illustration—One of the utensils for the priests in the Old Testament Tabernacle and Temple was the "flesh hooks." These metal tongs were used with the burnt offerings.

As the sacrifice was placed on the altar and began to burn, sometimes it would shift. The "flesh hooks" were used by the priest to keep moving the sacrifice back to the center of the altar. Even though we gave our lives to Christ at salvation (placing them on the altar so to speak), we must be watchful, lest that offering of ourselves shift away from total surrender. Like the burnt offerings in the Old Testament, our yieldedness to Christ must be maintained. Stephen's life was eternally significant, because he kept his life at that place of total surrender.

DISCUSSION: 30–40 MINUTES

A key objective in how you manage your discussion time is to keep the big picture in view. Your job is not like a schoolteacher's job, grading papers and tests and the like, but more like a tutor's job, making sure your group understands the subject. Keep the main point of the lesson in view, and make sure they take that main point home with them.

Main Objective in Day One: In Day One the main objective is to look at our introduction to Stephen as one of the seven of Acts 6 whom the apostles appoint to supervise the feeding of widows in the church. Start thinking now about what discussion starters you will use in your session devoted to Prayer. Review the question list below. Perhaps there is a question or two below that might be essential to your group time.

___ What do you think would have happened if the apostles had tried to care for the widows themselves?

___ Why do you suppose Stephen is mentioned first in the list of the seven men?

___ How do you think the congregation identified Stephen and the other men as good candidates for this task?

___ What grabs you from Luke's statement of verse 7?

Main Objective in Day Two: In Day Two, we look at Stephen's evangelistic ministry in Jerusalem. Check which discussion questions you will use from Day Two.

___ What did you learn in Acts 6:8 about Stephen's ministry?

___ Why do you think Luke makes reference to the "wisdom and Spirit" with which Stephen spoke?

___ What does verse 11 say about the spirituality of the religious men who opposed Stephen?

___ Did anything else in particular stand out to you from Day Two?

Main Objective in Day Three: Day Three focuses us in more specifically on Stephen's preaching before the high priest and leaders. Take a look at the discussion question list below to see if any are applicable to your group session.

___ How many references to God speaking do you see in those first 8 verses?

___ What common ground do you see between the story of Joseph and his brothers and what was happening in Israel?

___ What common ground did you see between the story of Moses and Stephen's situation?

___ What stood out to you from how Stephen closed his message?

Main Objective in Day Four: Day Four examines the actual martyrdom of Stephen. Choose some discussion starters for your group session.

___What stood out to you from the Sanhedrin's response to Stephen's words?

___Why do you think Luke makes a point of Stephen being "full of the Holy Spirit"?

___What are your thoughts about Stephen seeing Jesus "standing"?

___What did you learn when you compared Acts 7 with Luke 23:34 and 46?

Day Five—Key Points in Application: The focus of Day Five is to move us into evaluating where we are in making our lives a living sacrifice. Below, check any discussion questions that you might consider using for your application time.

___What sort of things get in the way of living a surrendered life?

___Do you ever struggle with being willing to yield yourself to the Lord?

___What is the biggest application point you observed this week?

CLOSING: 5–10 MINUTES

Summarize—You may want to read "The Main Point" statement at the beginning of the leader's notes.

Preview—If time allows, preview next week's lesson. Encourage your group to complete their homework.

Pray—Close in prayer.

TOOLS FOR GOOD DISCUSSION

One of the issues you will eventually have to combat in any group Bible study is the enemy of boredom. This enemy raises its ugly head from time to time, but it shouldn't. It is wrong to bore people with the Word of God! Often boredom results when leaders allow their processes to become too predictable. As small group leaders, we tend to do the same thing in the same way every single time. Yet God the Creator, who spoke everything into existence is infinitely creative! Think about it. He is the one who not only created animals in different shapes and sizes, but different colors as well. When He created food, He didn't make it all taste or feel the same. This God of creativity lives in us. We can trust Him to give us creative ideas that will keep our group times from becoming tired and mundane. In the "Helpful Hints" section of How to Lead a Small Group (pp. 189–90), you'll find some practical ideas on adding spice and creativity to your study time.

Lesson 8—The Sovereign Hand of God in Ministry - Acts 8

Memory Verse: Proverbs 16:9

"The mind of man plans his way, But the LORD directs his steps."

BEFORE THE SESSION

Your own preparation is key not only to your effectiveness in leading the group session, but also in your confidence in leading. It is hard to be confident if you know you are unprepared. These discussion questions and leader's notes are meant to be a helpful addition to your own study, but should never become a substitute.

As you do your homework, study with a view to your own relationship with God. Resist the temptation to bypass this self-evaluation on your way to preparing to lead the group. Nothing will minister to your group more than the testimony of your own walk with God.

Don't think of your ministry to the members of your group as something that only takes place during your group time. Pray for your group members by name during the week that they would receive spiritual enrichment from doing their daily homework. Encourage them as you have opportunity.

WHAT TO EXPECT

Every life is punctuated with situations that require wisdom and direction. God could have just given us a road map and told us to find our own way, or only given us our minds, making us dependent on our logic, but instead, He has chosen to give us a guide—His Spirit living in us. He does not want us to reject our own logic, but at the same time, we cannot lean only on that. In all these different and dramatic situations of Acts 8, the common denominator is the sovereign hand of God making use of circumstances and guiding His saints to those hungry for the gospel. Expect that your students will see each of the different situations, but not necessarily grasp the connection between them right away. Lead them toward the theme of God's sovereign working and guiding.

THE MAIN POINT

The main point in this lesson is how God sovereignly uses circumstances and His indwelling Spirit to lead His people to places of ministry.

OPENING: 5–10 MINUTES

Opening Prayer—A good prayer with which to open your time with is the prayer of David in Psalm 119:18, "Open my eyes, that I may behold Wonderful things from Thy law." Remember, if it took the illumination of God for men to write Scripture, it will take the same for us to understand it.

Opening Illustration—Admiral Sir Thomas Williams was a straight-forward, no non-sense leader who leaned on his keen intellect. He was in command of a ship crossing the Atlantic, and his course brought him in sight of the island of Ascension, at that time uninhabited and never visited except for the purpose of collecting turtles. The island was barely visible on the horizon, but as Sir Thomas looked at it, he was seized by an unaccountable desire to steer towards it. Though this desire made no logical sense to him, his desire became more and more urgent and distressing. After wrestling with the idea for a time, he told his lieutenant to prepare to "put about ship" and steer in that direction. The officer respectfully remonstrated that changing course would greatly delay them. This only increased the Admiral's anxiety, and the ship was steered towards the island. All eyes aboard were fixed upon it, and soon something was perceived on the shore. "It is white—it is a rag—it must be a signal!" When they neared the shore, they discovered that sixteen men, wrecked on the coast many days before, and suffering hunger, had set up a signal, although almost without hope of relief. It was only through the Admiral's responding to the "still, small voice" of the Spirit that sixteen lives were saved. While such experiences are not the norm, they cannot be dismissed altogether either.

DISCUSSION: 30–40 MINUTES

Remember to pace your discussion so that you don't run out of time to get to the application questions in Day Five. This time for application is perhaps the most important part of your Bible study. It will be helpful if you are familiar enough with the lesson to be able to prioritize the days for which you want to place more emphasis, so that you are prepared to reflect this added emphasis in the time you devote to that particular day's reading.

Main Objective in Day One: In Day One, the main objective is to show how God turned the negative of persecution into a positive by scattering the saints to new places of ministry. Choose a discussion question or two from the Day One list below.

___ Why do you think Saul was so much in agreement with Stephen being put to death?

___ Have you ever wondered why God didn't miraculously intervene in the persecution?

___ What do you imagine was going through the minds of believers who were being accosted by Saul?

___ Are there any other thoughts from Day One that you would like to discuss?

Main Objective in Day Two: We learn in Day Two some of the specifics of the first evangelistic efforts among the Samaritans. Check which discussion questions you will use from Day Two.

___ How do you think Phillip decided to go to Samaria?

___ Why do you think the apostles felt they needed to send Peter and John to investigate these Samaritan conversions?

___ Do you think the Holy Spirit operates differently today than He did in Acts? Why?

___ Did Day Two raise any questions in your mind?

Main Objective in Day Three: Day Three introduces us to the selfish motives of Simon the magician and his wrong understanding of ministry. In addition to any discussion questions you may have in mind for your group session, the following questions below may also be useful:

___ From what you know of Simon, why do you think he was so interested in this power to bestow the Holy Spirit?

___ What wrong thinking do you see reflected in his request?

___ What did Peter reveal of what is wrong with Simon's request?

___ Do you think Simon was genuinely saved?

Main Objective in Day Four: In Day Four, our study focuses on the promptings of the Holy Spirit that led Phillip to someone with a seeking heart. Place a checkmark next to the discussion question you would like to use for your group session. Or you may want to place a ranking number in each blank to note your order of preference.

___ What all did you see that indicated the Ethiopian wanted to know God?

___ What stood out to you as you looked at Isaiah 53 where the Ethiopian had been reading?

___ What do you think Phillip would have done if he hadn't responded to the promptings of the Spirit but instead, leaned on his own logic?

___ What principles of evangelism do you think we should apply from Phillip's example?

Day Five—Key Points in Application: The main goal of Day Five is to seek to put these truths about the Holy Spirit into application. Check which discussion questions you will use from Day Five.

___ What principles of evangelism do you think we should apply from Phillip's example?

___ Can you think of any ways God might be sovereignly using the trials in your life right now to bring about a positive result?

___ Where are some areas you struggle with prejudice as it relates to ministry?

___ What are some ways we err in our motives like Simon the magician?

___ What other applications did you see from this week?

CLOSING: 5–10 MINUTES

Summarize—You may want to read "The Main Point" statement at the beginning of the leader's notes.

Preview—If time allows, preview next week's lesson. Encourage them to be sure and do their homework.

Pray—Close in prayer.

TOOLS FOR GOOD DISCUSSION

From time to time, each of us can say stupid things. Some of us, however, are better at it than others. The apostle Peter had his share of embarrassing moments. One minute, he was on the pinnacle of success, saying, "You are the Christ, the Son of the Living God" (Matthew 16:16), and the next minute, he was putting his foot in his mouth, trying to talk Jesus out of going to the cross. Proverbs 10:19 states, "When there are many words, transgression is unavoidable. . . ." What do you do when someone in the group says something that is obviously wrong? First of all, remember that how you deal with a situation like this not only affects the present, but the future. In the "Helpful Hints" section of How to Lead a Small Group (p. 190), you'll find some practical ideas on managing the obviously wrong comments that show up in your group.

Lesson 9—The Life-Changing Power of God - Acts 9:1–31

Memory Verse: 2 Corinthians 5:17

"Therefore if anyone is in Christ, he is a new creature; the old things passed away; behold, new things have come."

BEFORE THE SESSION

- Pray each day for the members of your group—that they spend time in the Word, grasp the message God wants to bring to their lives, and that they surrender to what God is saying.

- Be sure you have searched the Scriptures carefully for each day's lesson.

- While preparing for this lesson, read through the discussion questions on the following pages, and select which questions you will use.

- Remain ever teachable. Look first for what God is saying to you. This will help you in relating to some of the situations your group members may be facing as they are seeking to make an impact on those around them.

WHAT TO EXPECT

The conversion of the Apostle Paul is one of the most familiar passages in the book of Acts, but few will ever have studied it in detail, let alone looked at it in the context of chapters seven and eight. Expect that your group members will gain new insights and appreciation for the miracle of God saving Saul of Tarsus. Take it as an opportunity to encourage them to believe God for the salvation of other "impossibles" in their life and in our world today.

THE MAIN POINT

The main point to be seen in the lesson on Acts 9 is the fact that if God could save the Apostle Paul, He is able to change even the most hardened and antagonistic of people.

DURING THE SESSION

OPENING: 5–10 MINUTES

Prayer—Remember to ask the Lord for His wisdom. He has promised to guide us into the truth.

Opening Illustration—One of the best-known hymns of all Christendom is the familiar song, "Amazing Grace." What you may not know is that it was written by a man named John Newton. His early life was characterized by rebellion and debauchery. As a young man, Newton worked his way up the ladder of success in the African slave trade, eventually becoming captain of his own slave ship. One stormy night in March of 1748, on a voyage from Africa back to England, God convicted him of his sins, and Newton was saved. At first, he tried to make a difference in the slave trade business, working for humane treatment of slaves and even holding religious services on board ship. Eventually he felt convicted of the inhuman aspects of this work and became a strong and effective crusader against slavery, as well as a devout and effective preacher. He shared his testimony across England and always found people willing to listen to the story of "The Old Converted Sea Captain." The lyrics of the old hymn come alive when you understand the context they were written from: "Amazing Grace, how sweet the sound that saved a wretch like me, I once was lost but now am found, was blind but now I see." The power of God to save Saul of Tarsus, the persecutor and John Newton, the slave trader is the same life-changing power that reached you and me. It truly is "Amazing Grace."

(taken from *Singing With Understanding* by Kenneth W. Osbeck, Kregel Publications, Grand Rapids, MI, p.64)

DISCUSSION: 30–40 MINUTES

Select one or two specific questions to get the group started. Keep the group directed along the main point. By this point in the course (Week 9), you know the talkative and the quiet. Continue to encourage each member in the importance of his or her input. Some of the greatest life lessons we ever learn may come from someone who has said very little up to this point.

Main Objective in Day One: In Day One, the main objective is to set forward the persecuting context of Saul just prior to his conversion. Review the question list below and decide upon some discussion starters for your group session.

___ Why do you think Saul took the lead in persecuting Christians?

___ What do you suppose was going through Saul's mind when he realized it was Jesus speaking to him?

___ How did you see Saul's blindness fitting into God's plan to save him?

___ What stood out to you from the other verses in Day One?

Main Objective in Day Two: Day Two focuses on the actual conversion of Saul. Check which discussion questions you will use from Day Two.

___ What do you think a three-day fast from food and water says about Saul's heart toward God?

___ Why do you think Ananias was hesitant to act on God's instructions?

___ How do you suppose he knew so much about Saul?

___ What spiritual parallels do you see in Saul gaining back his sight?

Main Objective in Day Three: Day Three introduces us to Saul's switch to advocate of the Christian faith. Some good discussion questions for Day Three include . . .

___ What did Saul do once he regained his sight?

___ What do you think it means that Saul "kept increasing in strength"?

___ How do you suppose the Sanhedrin received the news of Saul's conversion?

___ How long do you think it took for the Christians of Damascus to embrace Saul as a fellow believer?

Main Objective in Day Four: Day Four examines Saul's return to Jerusalem as a believer and advocate of the faith. Check which discussion questions you will use from Day Four.

___ Why do you presume the believers in Jerusalem responded as they did to news of Saul's conversion?

___ What stands out to you from Barnabas coming alongside Saul?

___ Why do you think God wanted to use Saul to reach Gentiles instead of Jews?

___ What role do you see Saul's conversion playing in the prosperity of the church at this point?

Day Five—Key Points in Application: The most important application point in this lesson is to recognize God's ability to change lives. Below, are some suggestions for discussion questions. Feel free to come up with your own questions as well.

___ What are some evidences in your life of the life-changing power of God?

___ Are there any areas where you struggle with believing God can change you?

___ Have you doubted God's ability to change anyone?

___ Why don't we close by praying for those we would like to see God change?

CLOSING: 5–10 MINUTES

Summarize—Restate the key points the group shared. Review the objectives for each of the days found at the beginning of these leader notes.

Focus—Using the memory verse (2 Corinthians 5:17), focus the group on the fact that Christianity is not us trying hard to be good people, but God changing us.

Ask them to express their thoughts about the key applications from Day Five.

Encourage—We have finished nine lessons. This is no time to slack off. Encourage your group to keep up the pace. We have three more lessons full of life-changing truths. Take a few moments to preview next week's lesson. Encourage your group members to do their homework in proper fashion by spacing it out over the week.

Pray—Close in prayer.

TOOLS FOR GOOD DISCUSSION

The Scriptures are replete with examples of people who struggled with the problem of pride. Unfortunately, pride isn't a problem reserved for the history books. It shows up just as often today as it did in the days the Scriptures were written. In your group discussions, you may see traces of pride manifested in a "know-it-all" group member. "Know-It-All Ned" may have shown up in your group by this point. He may be an intellectual giant, or he may be a legend only in his own mind. He can be very prideful and argumentative. If you want some helpful hints on how to deal with "Know-It-All Ned," look in the "Helpful Hints" section of How to Lead a Small Group Bible Study (p.187–88).

Lesson 10—The Greatest Miracle of All - Acts 9:32—10:48

Memory Verses: Colossians 1:13–14

"For He rescued us from the domain of darkness, and transferred us to the kingdom of His beloved Son, in whom we have redemption, the forgiveness of sins."

BEFORE THE SESSION

- Never underestimate the importance of prayer for yourself and for the members of your group. Ask the Lord to give your group members understanding in their time in the Word and to bring them to a new level of knowing Him.

- Spread your study time over the week.

- Remember to mark those ideas and questions you want to discuss or ask as you go through the study.

- Be sensitive to the needs of your group. Be prepared to stop and pray for a member who may be facing a difficult struggle or challenge.

WHAT TO EXPECT

Expect that your group will have tended to focus on the dramatic events of this passage, but the idea of salvation being the greatest miracle may be new to them. As they look at this section of Acts with that in view, expect that they will come away with a new appreciation for their own salvation. They may want to share their own stories as time allows. Expect that this will be a very motivating lesson with lots of interest.

THE MAIN POINT

The main point to be seen in the lesson is that of all the miraculous things that God does and has done, none is more miraculous than the gift of salvation.

DURING THE SESSION

OPENING: 5–10 MINUTES

Opening Prayer—Have one of the group members open the time with prayer.

Opening Illustration—Normally I encourage you to make use of an opening illustration as a hook to gain your group's attention and interest. This time, perhaps the best illustration will be a personal one. Why not BRIEFLY share your own personal testimony of coming to the Lord. Another option if you are not comfortable with this, or if you think it would be an encouragement to someone else, is to ask another group member to share their testimony. If you go this route, make sure you give them ample time to prepare, and that you emphasize the need for them to be brief (no more than 3–5 minutes) so as to allow time to discuss the lesson.

DISCUSSION: 30–40 MINUTES

Select one or two specific questions to get the group started in discussion. Continue to encourage each member in the importance of his or her insights and input.

Main Objective in Day One: Day One looks at an example of the miracle of physical healing in the person of Aeneas. Good discussion starters for Day One include . . .

___ What do you think was Peter's main ministry at this point in the development of the church?

___ What particulars stood out to you as you looked at the healing of Aeneas?

___ Why do you think Luke emphasizes the people of the region turning to the Lord?

___ Have you ever experienced physical healing or seen God heal others?

Main Objective in Day Two: In Day Two, the main objective is to consider the miracle of Dorcas being raised from the dead and to put that into the perspective of the context. Below are some suggested questions for your discussion on Day Two. Which questions will you use for your group session?

___ What impresses you most as you look at the character and ministry of the woman Peter healed?

___ How do you see prayer fitting in to the miracle of Dorcas being raised?

___ Why do you think Peter "presented" her to the saints and widows?

___ What resulted from this miracle other than the woman coming back to life?

Main Objective in Day Three: In Day Three, the main objective is to look at the miracle of the visions experienced by Peter and Cornelius. What discussion questions do you plan to use for Day Three? Below are some suggestions.

___ Why do you think God picked Cornelius as the first Gentile Peter would lead to faith in Christ?

___ What do you see as the significance of Peter's vision being repeated three times?

___ Why do you think a vision was necessary in this case?

___ Did anything else stand out to you from Day Three?

Main Objective in Day Four: Day Four zeros in on the greatest miracle of all being the miracle of salvation. Check which questions you will use for your discussion on Day Four.

___ What did Peter learn from his vision?

___ As you look at Peter's instruction to the crowd, what do you see as the essentials of the Gospel?

___ How do you see the salvation experience of these Gentiles comparing to Pentecost?

___ Why do you think it was important for there to be a contingent of Jews with Peter to witness this event?

Day Five—Key Points in Application: The most important aspect of each lesson is taking the time to seek to apply the truths to our own lives. Make sure you save time for this important part. Select a discussion question or two from the list below.

___ On the list of topics for this week (physical healing, raising from the dead, dreams and visions, and salvation) which would you have picked as most impressive before doing the lesson?

___ Which would you pick as most important after studying this passage?

___ Are there any who come to mind as those you don't think would ever be receptive to the gospel?

___ Let's close by praying for these we have mentioned.

CLOSING: 5–10 MINUTES

Summarize—Review the key points the group shared. You may want to review "The Main Point" statement for this lesson. Also, ask your group to express their thoughts about the key applications from Day Five

Focus—Using the memory verse, focus the group on the miracle of salvation.

Preview—Take a few moments to preview next week's lesson.

Pray—Close in prayer.

TOOLS FOR GOOD DISCUSSION

So, group leaders, how have the weeks of this study been for you? Have you dealt with anyone in your group called "Agenda Alice?" She is the type that is focused on a Christian "hot-button" issue instead of the Bible study. If not managed properly, she (or he) will either sidetrack the group from its main study objective, or create a hostile environment in the group if she fails to bring people to her way of thinking. For help with "Agenda Alice," see the "Helpful Hints" section of How to Lead a Small Group Bible Study (pp. 188–89).

Lesson 11—The Right Hand of Fellowship - Acts 11

Memory Verse: Ephesians 2:14

"For He Himself is our peace, who made both groups into one and broke down the barrier of the dividing wall."

BEFORE THE SESSION

- Pray for your group as they study through this week's lesson.

- Spread your study time over the week. This is like a large meal. You need time to chew each truth and digest it fully.

- Remember to jot down those ideas and questions you want to discuss or ask as you go.

WHAT TO EXPECT

Every culture in history has had some form of prejudice. All the way back to Cain and Abel we see people being judged because they were different. But the work of Christ unites what was divided by sin. As we grow in Him, that growth ought to result in laying aside prejudice. One of the biggest problems though of prejudice is that it is much easier to see it in others than in ourselves. Expect that this lesson will apply to everyone in your group, but that they might not immediately see that. Try to guard against them applying it only to others. Help them identify areas of application in their own life.

THE MAIN POINT

The main point to be seen in the lesson is that when Christ does a work in our hearts, we are able to lay down our biases and love even those who are different.

DURING THE SESSION

OPENING: 5–10 MINUTES

Opening Prayer—Have one of the group members open the time with prayer.

Opening Illustration—Fanny Crosby, the blind songwriter, was at the McAuley Mission in New York City (now the New York City Rescue Mission). She asked if there was a boy there who had no mother, and if he would come up and let her lay her hand on his head. A motherless little fellow came up, and she put her arms about him and kissed him. They parted; she went from the meeting and wrote that inspiring song Rescue the Perishing; and when Mr. Sankey was about to sing the song in St. Louis, he related the incident. A man sprang to his feet in the audience and said, "I am the boy she kissed that night. I never was able to get away from the impression made by that touching act, until I became a Christian. I am now living in this city with my family, am a Christian, and am doing a good business." Love makes all the difference in the world, and the greater the need to be loved the greater the impact it has. As the Lord works in our lives, He enables us to share His love even with those from different cultures, backgrounds and circumstances. ("Stories for Preachers and Teachers," AMG)

DISCUSSION: 30–40 MINUTES

When leading small group discussion, the most important temptation to avoid is doing most of the talking yourself. See yourself as the referee, always putting the ball back into play. Don't view yourself as the star player who always takes the shot. Your group will learn more from self-discovery than they will from anything else. If you guide the discussion properly, they will not realize how much you are directing the flow of discussion. It will seem to them as if they have been having a natural conversation. As you trek through the lesson, seek to keep the main point the main point. Emphasize what you clearly know and understand. Then you can move on to the things that are not as clear as the Lord gives you time and insight.

Main Objective in Day One: In Day One, the main objective is to see the prejudice which existed among the Jews toward Gentiles. In addition to any discussion questions you may have in mind, the list of questions below may also contain useful discussion-starter ideas.

___ What did you learn about circumcision from the Old Testament passages we looked at?

___ Why did "those who were circumcised" take issue with Peter?

___ What does this say of their attitude toward the uncircumcised?

___ Did anything else stand out to you from Day One?

Main Objective in Day Two: In Day Two, we examine the report Peter brings of his experiences among the Gentiles. Check which discussion questions you will use from Day Two.

___ Did you learn anything new by comparing Peter's report here with the previous account?

___ What do you see implied in how Peter says the Spirit came on the Gentiles?

___ How did Peter interpret what had happened with the Gentiles?

___ What was the response of the Jews to Peter's report?

Main Objective in Day Three: In Day Three, we are exposed to the work God does among the Gentiles with the planting of the first Gentile church in Antioch. Below, are some suggested discussion starters for you to consider.

___ What do you think motivated the men of Cyprus and Cyrene to start speaking the Gospel to Greeks?

___ How did the Mother Church at Jerusalem respond to the many Gentiles coming to Christ at Antioch?

___ What grabs you most as you consider this man Barnabas?

___ Why do you think "considerable numbers" were brought under Barnabas and then "considerable numbers" taught under Saul?

Main Objective in Day Four: Day Four's main objective is to focus on the gracious response of the Gentiles toward their fellow believers among the Jews. Check any questions that are applicable for your Day Four-discussion time.

___Why do you think the Lord chose to reveal what He did through Agabus at this time?

___What stands out to you from the response of the believers at Antioch?

___What can we learn from the example set for us by Antioch?

___How do you think this act of charity was received by the Jews in Jerusalem?

Day Five—Key Points in Application: The most important application point in this lesson is that how well we do at "loving our neighbor" and laying aside prejudice says much about how far we have come in our spiritual life. Check which discussion questions you will use to help focus the applications from Day Five.

___What kinds of prejudice did you grow up with?

___Who would you say are the main recipients of prejudice in your community?

___What are some ways the spread of the gospel is hindered by prejudice?

___What main application do you see from this lesson?

CLOSING: 5–10 MINUTES

Summarize—Restate the key points the group shared.

Focus—Focus the group again on the fact that we cannot love as we should or lay aside our prejudices in our own strength. Remind them it must be done by His power, wisdom, and grace.

Ask them to share their thoughts about the key applications from Day Five.

Preview—Take a few moments to preview next week's lesson. Encourage your group members to do their homework in proper fashion by spacing it out over the week.

Pray—Close in prayer.

TOOLS FOR GOOD DISCUSSION

Well, it is evaluation time again! You may be saying to yourself, "Why bother evaluating at the end? If I did a bad job, it is too late to do anything about it now!" Well, it may be too late to change how you did on this course, but it is never too late to learn from this course what will help you on the next. Howard Hendricks, that peerless communicator from Dallas Theological Seminary, puts it this way: "The good teacher's greatest threat is satisfaction—the failure to keep asking, 'How can I improve?' The greatest threat to your ministry is your ministry." Any self-examination should be an accounting of your own strengths and weaknesses. As you consider your strengths and weaknesses, take some time to read through the evaluation questions list found in How to Lead a Small Group Bible Study on pages 192–93. Make it your aim to continue growing as a discussion leader. Jot down below two or three action points for you to implement in future classes.

ACTION POINTS:

1.

2.

3.

Lesson 12—When God's People Pray - Acts 12:1–25

Memory Verse: Acts 12:5

"prayer for him was being made fervently by the church to God"

BEFORE THE SESSION

- You will certainly need to pray for your group as they walk through this last lesson in the study. Never underestimate the importance of prayer for yourself and for the members of your group. Pray for each of them by name.

- Spread your study time over the week.

- Remember to mark those ideas and questions you want to discuss or ask as you go through the study. Add to those some of the questions listed below.

- Be sensitive to the working of the Spirit in your group meeting, ever watching for ways to help one another truly follow God.

WHAT TO EXPECT

Prayer is one of the fundamentals of the Christian life, yet few Christians rate this as a strong point in their spiritual arsenal. Part of this may be due to the fact that no matter how diligent we are and how devoted we may become to prayer, there is always room for improvement. But for some, prayer is a weakness because they have never come to see it as the real work of the Christian life. It is viewed as a religious add-on instead of an essential. Expect that this lesson on "When God's People Pray" will build a vision in your group for the importance of prayer. Make sure in your talking about prayer that you allow some time to practice what you are preaching. Although it is always important to do so, this lesson in particular should certainly begin and end in prayer.

THE MAIN POINT

The main point to be seen in this lesson is that prayer can do what labor or striving or persuasion cannot do.

DURING THE SESSION

OPENING: 5–10 MINUTES

Opening Prayer—Psalm 119:18 says, *"Open my eyes, that I may behold wonderful things from Thy law."* Ask the Lord to open your eyes as you meet together. Have one of the group members open the time with prayer.

Opening Illustration—The person who wrote that electricity was one of the "mighty agents of nature enchained by the ingenuity of man" can scarcely have contemplated in his wildest dreams the full extent of that ingenuity. For instance, he would hardly have prophesied that a sick man, far from the habitations of civilization, would cut a telegraph wire in order to obtain assistance. And yet such a thing actually occurred. The whole of the vast continent of Australia was once practically cut off from European news for nearly twenty-four hours in consequence of an interruption on the line between Adelaide and Port Darwin. Inquiries were made, and it was found that the wire had been cut by a cyclist who had taken ill while on a journey across the continent. It is not related how he set about it, but he had the satisfaction, at any rate, of getting what he wanted. God has so made the human soul that none of us need cut off communication for others in order to reach the ear of heaven. Wherever a human heart turns toward God in simple prayer the unseen wire carries the petition to the Heavenly Father's heart.

DISCUSSION: 30–40 MINUTES

Select one or two specific questions to get the group started. This lesson on prayer offers many application points in which to look at how each of us is following (or faltering in following) God. Remember to look for those "Velcro" points where members can see something that applies to their own lives. Encourage them to share the insights the Lord has shown them during the week.

Main Objective in Day One: In Day One, the main objective is to introduce the surprise circumstance of Peter's arrest and how it moved God's people to pray. Place a check-mark next to the suggested discussion questions that you would like to use in your group session. Or you may want to use ranking numbers and rank the questions in preferential order.

___ Why do you suppose this wave of persecution came when it did in the life of the early church?

___ How do you think God not sparing James affected the church's prayers for Peter?

___ What do you perceive that God was doing through allowing this trial?

___ Is prayer our normal response when difficult times arise?

Main Objective in Day Two: In Day Two, the main objective is to look at Peter's miraculous release from jail. Check which discussion questions you will use from Day Two.

___ What stood out to you from the timing of God's deliverance?

___ What do you think was going through Peter's mind when the angel released his chains?

___ What reasons did you see explain why Peter thought he was having a vision?

___ How do you suppose the guards responded when they discovered Peter missing?

Main Objective in Day Three: Day Three continues to focus on Peter's release from jail and focuses in on the church's response when he shows up at their prayer meeting. Some good discussion questions for Day Three include . . .

___ How do you suppose Peter knew the church would be gathered at Mary's house?

___ What does the response of the gathering to Peter's arrival tell you about their expectations?

___ Why do you suppose Peter had others deliver his report to James and left town so quickly?

___ What do you think Herod would have done if he could have found Peter?

Main Objective in Day Four: In Day Four, the main objective is to introduce the unexpected answer to prayer through Herod's untimely death. Select a discussion question or two from the list of questions below.

___What sort of mood do you think Herod was in when he went to Caesarea?

___What stands out to you from Herod's address and the people's response?

___Why do you think God dealt with Herod the way He did?

___How was the church affected by Herod's death?

Day Five—Key Points in Application: The most important application point seen in this lesson is to recognize the resource we have in prayer as we face our challenges. Check which discussion questions you will use to help bring the applications from Day Five into focus.

___Are there any unexpected tribulations in your life right now?

___What are some of the factors that keep you from praying about things?

___Do you find it difficult to share your prayer needs with others?

___How can we pray for each other?

CLOSING: 5–10 MINUTES

Summarize—Restate the key points the group shared. Review the main objectives for each of the days found in these leader notes.

Focus—Using the memory verse, direct the group's focus to the reality that God wants us to pray for each other.

Ask the group to express their thoughts about the key applications from Day Five.

Pray—Close your time in prayer by thanking the Lord for the journey He has led you on over the past twelve weeks.

TOOLS FOR GOOD DISCUSSION

Congratulations! You have successfully navigated the waters of small group discussion. You have finished all twelve lessons in this study, but there is so much more to learn, so many more paths to take on our journey with the Lord, so much more to discover about what it means to follow Him. Now What? It would be wise for you and your group to not stop with this study. In the front portion of this leader's guide (in the "Helpful Hints" section of How to Lead a Small Group Bible Study, p. 191), there is information on how you can transition to the next study and share those insights with your group. Encourage your group to continue in some sort of consistent Bible study. Time in the Word is much like time at the dinner table. If we are to stay healthy, we will never get far from physical food, and if we are to stay nourished on "sound" or "healthy" doctrine, then we must stay close to the Lord's "dinner table" found in His Word. Job said it well, "I have not departed from the command of His lips; I have treasured the words of His mouth more than my necessary food" (Job 23:12).

When you purchase a Bible or book from **AMG Publishers, Living Ink Books,** or **God and Country Press,** you are helping to impact the world for Christ.

How? AMG Publishers and its imprints are ministries of **AMG International,** a Gospel-first global ministry that meets the deepest needs – spiritual and physical – while inspiring hope, restoring lives and transforming communities. Profits from the sale of AMG Publishers' books are poured into AMG International's worldwide ministry efforts.

For over 75 years, AMG International has leveraged the insights of local leaders and churches, who know their communities best to identify the right strategies to meet the deepest needs. AMG's methods include child and youth development, media evangelism, pastor training, church planting, medical care and disaster relief.

To learn more about AMG International and how you can partner with the ministry through your prayers and financial support, please visit **www.amginternational.org**.

AMG | MEETING THE
INTERNATIONAL | DEEPEST NEEDS

Made in the USA
Monee, IL
06 September 2024

64638708R00142